Home Improvement

Keith A. Butler Sr.
Deborah L. Butler

First Printing 2001

ISBN 1-893575-13-6

Word of Faith Publishing
20000 W. Nine Mile Road
Southfield, MI 48075-5597

Table of Contents

CHAPTER ONE

Family's Origin

Keith A. Butler Sr.

The first truth concerning the home and family that we will learn from the Word of God is one that is easy enough to accept — and that is that God, of course, is the author of homes. God is the author of families. But just because the family came from God and its origin is found in Him doesn't mean everything will be rosy all the time. We have a responsibility to accept God's blessing of the home and family, and to nurture and develop it into all that He has planned and purposed.

Whether we are fighting for the survival of our marriage and family, or just want to make our home life more like "heaven on earth," we can all stand to have our homes, our families, and our personal lives improved. And a person who is single has the distinct advantage of entering into marriage with a secure knowledge of how God wants a family to operate. That person can enter marriage prepared to handle the storms that come to every one of us, and he has the potential to go higher *faster* in the will of God for his home and family.

Our study is in-depth, but, first, I want to lay a foundation concerning God's original design for our home and family life. Let's go to the Book of Beginnings and look at the "First Family," Adam and Eve.

> **And God said, LET US MAKE MAN IN OUR IMAGE, after or likeness: and let them have dominion over the fish of the sea, and over the fowl of the air, and over the cattle, and over all the earth, and over every creeping thing that creepeth upon the earth.**
>
> **So God created man in his own image, in the image of God created he him; male and female created he them.**
>
> **And God blessed them, and God said unto them, Be fruitful, and multiply, and replenish the earth, and subdue it: and have dominion over the fish of the sea, and over the fowl of the air, and over every living thing that moveth upon the earth.**
>
> *GENESIS 1:26-28*

First of all, I want you to notice in verse 26 that it says, "*... Let us make man in our image, after our likeness....*" That word "image" means *resemblance; representation; figure*. God was saying, "Let us make man in our resemblance, representation, and figure."

The Family's Foundation
Began in Creation

Right after God said, "Let us make man in Our image," He said, "...*after our likeness*...." Now the word "likeness" in the Hebrew means *shape; pattern.* I want you to understand what God did when He created mankind. He created mankind to operate like He operates — to have His pattern, His form, His shape!

Believe it or not, human beings are made in the form of God. And God gave us His pattern or way of doing things. God's pattern is this: *God speaks and it comes to pass!*

We already know that God created the worlds by using words (Heb. 11:3). For instance, the Word says, *"And God SAID, Let there be light: and there was light"* (Gen. 1:3). Throughout the account of creation in Genesis chapter 1, we read over and over again, "And God said...." And we know that what God said *became*!

We've learned so far that we were created in God's likeness and that we have His pattern. He spoke words, and they came to pass. *We* are to speak words, and our words should come to pass too. Second Corinthians 4:13 says, *"We having the same spirit of faith...also believe, and therefore speak."*

What else characterizes God's pattern, which we were in the likeness of? *The right to choose* is another part of His pattern. God has the right to choose, and, as humans, so do we.

Did you know that human beings are the only species on the planet that has the right to choose? In fact, humans are the only entity ever created that has the right to choose. Even angels don't have that right. What got Lucifer, who is now called Satan, in trouble was that he attempted to exercise a right that didn't belong to him (Isa. 14:12-15).

And so it says in this passage in Genesis chapter 1 that God made us in His image and after His likeness. He told us, among other things, to be fruitful and to have dominion. Now I want you to notice what exactly God said here in verse 28.

> **And God blessed them, and God said unto them, BE FRUITFUL, AND MULTIPLY, AND REPLENISH THE EARTH, AND SUBDUE IT: and have dominion over the fish of the sea, and over the fowl of the air, and over every living thing that moveth upon the earth.**
>
> *GENESIS 1:28*

Another way we could say that is like this: "God said, 'I want you to develop a family. I want you to be fruitful. I want you to be productive. I want you to multiply yourselves and have children.'"

The word "replenish" in verse 28 means *to restock*. And so we can conclude from this passage of Scripture that it was God's idea to develop the family. *Family comes from God.* But if we're going to have homes that are representative of what God's idea or plan was, we're going to have to educate ourselves in this area according to His Word or we'll fall short, because God's plan was not for homes to be broken. His plan was not for there to be strife and division, which we see so often in families today. God's idea for the home was that it be a blessed place.

Now before you read any further, I want you to speak out in advance and say, "My family is blessed." Even if it doesn't seem that way right now, start saying what God says. You were created in His likeness; you have His pattern. And God's pattern is that He calls things that be not as though they were (<u>Rom. 4:17</u>). And He keeps on calling those things until they *are*! So say again out loud, "My family is blessed!"

'It Was Good'

Now let's go back further in Genesis chapter 1 and look at another important truth about our Creator God.

> And God saw the light, that IT WAS GOOD: and God divided the light from the darkness....
>
> And God called the dry land Earth; and the gathering together of the waters called he Seas: and God saw that IT WAS GOOD....
>
> And the earth brought forth grass, and herb yielding seed after his kind, and the tree yielding fruit, <u>whose seed was in itself,</u> <u>after his kind</u>: and God saw that IT WAS GOOD....
>
> And to rule over the day and over the night, and to divided the light from the darkness: and God saw that IT WAS GOOD....
>
> And God created great whales, and every living creature that moveth, which the waters brought forth abundantly, after their kind, and every winged fowl after his kind: and God saw that IT WAS GOOD....
>
> And God made the beast of the earth after his kind, and cattle after their kind, and every thing that creepeth upon the earth

**after his kind: and God saw that IT WAS
GOOD....**

**And God saw every thing that he had made,
and, behold, it was VERY good. And the
evening and the morning were the sixth day.**

GENESIS 1:4,10,12,18,21,25,31

✳ Everything that God made, God said, "It's good." From
the earth and the sky to every beast in water and on land, God
said, in effect, "I like it."

I have visited such places in this country as Alaska and
Hawaii. I've seen up close and in person the majestic bald
eagle perched proudly on a rock against a background of crisp
blue sky.

I've seen firsthand the elegant beauty of the sea. Whether
still and calm like crystal-blue stained glass or with white
waves thrashing against rocky shores, the ocean suggests a certain grandeur and majesty characteristic of its Maker.

I've witnessed with awe and amazement the creatures of
ocean and wilderness in their respective settings — the sea
lions, otters, whales, foxes, wolves, and bears — all the creation of God.

There are places on this earth that wondrously depict the
awesome beauty of creation. Anyone with even a little intelli-
gence would be able to conclude that such places and such
sights did not just "happen" with some big spontaneous
bang. No, there was a Creator. There was a grand design.
People flock to museums to see the creative works of famous
artists. But God is the Master Artist. There is none greater than
the Almighty. And He created the world and the fullness

thereof (Ps. 24:1). Then He looked at it all and said, "It is very good" (Gen. 1:31).

God's Crowning Creation

Genesis chapter 1 is a chronology of creation and of events leading up to the creation of man. Then chapter 2 talks about the sixth day of creation, the day on which He created man.

> And every plant of the field before it was in the earth, and every herb of the field before it grew: for the Lord God had not caused it to rain upon the earth, and there was not a man to till the ground.
>
> But there went up a mist from the earth, and watered the whole face of the ground.
>
> And THE LORD GOD FORMED MAN OF THE DUST OF THE GROUND, and breathed into his nostrils the breath of life; AND MAN BECAME A LIVING SOUL.
>
> *GENESIS 2:5-7*

The word "formed" in verse 7 literally means that God took that dust and molded it into the shape of the human body. But notice that God did something with this creature that He did not do with the cattle, with the fowl of the air, with the beast of the field, or with anything else. It says that God breathed into him *life*! The word "life" there means *life as God has it*. God breathed into man, and man became a living soul. God did not do that with anything else.

Animals are not the same as human beings. Now I realize that some people today want to say that we are animals (and you may want to believe that your great, great, great, great, great grandfather was an orangutan!). But animals are not in the same class as man.

I'm staying with the Bible. My God doesn't look like a monkey, and man didn't come from a monkey. Man came from God. And certain institutions of man, such as marriage, came from God. Therefore, to function optimally in the institution of marriage, we need to find out what God has to say about the union of a man and a woman as husband and wife and put what we learn into practice. Doing so is the foundation for a happy, successful home life, as we will see in the following chapters.

CHAPTER TWO

How To Be a Successful Man and Prepare Yourself For Marriage

Keith A. Butler Sr.

God's breathing into him the breath of life separated and distinguished man from the rest of God's creation. Animals do not have in them God's breath of life. God created the animals and everything else in creation for man's pleasure. Remember He said to Adam, in effect, "You have dominion over every thing that flies, that walks, that swims" (Gen. 1:26,28).

Then the Lord placed Adam somewhere. It says, "...*the Lord God planted a garden eastward in Eden; and there he put the man whom he had formed*" (Gen. 2:8). In this verse we find the first rule of success.

Rule Number One: Find Your *Place*

The first thing you need to know about a man is that he must allow himself to be placed where God wants him. God placed a man in Eden, and I'm here to tell you that if you're going to be a successful husband, father — or a successful man *period* — you're going to have to find out where you're supposed to be and get there! That's the first rule of success: *Find your place and get there!*

Rule Number Two: Find Your *Purpose*

Now at this point in Genesis chapter 2, there is no woman. God put the man there in Eden. Then after giving him a *place*, He gave him something very important — a *purpose*.

> **And out of the ground made the Lord God to grow every tree that is pleasant to the sight, and good for food; and the tree of life also in the midst of the garden, and the tree of knowledge of good and evil....**
>
> **And the Lord God took the man, and put him into the garden of Eden to dress it and to keep it.**
>
> *GENESIS 2:9,15*

After God gave him a place, God gave man a purpose. He said, "Your purpose in the garden is to dress and keep it. You are to guard this garden, and you are to till it.

So the second rule of success is, *find your purpose.* A person who doesn't have purpose doesn't know why he is here, and he is someone who is drifting. In other words, he's not stable.

You aren't ready for anybody else until you find out where you belong and why you are here. God has a plan for your life. He has a call for your life. He has a place of service for you.

God gave the man, Adam, purpose and He gave the man work — He gave the man a job! God gave Adam a job before He gave him a woman. You see, a man ought to be where he's supposed to be. He ought to know what he's about. He ought to have a job before he ever thinks about looking at a woman.

Now part of the problem has been that there are men who are engaging themselves with females before they are ready. They are involved with women before they are ready to deal with a family — before they have secured who they are, before they have found their place in life. And, invariably, the female is confused. Why? Because *he's* confused.

If You Truly Want God's Best, Don't Settle for Less

Single woman, you would be wise to follow God's pattern and design and not involve yourself with a man until you find one who has found his place and purpose. In other words, until a man has secured his employment, he's not ready for you. If you involve yourself with him before then, you'll find yourself hooked up with someone who is in a state of immaturity.

Oftentimes in counseling, we hear women complaining about the immature male in their lives as if they're genuinely surprised. But, you see, when she got him, he was immature. She was probably in fear, and her attitude was, *Well, if I don't take him as he is, somebody else may get him, and I may not get anybody.* She put herself in the position of taking whatever came along. But when you settle for immaturity, you should not be surprised that you reap the fruit of immaturity.

If you settle for less, don't turn around and want the best. If you really want the best, wait for the partner that meets God's qualifications according to His design. Remember, the family is of God, and He knows how to put two people together and develop a godly family from their union.

(Now I'm not talking about two people who are already married to each other. God is not advocating divorce. He can mature the person who wants to grow. Although a spouse may encounter rough patches in marriage and be disappointed in his expectations, he can seek God for growth and progress in the relationship. That progress may take longer to realize than if he had waited to begin with — before saying, "I do." But we have to go about these things according to the Word, not according to the flesh.

Divorce is not the answer. How many people have jumped out of the frying pan into the fire, so to speak, by trying to fix a problem themselves, in their own flesh and strength.)

Now let me paint for you a picture of the immature man. An immature man is intimidated by a mature woman. I've heard single professional women and women of some notoriety and wealth express their concern that no one will want them because they make too much money or because they're too successful or too educated. Well, certainly, they are going to have troubles with the immature man — one who doesn't know his place or purpose. He doesn't know who he is, so he is going to be intimidated by the woman who knows who she is. But a woman like that has no business with a man who isn't mature. *A mature woman belongs with a mature man.*

A mature man has found his place and purpose and is engaged in what he's supposed to be doing in life. And he knows it; he is not wishy-washy or uncertain. And he is not intimidated by you. He knows *who* he is and *why* he is. He knows what his purpose is. And when he sees your qualities and how well you do, he sees you as an asset and not a liability.

So if you as a single woman run up against a male who is insecure and uncertain, don't be disappointed; he is not the man for you to begin with. God has always had whatever it is you need in this earth. He is not in short supply, scrounging around to try to meet your need somehow. No, He's the God of provision, and He will *always* have provision for you if you can wait long enough for Him to send it to you.

This is why I don't advocate getting married too young. Men need time to develop — to find their place and purpose — so they can meet God's qualifications for success and bring joy to the marriage relationship as God intended.

Rule Number Three: Find Your *Reward*

Let's look again at Genesis chapter 2.

> **And the Lord God took the man, and put him into the garden of Eden to dress it and to keep it.**
>
> **And the Lord God commanded the man, saying, Of every tree of the garden thou mayest freely eat.**
>
> *GENESIS 2:15,16*

Now notice what God gave this man. First, God put him in the Garden and said, "Dress it and keep it." Then God said, "Of every tree of the garden thou mayest freely eat (except one)." God gave this man reward for his work. The third rule of success is, *find your reward.*

That's the way it's supposed to be. God intended that man have reward because of his work.

Notice so far in this passage that Adam still doesn't have the woman. God's still working on *him*. God is teaching Adam that there is reward for his labor. God said, "You're tilling this garden as I've instructed you. You're where I put you, and you're doing what I said to do. Therefore, you can have the fruit of your labor. Of every tree of the garden, except one, you may freely eat."

Effort and Reward:
The Cause-and-Effect Link to Success

There is a definite link between effort and reward. To receive fruit or reward without any effort is lust. It's sin. The definition of "sin" is *to miss the mark*. That's the reason God is against the casinos, the lottery, betting, and so forth.

It amazes me that Christian people will try to take numbers from the pastor's sermon and use them for betting at the races and so forth. They'll say, "Oh, he mentioned Philippians 4:9. I'm going to play number 49. I know I'm going to hit something." A person like that needs help!

No, the reward is not by chance. There must always be the link between effort and reward. For a society to have people rewarded without work always destroys the society, because it destroys the people in the society.

The Lord God said to Adam, in effect, "You can have everything in this garden while you're working the garden." Now it's important to note that God put the man in that garden. Then God gave him a job to do, and rewarded him.

You will have the most reward come to you when you have found out where God wants you to be. When you allow Him to place you where He wants you, and you're doing what He wants you to do, that's where the greatest reward is. Now God has called each of us to different things and different places. But regardless of what He has called us to, the reward will be great for you personally wherever you are and whatever you're doing *when you're where He wants you to be and you're doing what He wants you to do.*

Now let's keep reading from this passage in Genesis chapter 2.

> **But of the tree of the knowledge of good and evil, thou shalt not eat of it: for in the day that thou eatest thereof thou shalt surely die.**
>
> *GENESIS 2:17*

We know that God gave Adam a *place,* a *purpose* (a job), and a *reward.* But He also gave him *limits.*

Rule Number Four: Find Your *Limits*

We all have limits in life. There are places we should not go and things we should not get involved in, as in the case of Adam and the tree of the knowledge of good and evil. God told him not to eat of that one tree.

Many men have not learned this lesson yet. They still think, *If I see it and want it, I ought to have it.* But there are limits.

God has not given this man Adam a woman yet, but He's teaching him about limits. If you get a man who has not yet learned limits — if he has not yet learned to be content with where he is right now — he is going to have a problem. (Don't be surprised that he'll be looking to add someone else to your union.)

There are ways you can tell if a man has learned his limits. You can observe how he manages what he has. For example, is he content for the time being with the things he has, or does he just live in debt, buying everything he wants when he wants it? Does he know how to say no to his flesh? Or does he have the attitude, *Whatever I feel like I want, I go get it.*

This is something a female should look at in a man. In other words, she should pay attention to something else besides his muscles! You see, success is not measured only by outward appearances. Success is measured by what's in a person's heart. *Success begins on the inside.* But an inwardly successful man will eventually manifest success on the outside as well, not in his stature or build, but in his character and the rich quality of his life in *every* area.

CHAPTER THREE

Man's Need Was Woman's Purpose

Keith A. Butler Sr.

We read in the first chapter that God created the earth, all the beasts of the earth, and then He created man. We learned from Genesis chapter 1 that each time after God created something, He stepped back and said, "It's good."

Now let's look at Genesis 2:18 at a shift in God's remarks about His creation.

> **And the Lord God said, It is NOT GOOD that the man should be alone; I will make him an help meet for him.**
>
> *GENESIS 2:18*

Everything we've read about so far, God said, "It's good." This is the first time we hear God say something is not good. What is it that God said was not good? *That the man should be alone.*

Most Men Are Not Called to Singleness

God was saying, "Look, you need somebody, man." You see, it's not good for a man to stay single all the days of his life unless God especially calls him to a life of singleness. Now Jesus said in the Book of Matthew that there are men who are called to be eunuchs for the Kingdom of God's sake (Matt. 19:12). The eunuch has no desire or need for a woman. He is totally dedicated to the service of God. That definition rules out most men! Most men are not called to singleness.

Now I'm not saying that a man who needs and wants a woman cannot be totally dedicated to God's service. His wife should serve God with him. But a eunuch isn't concerned with pleasing a wife; his total focus is the Lord.

Now there are men who are not eunuchs but who remain alone because they don't want anybody to change anything about them! They want to go fishing or play ball when they want to without having to answer to anyone. If they want to buy a new car, they can just do it. They don't have to discuss it with their wife.

These men think they're living the high life, and some of the married brothers might agree with them. But most married men are laughing at them, because they know firsthand, in a way single men can't know, that they're living a much happier existence in the bonds of matrimony!

God said, "It's not good for the man to be alone" (Gen. 2:18). But then He said something else in that same verse: "...I will make him an help meet for him."

Woman's Divine Purpose

Now there are a couple of words in that phrase that we need to understand. Number one, God said, "I will make a help for him." Now the word "help" means *assist*. In other words, God was saying, "I will make one that will assist him."

God was beginning to lay out what the wife's role was to be before she was ever created. He was communicating what His design for her was. God said, "... *I will make him an help meet for him.*"

So, number one, God said He was going to make Adam someone who would help him. Number two, God said that she would be "meet" for Adam. The word "meet" in Genesis 2:18 means *adaptable; suitable; and completing.*" In other words, God said, "I will make one who can assist him. She can adapt to him, and she'll be suitable for him. She'll be just right for him. And she will complete him."

Now why did God say that the woman would complete the man? *Because a mature man without a woman is incomplete!*

How To Obtain More Favor From God

Let's look at another Old Testament passage concerning the woman as a wife.

> **Whoso findeth a wife findeth a good thing,**
> **and obtaineth favor of the Lord.**
> *PROVERBS 18:22*

Now why would you as a man get more of the favor of God by finding a wife? Because you are now complete! And now that you are complete, God can have total recourse. He can have the full expression in the earth from you that He wants.

Now don't tell me that there are not enough good women and good men available, because in doing so, you're telling me that God was not smart enough to create what was necessary.

Once when my son was in school, I attended one of his classes (as a good parent should, and we'll talk about parenting later in this book). I wanted to know what they were teaching my boy in science class. I wasn't just going to trust the teacher. I was going to read the book myself and hear what the teacher had to say about it. One of the things I heard this teacher say was, "There's not enough food on the planet," and then she proceeded to talk about what should be done because there's not enough food to sustain our growing population.

Afterward, I said to her, "From the beginning, God knew that this time — this specific year in time — would exist. He has always known what the population would be, and He created enough food for everybody on the planet. Food shortage is not the problem. Food-*hoarding* or food-*destroying* might be issues, but a lack of food isn't the problem."

So when I hear single people saying there aren't enough men and women available, I take issue with them. God has created enough wives for husbands, and enough husbands for wives. It's not that there aren't enough; the issue is whether they've been *developed*.

What Woman Is *Not*

So we know that woman's divine purpose was to be a help *meet* for her husband; she was to be made an "assister" *suitable* for him. Now since she's supposed to be what we refer to as a "helpmeet" for him, that means she is not his mama! Her role is to *assist* him, not *dominate* him.

Let's look at First Corinthians chapter 11 at God's divine order for the home.

> **But I would have you know, that the head of every man is Christ; and the head of the woman is the man; and the head of Christ is God.**
>
> *1 CORINTHIANS 11:3*

Let's look at the first part of that verse first: *"But I would have you know, that the head of every man is Christ...."* That's the way it ought to be. Every man should be submitted to God first and foremost. And if he's where God wants him to be, doing what God wants him to do, then he is submitted to Christ.

Let's continue reading in First Corinthians 11.

> **. . . the head of every man is Christ; and the head of the woman is the man; and the head of Christ is God. . . .**
>
> **For the man is not of the woman; but the woman of the man.**
>
> **Neither was the man created for the woman; but the woman for the man.**
>
> *1 CORINTHIANS 11:3,8,9*

Now when we go back to Genesis chapter 2, we can clearly see what these verses are saying. The man is submitted to Christ. The woman is submitted to the man, to her husband. Woman was created *from* man *for* him. That's what the Bible says. God said, "I will make a helpmeet, an *assister*, for Adam who will be *adaptable* to him, *suitable* for him, and who will *complete* him" (Gen. 2:18).

Now God said that in verse 18, but notice He didn't do it right then.

> **And the Lord God said, It is not good that the man should be alone; I will make him an help meet for him.**
>
> **And out of the ground the Lord God formed every beast of the field, and every fowl of the air; and brought them unto Adam to see what he would call them: and whatsoever Adam called every living creature, that was the name thereof.**
>
> **And Adam gave names to all cattle, and to the fowl of the air, and to every beast of the field; BUT FOR ADAM THERE WAS NOT FOUND AN HELP MEET FOR HIM.**
>
> *GENESIS 2:18-20*

Now God said in advance what He was going to do, but He didn't create the woman yet. He then gave the man some more chores and responsibilities. God tells him, "I'm going to create a helpmeet for you," but He first continues to work on the man. The man is still developing his role. Adam gave names to the cattle, the fowl of the air, and the beasts of the field, but there was not one among them that was suitable as a help for Adam (v. 20).

In other words, God looked at that bear and said, "No, that isn't going to work"! There was nothing on earth of God's creation that was right for Adam.

> **And the Lord God caused a deep sleep to fall upon Adam, and he slept: and he took one of his ribs, and closed up the flesh instead thereof;**
>
> **And the rib, which the Lord God had taken from man made he a woman, and brought her unto the man.**
>
> *GENESIS 2:21,22*

Now I want you to notice that God did not take this woman from Adam's head to be over him. And He didn't take this woman from his feet for him to stand on her. He took her from his rib to stand beside him.

The Woman as a Protector

The ribs cover the heart and other vital organs. A rib has the ability to expand and contract according to the body's needs. And that's what woman's role is. She is made of the rib. She's made to be able to move left and right with her husband. Whichever way he needs to go, she can go. She can bless him and help him. And she covers or protects him.

Now I don't care how big and strong or rough and tough a man is, he still needs protecting. Sometimes you see a man who has huge biceps, a big, thick neck, and who is strong as an ox — but on the inside, he could be as soft as a kitten.

Recently, I was ministering to the men of my church at a men's meeting. At the end of the message, many of them came up to talk to me. Some of them had tears in their eyes, crying before God because He touched their hearts. One guy hugged me, and he was a big brother — one of those fellows with no neck! He was crying like a baby.

But, you see, just because a man may appear strong, he can be soft on the inside. Men may look rough and tough, but they still hurt and bleed emotionally. And they need to be protected. Since God knew that, you as a man ought to allow yourself to be protected by what He sent you to protect you — *your wife*!

Different Roles — One Purpose

God made men and women different. Anybody notice that? Some psychologists and sociologists have tried to make them out to be the same. But they are quite different. Not only do they *look* different, their *roles* are different. They were made for different purposes. They have different jobs, and God gave them the equipment for each of their jobs.

The 'Sense' of a Woman

Your wife has the equipment to see things you need protecting from. She can see danger coming that you don't always see. You might be just marching blindly on your merry way, but she senses when there's trouble lurking ahead. She may not be able to articulate exactly what it is in a way that you'll understand it, because men like things that are logical. They don't like, "Well, I *sense* such-and-such."

Men like *a-b-c* or *1-2-3* or *1 plus 1 equals 2*. They don't delve in things that aren't logical! But sometimes in life, things don't quite work that way. Everything is not as simple as *1-2-3*. A woman may not be able to lay it all out logically, but she knows. God made her that way. And a wise husband will allow his wife to function in her role. He will trust her in her role as an assister, a helpmeet.

Let me tell you what a good manager in the work world does. A smart boss will recognize the abilities of those who work with him, and he will utilize those people according to their abilities instead of trying to do everything himself.

It is deception for a person to think he is self-sufficient, needing nothing or no one. You've heard it said, "No man is an island." The same is true in marriage. A smart husband will recognize his wife's gifts and abilities and will listen to her when she's trying to function in her role.

When a wife is not listened to, she gets frustrated. And when the husband keeps banging his head against the wall, so to speak, and messing up, *he* gets frustrated. But God made them as one unit; together you have the entire package. That's why husband and wife need to understand each other's role and allow the other to function in that role.

Don't Deprive a Man
Of the Thrill of the Chase!

We already read Proverbs 18:22, which says, *"Whoso findeth a wife findeth a good thing, and obtaineth favour of the Lord."* Notice that this verse says, *"Whoso findeth a wife...."* That "whoso" has to be talking about the man, so we can conclude that the man does the finding, not the woman.

God intended that the man do the chasing and that the woman be pursued. Unfortunately, today you oftentimes see it happening the other way around. A lot of women are doing the pursuing, and the men are doing the running! Then many of these women wonder, *How come he doesn't want me?* It's probably because they are out of their role.

Men like the chase. They like a *good* chase! They like to feel as if they have to work for this "finding a wife" thing, because men like to conquer. Well, there's nothing left to pursue and conquer when a man attends a church as a first-time visitor, for example, and before he sits down, five ladies give him their phone numbers! He doesn't want that.

Right after I surrendered my life to Jesus, I went to a certain church, and during the first month I attended there, I had more phone numbers given to me by ladies than you could imagine! Now I didn't ask for the phone numbers. Ladies would just walk up and say, "Here's my number."

The woman I eventually married attended that same church, but she acted as if I didn't even exist! Once a single buddy of mine and I were discussing the women in the church, going down the list, so to speak, talking about their attributes as well as potential liabilities. When my wife's name was mentioned, I said, "I don't know what her problem is. She acts like we don't even exist."

But I'll tell you what. That made her *real* interesting! It made her very mysterious to me, and I wanted to solve that mystery! I knew the very first time I saw her that I liked the way she looked. I liked the way she walked, the way she carried herself. I was amazed at how God assembled that woman!

But she never paid me any mind. I mean, she was cool and collected. I tried to talk to her, and she'd just say, "Hello" and keep walking. If you tried to say hello to some of the ladies, they'd answer, *"Oh, hi! Hi! Hi!"* They were *too* eager, and they left nothing to the pursuit.

But Deborah would say, "Hello" and then not hang around. Finally, I said to my buddy, "She's the one I've got to get!" It took a year to even get her to go out with me. But once she did, it was all over. She was smitten! And I got her. She was and still is worth the pursuit. (It was a *good* chase!)

'Bone of My Bone, Flesh of My Flesh'

What is woman to man and what is her purpose? The woman is the glory of man (1 Cor. 11:7). We read that God put Adam in a deep sleep and made from one of his ribs a woman (Gen 2: 21,22). Let's read how Adam responded when God presented her to him.

> **And Adam said, This is now bone of my bones, and flesh of my flesh: she shall be called Woman. . . .**
>
> *GENESIS 2:23*

Now before God made woman, He looked at the bear and said, "The bear is not right for you." I can also imagine God looking at the giraffe and saying, "No, that's not it, either." (And Adam probably answered, "You got that right!")

But when Adam woke up from that deep sleep, I can just hear God saying, "Adam, I made something for you." And then He brought woman out to Adam. I believe that's when Adam exclaimed, "*Whoa! Man!* She shall be called *Wo-man!*" (That's my theory on how woman was named!)

The Bible makes clear a woman's glorious purpose. She was created to help man. The first woman, Eve, was God's crowning creation to be a helpmate to Adam. And she was created well-suited for and capable of fulfilling that divine role.

CHAPTER FOUR

A 'Help' Meet For Him

Deborah L. Butler

Notice that before God told Adam to replenish the earth, He talked about creating the woman, because there was no way man could replenish the earth without the woman (*see* Genesis 1:27 and 28).

In Genesis 1, for everything that God made, He said, "It is good." However, Genesis 2:19 and 20 shows us that when God created all the animals and brought them to Adam to name, among all the animals, there was not a help meet, or suitable, for Adam.

> **And out of the ground the Lord God formed every beast of the field, and every fowl of the air; and brought them unto Adam to see what he would call them: and whatsoever Adam called every living creature, that was the name thereof.**

> **And Adam gave names to all cattle, and to the fowl of the air, and to every beast of the field; BUT FOR ADAM THERE WAS NOT FOUND AN HELP MEET FOR HIM.**
>
> *GENESIS 2:19,20*

No matter what you have heard, a dog is *not* a man's best friend! No dog — no animal — can help a man the way God intended. That is why when God made man, and looked at Adam standing there alone, He said, "That is not good."

> **And the Lord God said, It is NOT GOOD that the man should be alone; I will make him an help meet for him.**
>
> *GENESIS 2:18*

God said, "It's not good for man to be alone." Man needed a "helpmeet." This verse is an important one to remember in our study. If you as a woman catch on to what it is telling you, your attitude toward men will change.

As my husband said previously, not one of all the animals God created was a suitable help for man. A dog can't be man's best friend, because a dog can't help a man do anything, really, and God has already said, after "dog" was created, that man needed a helper!

Then the Lord God said, "I will make him a help that's meet for him."

> **And the Lord God caused a deep sleep to fall upon Adam, and he slept: and he took one of his ribs, and closed up the flesh instead thereof;**

> **And the rib, which the Lord God had taken from man, made he a woman, and brought her unto the man.**
>
> **And Adam said, This is now bone of my bones, and flesh of my flesh: she shall be called Woman, because she was taken out of Man.**
>
> *GENESIS 2:21-23*

What every woman needs to see is, if it wasn't for the fact that God's man needed help, she wouldn't be here! She would not exist.

Woman is here for man. And you as a Christian woman are here for a man of God. Don't search for a man out in the world. If you get a man from the world, you're going to end up with the wrong one. You need a man of God in your life, so you need to wait until God presents you to him.

That's very important, because some women try to present *themselves*. But even if you as a single woman believe God told you who your husband is, you need to keep it quiet, between you and God. Don't go tell the man, "I think you're my husband." That's very unbecoming and, really, it's unbelieving. The Bible says that he (or she) that believes shall not make haste" (Isa. 28:16).

If you really believe God has spoken to you, you will wait patiently and let God work out the arrangements, just as He did for Adam when He formed Eve — a help meet for Adam — and presented her to him.

Men Need Help!

Bishop Butler talked about a man's need to find his purpose. But a woman needs to know her purpose too. She needs to realize that women are on this earth because men needed help! And some men need *help help*! (And I'm not talking about him needing two women; it only takes one.)

Genesis 2:18 says, *"...It is not good that the man should be alone; I will make him an HELP meet for him."* The word "help" there means *assist*.

Then verse 20 says, *"And Adam gave names to all cattle, and to the fowl of the air, and to every beast of the field; but for Adam there was not found an HELP MEET for him."* The phrase "help meet" in this verse means, in essence, *one who assists and is adaptable, suitable, and complementary to another*. Therefore, as a wife, you are to assist your husband and be adaptable, suitable, and complementary to him.

A Wife Is To Complete Her Husband

Now when I say "complementary," I'm not talking about the word complimentary (although it is important, as we will see, that wives pay compliments to their husband). To complement means *to fill; supply for a deficiency;* or *complete*. We need to understand that every man has a deficiency, as does every woman. This is one reason why it is so important that a woman not present herself to a man as a prospective help-meet. She does not know what his particular deficiency is. She may be deficient in the same area! That is why we have to let God do the presenting.

As a man, you need to be wary of women who chase after you. Do not fall into the devil's trap made to keep you from fulfilling God's will in your relationships and in your calling. You need a woman who will *complete* you. You need someone who will supply for your deficiency, not bring more attention to it because she is deficient in the same area.

As a word to men, if you get the right woman, you don't need to look for another one. And if you get the wrong woman, you *still* don't need to look for another one! You need to get on your knees and talk to God about making that relationship right. Stop looking for somebody else; stop looking to throw your woman away. She is yours now.

You see, God gave us free choice — the right to choose. So, although He had a woman out there for you, if you decided to supercede what God had for you, you made your choice, and now you have to live with that woman. That seems hard, but the good news is, God is an awesome God. He's an excellent God. And if you'll take your part and do what you're supposed to do, God will turn your mess into an excellent, beautiful marriage.

So if you as a married man feel you married the wrong woman, you can't say, "Well, she's not the right one. I'm going to get rid of her and start over." No, you married her. You said, "I do"; she is now the right one!

The same thing is true for women. You married him; you're the one who said, "I do." Nobody opened your mouth and made you say it. So now he's the right man for you. You made a choice. You may feel unhappy, but the first thing you need to do is *not* run to divorce court! No, the first thing you need to do is seek God so you can get to the point where you can pray for him. Through prayer and your fellowship with God, you'll begin to see that man the way God sees him, and things will be so different for you.

See Them As God Does

The best thing we can do to make things right in our marriage is to pray for our spouse so we can begin to see them the way God sees them. When we see through God's eyes, we will see our mate as valuable and precious. That is how God sees us, no matter what we have or haven't done.

We should not talk about ourselves or our husband or wife as anything less than valuable and precious. Anyone who demeans himself or anyone else, whom God has made, is actually calling Him a liar.

Don't talk negatively about yourself, and don't hang out with someone who talks negatively about you. God says you are valuable and precious. That means it's settled: You *are* valuable and precious. You may not act that way at first, but the evidence will come by faith as you pray for yourself and for your spouse.

When you begin to see your husband or wife as valuable and precious, your attitude toward him or her will change and, along with that, your outlook will change. You will think and act differently.

A Wife Should Compliment Her Husband

As a woman begins to see her husband through God's eyes, she becomes skilled in giving him compliments. This is something a help meet for her husband does well. Sadly, many women do not compliment their husband because their own egos get too big. This is not only selfish, but also risky behavior.

The Lord once told me that one of the most successful ways other women draw men away from their wives is by complimenting them. It works especially well when the man's wife is not complimenting him.

Many women will not compliment a man unless she is out to get him. Then when they get him, they don't want to compliment him anymore. Their attitude might be, "Well, I'm married now, so I can take it easy."

If you are a married woman, you may sometimes feel as though your husband is not worth a compliment. Well, the Word has the answer for you: "Call those things which be not as though they are" (Rom. 4:17)! Compliment him all the time. Discover different ways to use your words to draw attention to something you find that he does right. Become skilled in complimenting him.

A Wife Should Be a Companion to Her Husband

Finally, in order to help your husband, you need to spend time with him. Some women spend more time with other people than with their own husband. That is not right. We need to spend the majority of our time with our spouse. Your husband should be your best friend. If your spouse is not your best friend, then read on and discover how you can develop that friendship so that you can enjoy the kind of marriage God wants for you!

CHAPTER FIVE

The Basics of a Harmonious Home

Keith A. Butler Sr.

Earlier, we read that God made woman and presented her to the man Adam. Adam responded, *"...This is now bone of my bones, and flesh of my flesh: she shall be called Woman, because she was taken out of Man"* (Gen. 2:23).

Then notice what the next verse says. *"Therefore shall a man leave his father and his mother, and shall cleave unto his wife: and they shall be one flesh"* (v. 24).

'Leave and Cleave' — Some of God's First Instructions on Marriage

Now those were inspired words: *"...a man [shall] leave his father and his mother, and shall cleave unto his wife: and they shall be one flesh."* In this verse, a man leaving father and mother means that he is now going to be exclusive to his wife. And leaving father and mother doesn't just mean leaving their home to make a new home with your wife. It means leaving father and mother's home, their money, their protection, and even their counsel. In other words, when a man marries, he cuts ties, in a sense, with his family. He has a new family now.

Now if you try and keep the strings of the old family attached to the new family, you are going to have trouble. It's called "interference" when you have a man's mother trying to dictate certain things to his wife.

Mother, you must understand that when your son takes on a wife, you are no longer the woman in his life. You must "cut the cord" and let him go to her whether you like her or not. It's not your decision; it's his decision. And once he makes the decision to choose her, your attitude should be, *That's his choice, and I'm going to support my boy.*

Someone said, "That seems kind of hard. I mean, surely you've heard the classic rebuttal of a mother about her son, 'But nobody's good enough for my Johnny.'"

Well, that might seemingly be the case. But Johnny thinks she's good enough! And if Johnny thinks she's good enough, that's good enough! Johnny's mother really has no more comment to make. She should have nothing but good to say about his wife. If she's concerned, she should pray. She should talk to God, not to Johnny, about it.

So Mother (and Father too), you have to let your son go when he finds a wife. If he's a man, he must separate himself from you. Now he'll visit you and call just to talk to you and fellowship with you sometimes. But his first responsibility becomes his wife and the care of his new family.

There should never be a collision in a man's life of his mother and his wife. A man should not have to be "whip-sawed"— played against from both sides — by having to choose between his wife and his mama. In other words,

Mama should not move into son's house! If the situation dictates, Son should spend the money to set Mama up somewhere. But keep Mama out of the house. Get her a house of her own.

There can only be one woman of the house! You could put Mama in the house with Wife and, even if they're both saved, sanctified, and filled with the Holy Ghost, you are still going to have a manifestation of the devil! For example, Mama likes *this* décor; Wife likes *that* décor. Mama likes the kitchen set up *this* way; Wife likes it set up *that* way. Mama likes the furniture arranged *this* way; Wife likes the furniture arranged *that* way.

No two women are the same. They don't look the same; they don't think the same; they don't have the same tastes. They don't do *anything* exactly the same. And if you put them both in the same household together, you are going to have a problem.

So if necessary, if you as a husband must assist your mother (and you should help your mother), do it with wisdom. The Word of God tells us that we should honor our parents (Eph. 6:2). And you as a married couple should help each other's mothers. But use wisdom and discretion. Don't put two women who could potentially be the head of the house in the same house together!

Many times you'll hear a mother-in-law say about her daughter-in-law, "She doesn't respect me." But more often than not, what she really means is, "She doesn't do what I want"! More marriages have been wrecked and lives destroyed over interfering parents and by children who *allowed* parents to interfere because they didn't "leave and cleave" as the Bible says.

A house will become a home where there is peace and joy when people just obey the Bible. And one thing the Bible says regarding a harmonious home is, *"...a man* [shall] *leave his father and his mother, and shall cleave unto his wife..."* (Gen. 2:24).

Now the Hebrew word "cleave" in this verse means, in effect, that he runs after her — pursues her — and sticks to her. He runs after his wife. He's always chasing her, which means she's always doing things that warrant the chase.

Some women don't encourage their men to continue to chase them once they are married. For example, before she married that man, she smelled good, looked good, and she never let him see her in rollers! She was always her best. But after the man marries her, it's rollers all the way, baby! She "got" him, so now she just sits back.

Some women work diligently on maintaining their proper weight and shape before they get married. They watch what they eat, and they go to the gym. They want to make sure they're at the top of their game. They want to get that man!

But after they get married, they don't seem to care about their weight anymore. They don't care that they've put on thirty pounds. Well, of course, he wanted to chase you before you were married; he liked what he saw. You kept him interested, because you looked different every time he saw you. You took great care with your appearance.

The same can be true with men. Before he married that woman, he opened doors for her. He talked to her nice and treated her with kindness. He was a perfect gentleman! He may have even put on cologne for the first time in his life! He thought about places to take her that would get her attention and impress her. He couldn't wait to get home from work so he could call and talk to her. Why? *Because he was on a mission to get that woman!*

Then after he got her, no more cologne, no more romance, and no more pursuit. He doesn't spend time with her, and she's thinking he doesn't love her anymore. He's just enjoying his hot meals in the evening and getting fat and sassy. He won't talk to her all day long, except for when it's time for bed. Then he says, "Come here, baby," but she says, "I don't know you!"

"Therefore shall a man leave his father and his mother, and shall cleave [pursue, stick] *unto his wife: and they shall be one flesh."*

The last part of that verse is important: *"...and they shall be one flesh"* (Gen. 2:24). Family is about oneness. We become one in name and in aim, purpose, thought, and direction. (We will look at this further in another chapter.) We also have the potential to become unstoppable for the Kingdom of God. Agreement and unity between a husband and wife create a powerful force through which God can move.

That's why Satan attacks Christian marriages. He wants to stop the plan and purpose of God from being fulfilled. He wants to destroy homes, rob men and women of their Christian witness, and shipwreck their faith.

The Battle for Independence

Keith A. Butler Sr.

God made the woman to help man, but He also made her to be dependent upon him. This interdependence is God's plan and design, as we will study in more detail in the next chapter. However, when one or both parties in a marriage battle for their independence, there will be trouble. Adam and Eve found this fact out the hard way, and we have been seeing the result of their error played out ever since.

As we already read, Genesis 2:22 says concerning the creation of woman, *"And the rib, which the Lord God had taken from man, made he a woman, and brought her unto the man."* That word "made" there means *built*. God had formed Adam's body out of the dust of the ground, and then He removed a rib from that man. In quick review of material I discussed previously, the rib's job is to cover the vital organs, and ribs can contract or expand based upon the need. God built woman from that rib; she is built to adapt to her husband.

Woman is different from man. He is formed out of the dust, whereas she is formed from his rib. She is made out of dust only in the sense that she is made out of *man,* who is made out of dust. However, God handcrafted her. She is the most beautiful thing God ever made.

God's Command for Marriage

Then God presented Eve to Adam, and performed the first marriage ceremony. Verse 24 records God's command regarding not only their marriage, but the very institution of marriage.

> **Therefore shall a man leave his father and his mother, and shall cleave unto his wife: and they shall be one flesh.**
>
> *GENESIS 2:24*

Notice from this verse that a *man* shall leave his father and mother. God was not talking about a *boy!*

Did you know that age, height, and weight do not distinguish a boy from a man? Just because a human male happens to be twenty-five years old, six feet tall, and 200 pounds does not make him a man. If he is immature, he is merely a full-sized male! He is not the kind of person to whom God addressed this command. God was speaking to *men.*

A Man Shall Cleave to His Wife — The Two Shall Be One

God said in Genesis 2:24, "…[a man] *shall cleave unto his wife: and they shall be one flesh."* The word "cleave" means *to run after; pursue; stick to hard.* A man should always be running after his wife, and, of course, she should always be making it easy, desirable, for him to do so.

God also said in Genesis 2:24 that a man and a woman shall become "one flesh." Of course, He meant they would be one physically. When a man and a woman are legally, publicly, properly married to each other, God wants them to be one sexually. Additionally, they shall be one in name, purpose, and direction.

In the first two and a half chapters of Genesis, Adam and Eve shared the name "Adam." He is the male Adam, and she is the female Adam. Her name did not become Eve until after they sinned (Gen. 3:20). Until that point in time, they were one in name, purpose, and direction. They were one, *period*.

The whole issue of names is important according to Scripture. When a woman joins herself to a man in holy matrimony, she takes his name. They become one in name. When a person becomes so independent that she decides, "I don't want his name," she has already made a decision not to operate in unity. This can be detrimental to a marriage, because unity is the whole basis for a successful marriage and family.

Marriage is about oneness. It is not about two people going in different directions. It is not about two individuals' spheres of influence.

Each single person has a sphere of influence. Such a person operates as "me." However, *married* people operate as "we." There is a big difference between "me" and "we." When it is "me," I do not have to consider, share with, or consult anybody except God. When it is "we," I am attached. If I want to move in a certain direction, I have to consult the other half of "we." I may have to wait until the other part of "we" is ready to go that way.

Oneness is also what *family* is about. A husband and wife are not only accountable to one another, but to their kids, because the building and maintaining of a family is a group effort.

When our kids were old enough, we gave them phones and pagers so that they could check in with us. We also had phones and pagers so that we could check in with them. It is a two-way street, so to speak. Not only do *we* know where our children are; *they* know where we are. We hold each other accountable. You see, family is not about independence; it is about unity.

The First Attack on the Family

Satan's goal is to divide and conquer. In the beginning of Adam and Eve's relationship, as recorded in Genesis 1 and 2, God said, "They shall be one. She will help him, and they will operate as one together." As we read further in Genesis, though, we see Satan's first attack on the family. Satan's attacking marriages is nothing new. He came against the first family, Adam and Eve, and he is still coming against families today.

> Now the serpent was more subtil [cunning] than any beast of the field which the Lord God had made. And he said unto the woman, Yea, hath God said, Ye shall not eat of every tree of the garden?
>
> And the woman said unto the serpent, We may eat of the fruit of the trees of the garden.
>
> *GENESIS 3:1,2*

Notice how Satan attacked: "He said unto the woman." The enemy did not come up against him *and* her. He chose to come at just one of them.

Satan's tricks have not changed; he does not have any new tricks. He still wants to divide husband and wife in order to conquer them and their seed. In order to overcome his attacks against our families, we must always remember that family life is not about independence; it is about being dependent on each other. *Independence causes the collapse of families.*

This is why Satan immediately came and tried to split the first woman off from the first man and appeal to her independence. After successfully drawing Eve apart, Satan said, "*You* shall not eat of every tree of the garden?" The woman said unto the serpent, "*We* may not eat of every tree in the garden. "

Remember, Genesis 2:25 says about Adam and Eve, *"And they were both naked, the man and his wife, and were not ashamed."* God performed the first wedding union whereby Adam and Eve were made husband and wife. They were made one flesh. But notice that when Satan came to attack, he said to Eve, *"What about you?"* He said to her, *"...Yea, hath God said, YE shall not eat of every tree of the garden?"*

When you're single, it's *"me."* When you're married, it's *"we."* But Satan said, "Has God said that *you* shall not eat of every tree?"

Eve responded properly that time, saying, *"...WE may eat of the fruit of the trees of the garden: But of the fruit of the tree which is in the midst of the garden, God hath said, Ye* [talking about both Adam and Eve] *shall not eat of it, neither shall ye touch it, lest ye die"* (Gen. 3:2,3).

Satan said to Eve, "*You* shall not eat of every tree of the garden? Is that what God said?" She replied, "*We* shouldn't." Now Eve spoke properly, because the command or order given by God was for him and her. She had not yet been created when God had told Adam not to partake of this tree in the midst of the garden. Her husband was the one who had communicated to her what God had said.

Man Discovers God's Order for the Family

This tells us who should be the first one seeking the face of God concerning His will for the family: the husband and father. The husband and father should be the one who prays and seeks the face of God to receive instructions from God about what the family is to do. This further indicates that a single man who has not yet learned how to hear from God is not ready to lead a family.

Adam was fit for the task of listening to God and telling his family God's will for them. He heard from God and communicated God's command to Eve. And Eve is responding properly at this point to Satan's temptation as she tells him, "We may not eat of the fruit of tree in the midst of the garden."

Now this is very important to note, because so often the problems in the marriage, which filter down into problems with the children and with finances and so forth, are a result of married people still trying to act as though they are single.

Marriage is about "*we*," not "*me*." But notice that the first thing Satan did was show up and say, "Now what about *you*? What do *you* think about this?"

I've dealt with this same issue in the more than twenty years I've been a pastor. I've seen over and over again people who are legally married trying to function as though they are single. They make independent decisions, independent money, and they live independent lives. And it gets them in trouble.

I've even seen couples take independent vacations! Now I've got news for you, when you go on vacation, you need to go with your husband or wife. Husband, you have no business out there on the beach by yourself! That's how you get in trouble. When your wife is sitting next you, it keeps you in check. Left to yourself, you could be as dangerous as an out-of-control machine gun!

One of the first things that the enemy will attempt to do with your new marriage union is sever you from being one with your mate. He'll try to get you thinking, *It's what I want.* But, no, you do what *you* want *before* you get married! When you get married, it's not just what *you* want anymore. Now most people will say, "Of course. We know that." But in reality, many of them are not living it.

We said before that Christ is the head of the man, and man is the head of the woman, his wife (1 Cor. 11:3). The man should be the first in a marriage who seeks the face of God. He should hear from God about his family. I'm not saying that God won't speak to the wife, because, of course, we know He will. But the husband is supposed to be the leader, and he should be the one spending time before God to get the direction his family needs.

I'm talking about God's order of things, not just some good idea. When a household is in divine order, God's blessing is on that house. Direction is flowing because the head of the house, the husband, is taking his place of leadership.

Notice that when God said, "… *Of every tree of the garden thou mayest freely eat: But of the tree of the knowledge of good and evil, thou shalt not eat of it: for in the day that thou eatest thereof thou shalt surely die*" (Gen. 2:16,17), He said it to

Adam. Eve had not even been created yet. How did Eve find out what God had said? *Through her husband.* He shared with her what God said, but he added a little extra to it.

Eve told the serpent, the devil, in the garden, "*...of the fruit of the tree which is in the midst of the garden, God hath said, Ye shall not eat of it, NEITHER SHALL YE TOUCH IT, lest ye die*" (Gen. 3:3). But when God told this to Adam in Genesis chapter 2, He did not tell Adam that he couldn't touch it. God said, "*... of the tree of the knowledge of good and evil, THOU SHALT NOT EAT...*" (Gen. 2:17).

So God did not tell Adam that he couldn't touch the tree, but Eve told the devil that that's what God had said. Adam received direction from God, and Eve received God's direction from Adam. But, apparently, Adam told Eve, "We're not to eat of this tree, and don't you touch it, either." So that's what she told the serpent.

Notice how the serpent immediately challenges God's Word and tries to divide Eve and her husband.

> **And the serpent said unto the woman,**
> **Ye shall not surely die.**
>
> *GENESIS 3:4*

The devil said, "No, you're not going to die." He blatantly challenged God Almighty! The devil said, "Well, God didn't really mean that. He didn't really mean what He said. It's not like that at all. No, things are going to be better when you eat of that tree."

Let's continue reading what the devil said to Eve.

> **For God doth know that in the day ye eat
> thereof, then your eyes shall be opened,
> and ye shall be as gods, knowing good and
> evil.**
>
> *GENESIS 3:5*

What was the devil trying to do? He was trying to cut Eve off from her husband to make her independent of him. He basically told her, "You can make your own decisions; you can be your own god."

That attitude has prevailed to this day. And in marriage, instead of couples operating together in unity and oneness, they're operating as separate entities. They've decided to make their own decisions and become their own gods. Whether they realize it or not, their attitude is, *Forget what God said about what I'm supposed to do in marriage. I don't need anybody to tell me what to do. I'm going to do my own thing. I'm going to do what I think I should do.*

That's the way the devil went at Eve to cut her off. And she fell for it.

> **And when the woman saw that the tree
> was good for food, and that it was pleasant
> to the eyes, and a tree to be desired to make
> one wise, she took of the fruit thereof, and
> did eat....**
>
> *GENESIS 3:6*

Several things happened here. First, Eve allowed her attention to be diverted from what God had told her husband. She became fixated on that tree when she shouldn't have, and she became attracted to it. (That same kind of thing happens today. You need to watch what you give your time and attention to.)

The Day 'Ye' Won Out and 'We' Fell

When the enemy tempted Eve, for a time she stood strong on God's command that came to her through Adam, saying, "We may not eat." But Satan was not moved by that "we" business at all. He addressed Eve as an individual "me" rather than as a family member "we." He appealed to her independence. His plan of attack was to cut the woman off from the man, to isolate her. He caused her to become focused on herself and to forget her husband. Satan said to her, "Look, Honey, this is what you can have. This is what you can be. You are independent."

Although Eve started off all right answering Satan's temptation, when the devil kept saying, "Ye," eventually "ye" won out and caused "we" (both of them) to fall. She bought into the devil's trick; and in buying into it, both she and her husband were sunk (Gen. 3:6).

Eve took of that tree and ate. And the rest of that verse says, *"… and gave also unto her husband with her; and he did eat."* Both of them died spiritually.

So we know that Satan attacked the first family, and the way he did it was by trying to divide them. He brought Adam and Eve from living as one flesh to living as two singles — from oneness to singleness.

What can we learn from that situation today? When you are a single adult, you have to account to no one. But when you are a married person, you must account to your mate. That's the way the family is made. We have to protect harmony in the home by following God's divine order. When we function in our God-given roles and follow God's order, we

won't be divided. We might be attacked, but we won't suc-
cumb to those attacks. We won't give in and be defeated.
We'll stay as one and live in God's blessings for our home
and family.

Family Is About Teamwork

Independence is still the enemy of marriage and family.
But we know that marriage and family is not about independence; it is about interdependence. It is about depending
on one another, working as a team.

When a team member decides to operate on his own,
without his teammates, he prevents the team from winning.
It works the same way in "family teams" as it does in sports
teams. If the "Coach," who is God, draws up a play but one
member of the team says, "I don't care what the rest of you
are doing; you can go over there if you want, but I'm going
over here to do what *I* want to do," that team will be short a
player. That team will have chaos on the court, so to speak,
and will be unsuccessful as a family.

If you are a single person who wants to be married, you
need to recognize that you must be willing to give up your
independence. If you are not willing to give up your independence regarding your money, career, time, body, and so
forth, you are not yet prepared for marriage and family.

The enemy has understood this since the introduction of
the family to the earth. That is why he drew Eve apart and
emphasized her individuality.

"You, you, you," the serpent said. "Look what you can do
when you stand on your own, by yourself."

Have you ever heard him saying that to you? If so,
remember that even if you are a single person, you cannot

make it on your own. No matter who you are, you need to be dependent on God to be successful.

The same principle applies to the marriage union. Certainly, both the husband and wife must look to God and trust Him and His Word. But they need to look to each other, too, instead of outside the marriage relationship to try and meet their needs.

This is the way God views marriage: A wife is here to please her husband; a husband is here to please his wife (1 Cor. 7:33,34). When a married person pleases one's spouse, he or she is pleasing the Lord!

We are not here to please ourselves. Our unwillingness to view marriage this way is what creates the tension and strife in marriage and family. Our desire for independence is what tears the structure of our families apart. However, if we will read the Word and adjust our thinking to God's way of thinking about marriage and family, we will be successful. The devil will never again defeat us if we will stand up in the Name of Jesus and fight the battle for unity and dependence upon one another in our marriages and in our families.

CHAPTER SEVEN

God's Structural Design
For the Family

Keith A. Butler Sr.

We know that God instituted the family unit; God is the author of the home and family. And He has a carefully structured design for the family that, if followed, would eliminate much of the heartache and difficulties we have in families today. For example, one person's act of disobedience to God's plan for the way a family should run could cause untold consequences to that family unit that could even affect the family's future generations.

That's why it's so important to discover how God intends the family to operate and then to operate accordingly. We will be blessed, and our loved ones will be blessed, if we do.

Satan does not want families to be blessed and to honor and glorify God in the earth. His goal is to destroy the family structure as instituted by God because he knows that weakened families will weaken the Church, the Body of Christ, as well as weaken a nation. That's why Satan attacks families so much. We should not be surprised, but we *should* be ready so we can withstand those attacks and remain strong in the blessing of home and family that God has given us.

As we found in Chapter 6, Satan's first plan of attack on the first family was to get the woman to be independent of her husband. We discovered that family is about depending on one another, not being independent of each other. We know that Eve gave in to the devil's temptation to step out of her dependent role.

Genesis 3:6 records her first independent act.

> **And when the woman SAW that the tree was good for food, and that it was pleasant to the eyes, and a tree to be desired to make one wise, she took of the fruit thereof, and did eat, and gave also unto her husband with her; and he did eat.**
>
> *GENESIS 3:6*

Notice what happened to Eve. First of all, she *looked.* When a person becomes independent, instead of depending on one another according to God's way, that person's eyes will start looking where they should not.

Furthermore, when that person starts looking, the "eye candy" that the enemy has provided for the individual will look good! It won't be an eyesore. This verse says that the fruit was "pleasant to the eyes." The Word of God tells us that after Eve saw the tree, she then partook of it. Once the enemy can get our attention and divert our eyes from God's way, and then get us looking at *his* way, it will not be long before we are partaking of Satan's way of doing things.

Adam Was Left With a Choice

When Eve ate of the forbidden fruit, of course, she died spiritually. Now the man was left with a choice. The woman had died spiritually and lost the glow of the anointing. She no longer looked like him; she was not like him anymore. There was a visible and spiritual difference between him and her. They were unequally yoked. She had lost the anointing, and he still had it.

Now Adam had a decision to make. He looked at Eve and, no doubt, thought about what God said. He probably reasoned within himself, *If I eat this, I'm going to die spiritually.* Again, he looked at the woman and thought about what God said. Then he made a decision: He chose to go with the woman.

God Is Our True Source of Everything We Need

Now you know a person is in trouble when he will choose some other person ahead of God. When a person thinks, *Whatever he or she can do for me is more than what God can do for me*, that person has become deceived. God is the source of all things we need in this life.

As a result of Adam's choice, of course, he died spiritually as well. Eventually, physical death would follow spiritual death.

Eve Stepped Out of Her Dependent Role

First Timothy 2:13 and 14 retells the story of Eve's demise.

For Adam was first formed, then Eve.

> **And Adam was not deceived, but the woman being deceived was in the transgression.**
>
> *1 TIMOTHY 2:13,14*

I want to point out two truths from this passage of Scripture. First of all, we know that the woman was deceived or tricked. However, that did not *excuse* her, because the reason she was tricked was that she became independent. That is the first truth we learn from these verses. Eve got out ahead of her husband. She got out of her role. She got out of what God created had her for. She was to be a help meet for Adam. She was supposed to assist him and not be out in front of him.

Nevertheless, she did get out ahead of him where she was not supposed to be, and the enemy was able to deceive her.

When a person is deceived, he or she sees something different than what is truly the case. Thus, in her deceived state, as Eve offers her husband the forbidden fruit, she thinks she is doing the right thing. Genesis 3:6 says that Adam was with her while she took of the fruit. However, she was acting first, ahead of him. Then she said, "Now partake of this with me." She thought she was doing the right thing, but she was wrong.

A woman's place is not to get out ahead of her husband; it is to be *beside* her husband. Eve was out there, leading Adam instead of him leading her. Consequently, what happened was shipwreck for the whole family.

Adam Made a Conscious Choice

The second truth we learn from First Timothy 2:13 and 14 is that Adam was *not* deceived; *his* disobedience was a result of his conscious choice.

> **And Adam was not deceived, but the woman being deceived was in the transgression.**
>
> *1 TIMOTHY 2:14*

Adam understood exactly what was happening here. He heard that serpent talk to Eve. He saw her partake of that fruit. He saw her die spiritually. Then, when it was offered to him, he made a conscious choice to eat of the forbidden fruit. Therefore, God held Adam even more responsible than Eve for what took place.

You see, if you are going to be the head of the home, what comes along with that leadership is *responsibility.* Men generally have no problem wanting to be the boss and to call the shots. But they must realize that there are responsibilities that go along with leadership.

Do you want a definition for a real man? *A real man is one who will take responsibility for his actions.* A real man will take his rightful place, and if he messes up, he will stand up and say, "I messed up." Then he will get up, dust himself off, and straighten up. He'll make things right. Furthermore, no one will have to boost him up or coax him to do it!

Run to God When You Sin

After Adam and Eve sinned, they both became dead spiritually. Spiritual death has a two-fold definition: *First,* spiritual death is *being separated from God*. Sin separated them from God; *second*, spiritual death causes a person to have Satan's nature, the nature of death, in him.

Genesis 3:8 tells us that Adam and Eve tried to hide themselves from God when He came to look for them afterward.

> **And they heard the voice of the Lord God walking in the garden in the cool of the day: and Adam and his wife hid themselves from the presence of the Lord God amongst the trees of the garden.**
>
> *GENESIS 3:8*

That is what happens with people sometimes. They mess up, and then they go hide! However, I want you to know that you need not run away from God when you sin. Run *to* Him. Own up to your sin. The Word says in First John 1:9 that if we confess our sins, God is faithful and just to forgive us.

Not only should you run to God instead of away from Him when you miss it, you shouldn't wait till you've been caught at something and exposed to repent. No, if you sin, repent now.

Of course, this is not what Adam and Eve did. There they were, hiding from the Presence of God as He walked through the garden.

God said, "Adam! Where are you, man?"

Adam didn't answer.

"Adam! Where are you?"

Finally, Adam answered and said, "Here I am."

God was used to talking to this man every day. They had conversed with one another every single day since man's cre-

ation! Therefore, God noticed when Adam behaved differently that day when He went to him in the cool of the day (Gen.
3:8).

Adam said, "I hid myself because I was naked."

God said, "Well, who told you that? Did you do what I
told you not to do?"

Take Responsibility for Your Own Actions

Then we find in Genesis 3:12 that immediately the man
started blaming God *and* the woman for his own act of disobedience.

> **And the man [Adam] said, The woman
> whom thou gavest to be with me, she gave me
> of the tree, and I did eat.**
>
> *GENESIS 3:12*

First, Adam blamed God: "Well, it's Your fault. You gave
this woman to me to begin with." Then Adam blamed Eve:
"It's the woman's fault! We wouldn't be in this situation if it
wasn't for her. If only I'd had a different woman!"

No, Adam's problem was not that he needed another
woman. His problem was that he needed to step up and be a
man. He was refusing to take responsibility for his own
actions. He started blaming God right off the top! "You're the
source of this mess," he intimated. It almost sounds comical,
but it's serious. I mean, just before that incident, he was saying, "*Whoa*, man! This is *wo-man* — bone of my bone and
flesh of my flesh! Oh, yeah! Thank You, Lord!"

But now Adam was saying something altogether different. First he tried to blame God. Then he said, "*She's* the problem!"

Then the Lord said to the woman, "Now, what did you do?"

The woman immediately started blaming the serpent: "The serpent's the one! He did it. He beguiled me and caused me to fall!" She started blaming somebody else too. Neither Adam nor Eve were taking responsibility for their actions.

Now let me give you a little tip: When you are blaming everybody else for your problems, just know that the problem is yourself. You know you are deceived when you are thinking, *Everybody's against me, and everybody's wrong.* You *know* everybody is not wrong! You have to own up to your mistakes and take responsibility for your own actions.

The Consequences of Sin

Genesis 3:14 and 15 shows us how God responded to the serpent.

> **And the Lord God said unto the serpent, Because thou hast done this, thou *art* cursed above all cattle, and above every beast of the field; upon thy belly shalt thou go, and dust shalt thou eat all the days of thy life:**
>
> **And I will put enmity between thee and the woman, and between thy seed and her seed; it shall bruise thy head, and thou shalt bruise his heel.**
>
> *GENESIS 3:14,15*

God then dealt with Eve and Adam for their sin. They were about to hear the consequences of Eve's being out of her place and Adam's being out of his place — for their stepping out of what God had originally said were their roles. They had already suffered in the fact that they had died spiritually. The "light" had gone out; they had lost the anointing. However, losing that anointing resulted in even more loss.

Sorrow in Childbirth

In verse 16, God pronounced the results of sin to the woman.

> **Unto the woman he said, I will greatly multiply thy sorrow and thy conception; in sorrow thou shalt bring forth children; and thy desire shall be to thy husband, and he shall rule over thee.**
>
> *GENESIS 3:16*

God created the woman to have children. However, until this point in time, giving birth to them would not have been a "sorrowful" experience. Sin is what brought it about.

No More 'Sweatless' Work

Then God told Adam how he would be affected by this spiritual death.

> **And unto Adam he said, Because thou hast hearkened unto the voice of thy wife, and hast eaten of the tree, of which I commanded thee, saying, Thou shalt not eat of it: cursed**

is the ground for thy sake; in sorrow shalt
thou eat of it all the days of thy life;

Thorns also and thistles shall it bring forth
to thee; and thou shalt eat the herb of the
field;

In the sweat of thy face shalt thou eat
bread, till thou return unto the ground; for
out of it wast thou taken: for dust thou art,
and unto dust shalt thou return.

GENESIS 3:17-19

God had already given Adam the job of taking care of the
land before He had given him a woman. However, up until
this point in time, the task was different. The land had always
simply produced for the man. The man had worked, all right,
but there had been no "sweat" to it. It had been relatively
easy.

God intended work to be a reward, not a hardship.
However, as a result of sin, God said, "Now when you work,
it will be difficult to you. It will make you sweat."

Now I want you to notice that this is what happens when
a man is not flowing in the anointing. Adam was outside of
the anointing of God, so now work would be difficult.
Conversely, when a person today is operating in the anointing, work can be "sweatless" or easy.

We can do things our way or we can do things God's way.
Depending on what we decide to do with the anointing, we
can either make our work easier or we can make it harder. We
can flow in the anointing by obeying God, or we can do
things our own way. However, if we do choose to do things
our own way, it will be a "sweat field"! The way of the flesh is
always hard.

Furthermore, God said, "Thorns and thistles will be produced. Instead of just producing *good* things abundantly, you
will have a lot of stuff in there that shouldn't be" (Gen.
3:18).

Sin is what brings about this kind of mixed result. I know
I do not want a mixed result. I want my work and my faith to
always be flowing and to produce positively. I want it to be
such that when I speak, it just comes to pass. However, in
order to have these results and to keep the anointing flowing,
we need to keep sin out of our lives.

For Adam, working with the anointing was easy. Without
the anointing, it was hard. Notice, though, that both with the
anointing and without it, Adam always had a job. Providing
for his family by working the land was one of the responsibilities God specifically designed for Adam.

Man's Responsibility
To Take Care of the Family

First Timothy 5 shows us that a man's responsibility to
provide for his family extends beyond his immediate family
members. He is also to take care of his relatives, specifically
widows.

> **But if any provide not for his own, and spe-
> cially for those of his own house [kindred],
> he hath denied the faith, and is worse than
> an infidel [unbeliever].**
>
> *1 TIMOTHY 5:8*

One of the reasons things are going wrong in our homes
today is that we do not fulfill this scripture. It is the man's
responsibility to work and provide not only for his wife and

children, but also for widows in his family. Notice, however, that God talks about a certain *type* of widow for whom we are to provide. Verse 5 describes a widow who is trusting in God, continuing in supplication, praying night and day.

Then First Timothy 5:9 says, *"Let not a widow be taken into the number under threescore years old, having been the wife of one man."* In other words, provide for a woman who is no less than sixty years old and who has been a faithful wife.

Verse 10 further describes her.

> **Well reported of for good works; if she have brought up children, if she have lodged strangers, if she have washed the saints' feet, if she have relieved the afflicted, if she have diligently followed every good work.**
>
> *1 TIMOTHY 5:10*

The type of widow God is talking about is not just sitting around, but is doing some profitable things with her life. She has been faithful to her family, to strangers, to the Body of Christ. She has been in prayer and service to God.

The following verses show us what kind of widow for whom we are *not* to provide.

> **But the younger widows refuse: for when they have begun to wax wanton against Christ, they will marry;**
>
> **Having damnation, because they have cast off their first faith.**
>
> **And withal they learn to be idle, wandering about from house to house; and not only**

idle, but tattlers also and busybodies, speaking things which they ought not.

I will therefore that the younger women marry, bear children, guide the house, give none occasion to the adversary to speak reproachfully.

For some are already turned aside after Satan.

1 TIMOTHY 5:11-15

The reason God lays that out is that He has specific people in mind whom He wants us to bless: widows who do not have ex-husbands all over the place who should still be providing for them. If these women have not been serving God, and they are not living for God now, we are not required to help them.

Then verse 16 says, *"If any man or woman that believeth have widows, let them relieve them, and let not the church be charged...."*

A man is supposed to work and care for his wife and children. Then if there are seniors who meet the qualifications — widows who are honest, whose lives have been faithful, and who are still now praying and ministering — the believing man or woman should assist them. Now God did not say that we have to pay for one-hundred percent of their support. However, we should provide some assistance.

We Must Follow This Scripture Along With the Rest of the Bible

As a rule, we do not do this today. When we see an individual who meets all of the qualifications for our assistance, we just kick her to the curb, slam her into some nursing home somewhere, and forget all about her. We say, "You've got Social Security, don't you? If you don't, that's too bad. I'm sorry."

Then we go to God and say, "Lord, bless me! I want prosperity now! Let the money come to me!"

We have to understand that we cannot accept some of the Scripture and then leave out all the rest. In other words, if God is telling us we have a responsibility to our seniors, then we had better fulfill our role as their assistants. Otherwise, we do not qualify for His promises.

Now my mama is not going into any nursing home. Should Jesus tarry and she live a whole lot longer and I live a whole lot longer, she is not going to a nursing home. My job is to work. My job is, first, to provide for my wife and to set aside for my children. ("A good man leaves an inheritance to his children's children" [Prov. 13:22].) Finally, my job is to assist my mother or my wife's mother if they are widows who have been faithful and are faithful now. My job is to assist them and not just kick them to the curb.

God particularly holds the man, who is the head of the home, accountable to this. Note what He said here: "If you don't provide for your own house, you have denied the faith! You are worse than an unbeliever, because there are unbelievers who take care of their own!"

If we are assisting and helping take care of our own, that means people will not be in positions of poverty. However, our society today places so much significance on independence that we seem to have forgotten how to be assisted or to assist others. God's Word teaches us to be dependent upon God and dependent upon each other as a family.

Believing family should assist believing family. Now we have no obligation to assist family members if they are going

Furthermore, work is not playing the lottery. It is not gambling. It is not playing the numbers. It is not trying to get some number out of a dream book. That is against God's system. In God's structural design for the family, the man is to provide for his own by the sweat of his own brow, *period.*

Even when a man and a woman have a child out of wedlock, or they divorce after bringing a child into the world, that man still has to take care of his own. Of course, God never intended for those things to happen in the first place. That is one reason why God is against divorce and sex outside of marriage. Divorce and extramarital sex often produce children who do not have what every child should have: a father who is there to teach, train, nurture and guide, and support and provide for him financially, emotionally, and spiritually.

When this is not the case, we have women in positions they should not be in. While God's intention for a woman is to be a help to a husband and to have a husband as her covering, providing for her needs, she now has to take on double roles. Then she is certainly not able to help her mother when she becomes a widow. Do you see the "chain effect" that one act of disobedience can perpetuate? Eventually, we wind up with a whole lot of needy people because of one person's failure to fulfill his or her role in God's structural design for the family.

You see, God wants order. He does not want anybody hurt. He does not want you to be hurt; He does not want your spouse to be hurt; He does not want your kids to be hurt. He does not want seniors to be in poverty, but to instead be provided for.

If we follow our flesh, somebody always gets hurts. As we have seen from Adam and Eve's example, it is usually not just one person but multiple people who suffer because of one person's act of indiscretion. That is why God gave us so much instruction in His Word about fulfilling our roles in His structural design for the family. If we will follow God's system, if we will do things God's way, everyone's needs will be met. We will be a blessing, and we will be blessed because of our obedience.

Friendship in Marriage: The Basis for a Home That's Heaven on Earth

Deborah L. Butler

Some Christians attend church two or three times a week and enjoy the Presence of God. They hear about the victory that God provided and Jesus guaranteed. But when they go home, "hell" is waiting for them. In other words, their home life is in shambles.

But it doesn't have to be that way. God doesn't want any of His children to experience failure in his or her family life. And He has an answer to get your home on track.

Someone might say, "But you don't know what a mess my marriage is in." No, but I'm telling you that there is a way. If you can yield to God and let Him help you get your heart right and your attitude together concerning your spouse, you can experience the "divine" in your house. It doesn't always have to be someone else who's blessed. What seemed impossible can be made possible, and the supernatural can happen for *you*!

The Four Stages of Friendship

God wants each of us to marry someone with whom we can share a lifelong friendship — a true friendship that has gone through the four stages of deepening intimacy. In this chapter, I want to show you the stages that every true friendship must go through: *acquaintanceship, casual friendship, close friendship,* and *intimate friendship.*[1]

Sadly, many people marry someone who is not their friend. Far too frequently, people marry an acquaintance — someone they met and decided they liked. As you read about the four stages of friendship, you'll realize that if you're married, you may have skipped some of these stages in your relationship with your spouse. You'll have to make some adjustments and correct some things in your marriage to align it with God's will.

On the other hand, single people have the ability to walk in the things of God in the correct way from the very beginning of their relationship with their future mate. Single people who follow God's way in their relationships will, of course, still have to make some adjustments when they get married. However, they will have gone through the necessary steps before marriage to gracefully deal with those adjustments.

First, Be a Friend of God

If you are single, you can avoid the messes in which many married people find themselves by simply following God's plan in relationships. The first thing you must learn is that it's only as you become a successful *single* Christian that you can become a successful *married* Christian!

God wants you to be successful in your single life so that you will be a blessing to the man or woman He gives you.

The first step to achieving this is to go through the stages of friendship with God. The Bible tells us in First Corinthians 7:32, *"...He that is unmarried careth for the things that belong to the Lord, how he may please the Lord."*

I want to ask you a question. What do you do when you care deeply about something? *You spend time with it.* For example, when two people really care about each other, they spend every spare moment together. According to this verse in First Corinthians 7, an unmarried person cares for the things of God; therefore, a single person should be spending his or her time with God and the things of God.

In a practical sense, a single person can show that he cares for God by giving Him his time, for example, at his local church. This tells me that no church that has single members should ever have a problem finding volunteers! Single people are to spend time around the things of God, helping take care of the church to which God sent them, working in the ministry. They should spend time praying and listening to God, learning His voice for themselves.

Now some single women believe the world's lie and say, "There just aren't enough men." First of all, you only need *one*! Secondly, for you to say that there are not enough men for you to be able to find one is to say that God doesn't know what He's doing. It's unbelief, really. God created you for a man. However, if you go out looking in all the wrong places, you will get the wrong one. So instead of spending your time in pity parties over whether or not you will get married, spend your time fellowshipping with God. Care about the things of God. Get busy doing the work of God. (Besides, you will likely find your future mate as you're both busy doing something in the church.)

Single People Should Care About Their Reputation With God — Not About What Others Think

If you are a single person, do not be concerned if people say to you, "It seems like all you ever do is work at the church." Do not get down on yourself and say, "Well, I don't have a life." You *do* have a life! You are living the life God intended! You are caring for the things of God. You are the one doing it right, not those who are out in the world pursuing their own selfish interests.

So if someone gets down on you, saying you spend too much time with the things of God, you tell them, "Yes, you're right. That is what God wants me to do." Then when it is time to enter into a closer relationship with someone else who has also been doing God's work and becoming a friend of God, you will be able to move forward with assurance that you have the right one.

According to the Word, it is important for a single person to develop a relationship with God and to care about what He wants him to be and do. If you are a single person, God's Word tells you that the only One you should be interested in pleasing is the Lord. You do not have to worry about what anyone else thinks about you.

That's liberating, because you can't please people, anyway, even if you tried. If you wear your hair short, people will say your hair is too short. If you wear your hair long, people will say your hair is too long. If you drive an expensive car, people will say you spend too much money. If you drive a little thrifty car, they say you are a miser. If you talk a lot, they say you talk too much. If you keep quiet, they say you are stuck up.

No matter what you do, you cannot please folks. It is a waste of time and energy to be concerned about what people think about you. There is only One whose thoughts need to be of your concern — and that is God.

You know, concern for what other people think and do is one thing that drives many people into getting married prematurely. Some people think, *A few of my friends have gotten married, but I haven't. I feel the pressure to get married.* Pressure from whom? It is not God who is pressuring you, and what He thinks and says of you should be all that matters.

We talked about the fact that single people are to care for the things of the Lord. Well, what about married people? *"But he that is married careth for the things that are of the world, how he may please his wife.... She that is married careth for the things of the world, how she may please her husband"* (1 Cor. 7:33,34).

Here is the difference the Word makes between a single person and a married person: Those who are single should be looking to please the Lord; those who are married should be looking to please their spouse. God says, "He who is unmarried cares for the things of the Lord, how he may please the Lord." If a Christian single person is caring for the things of the Lord, he will never say, "I don't have any kind of a life. All I do is go to church, work in the church, and read the Word."

God tells you in His Word that this is how your life is *supposed* to be. Seeking the things of God is supposed to be your life. In fact, the largest group serving in the church should be single people because they can arrive earlier and stay later than anybody. Unless they are single with children (a topic which we will address in another chapter), they do not have to "drag" children to their classrooms and then pick them up in a timely manner after the service. Single people who have not yet been given the responsibility of child-rearing and of caring for a family are the people who should be working more than anybody else in the church.

How Singles Are To Stay Holy in Body

First Corinthians 7:34 says, *"There is difference also between a wife and a virgin* [an unmarried woman]. *The unmarried woman careth for the things of the Lord, that she may be holy both in body and in spirit...."*

This verse tells a single person how to stay holy in body. It says that if a single woman cares about the things of God, as opposed to things of the world, then she will stay holy in body and in spirit. When a man tells such a woman, "If you love me, you will have sex with me," she will know that this man is no friend of hers. She will know he is someone who just wants to use her. She will save herself for her husband. Likewise, a single man who cares about the things of God will save himself for his wife.

A single person should not date anyone or even think about marriage until he has gone through the four stages of friendship with God. He should have a vital, intimate friendship with His Heavenly Father. I always admonish single Christians that one of the very first things they need to watch about someone of the opposite sex is his or her relationship with God. If they cannot relate to God right, they will not be able to relate to you.

Many of us have just *met* Jesus and we like what He can provide for us, but we are still at the acquaintanceship level with Him. We have not made ourselves His friend. He has laid Himself out for us so that we can pursue a closer walk with Him, yet we often do not accept His invitation. But we need to make the Savior our friend.

Why God Will Always Stand Out as a Friend

I want to point out that there is one significant difference between relationships with people and a relationship with God. It does not take a long time to develop an intimate friendship with God if we are serious about it. That is because everything we need to know about God is already in His Word. We do not have to be concerned about whether or not God is telling us the truth, what He means when He says something, or whether He understands us.

Furthermore, before we even become acquainted with God, He already knows everything He needs to know about us! He has already decided He wants us to be His intimate friend. He is just waiting for us to choose Him.

Yes, God wants to be our friend. The Bible says in Proverbs18:24 that He is our friend who sticks closer than a brother. That means that once we have accepted Jesus Christ as our Lord and Savior, we can go no place where He is not! He is with us all the time. That is His promise. We may forsake Him and leave Him, but He is still there, just a prayer away.

Jesus is inviting you to be His friend. Do you know what it means to be a friend of Jesus? A friend of Jesus likes to hang with Him. He likes to go with Jesus wherever He goes. He likes to take Jesus with him wherever he goes, unashamedly.

Have you ever gone somewhere and seen a fellow believer doing something he should not have been doing? Such a person has likely forgotten that God is with him all the time. Hebrews 13:5 says He never leaves us or forsakes us, no matter how we act. Unfortunately, too few of us are conscious of Him, because we have not made Him our friend. We do not talk to Him as we talk to our friends.

If we want to be a friend of God, we need to stand up for Him. James 4:4 shows us just how important it is to choose between God and the world.

> **You [are like] unfaithful wives [having illicit love affairs with the world] and breaking your marriage vow to God! Do you not know that being the world's friend is being God's enemy? So whoever chooses to be a friend of the world takes his stand as an enemy of God.**
>
> *JAMES 4:4 (Amplified)*

When we choose to hang out with the world, we choose to be God's enemy. We have to realize that and stop treating God like an acquaintance. We can no longer approach Him with the kind of attitude that says, "Okay, I met You, and I like You. But I've got other things to do." We have to grow up.

God is our source for everything. He is our victory, our success. We cannot be victorious without Him. Victory and success do not come apart from God. Only counterfeit success comes apart from God. People who have counterfeit success have broken marriages, broken hope, broken lives. They are looking for something. They are looking for God.

Matthew 5:16 says, *"Let your light so shine before men, that they may see your good works, and glorify your Father which is in heaven."* Too often, we hide our light from the very people who are looking for God and looking to us for help. We miss so many opportunities to offer the healing hand of God to others because we are afraid to let them know that we are Christians.

Choosing between Christ and the world is not a game. It is a choice between life and death, Heaven and hell. It is a choice that will determine how many people we will take with us to Heaven. What a disappointment it would be to realize that we had not helped bring anybody with us to Heaven, that we had no jewels in our crown because we kept our light hidden (*see* Proverbs 11:30, Daniel 12:3, and Revelation 2:10).

If we want to have effective relationships in this earth that will make an eternal difference, it is so important that we spend time doing what God wants us to do. We must get to know what He has done for us, what He has promised us, and what His purposes are for our lives. This is what it means to care about the things of God.

A Friend of God Knows His Will in Relationships

In God's design for marriage, both the bride and groom come to the relationship with hearts that are pure before Him. The moment a person's heart becomes pure before God, he must not get away from it. Maintaining such purity takes a decision and commitment that a person has to stand by.

If a single person will follow the simple instruction to "care for the things that belong to the Lord" — to be a friend of God — he will know God's will regarding relationships. He will not fall into the enemy's traps in his dating relationships. If he will spend time with God and become attached to Him emotionally, then he will not likely become attached to anyone who is ungodly or who is not the one God has chosen for him as a mate.

In fact, a single person who lives caring for the things of God, developing a divine connection between himself and

God, does not even have to ask, "Well, is this God or not?" When he meets someone, he will know. He will automatically recognize whether God is in it or not, and If He is not, that person will want no part of that relationship. Nobody else will be able to talk him into doing something against God. Then when God introduces such a person to someone else for the purpose of joining their hearts in the deepening stages of intimacy, both will be prepared to take those steps according to His plan.

Married person, as you read on, I do not want you to get into confusion or condemnation. Whether you and your spouse have been married five years or fifty, you can still go back and develop the stages of friendship in your marriage.

Let's take a closer look at each of those stages.

Stage One: *Acquaintanceship*

The first stage of friendship is *acquaintanceship*. An acquaintance is an occasional contact, such as a classmate, a co-worker, or a fellow churchgoer. Once you have introduced yourself to someone and have learned each other's name, you are acquaintances. In this stage of friendship, it is proper to speak with the other person about common interests or other casual topics.

Sometimes people mistake acquaintances for friends. In other words, as soon as they meet somebody, because they like him, they now become his "friend." However, he is not really their friend. They know nothing about him.

Friendship is not just meeting somebody and liking him or her. When we mistake an acquaintance for a friend, we give him information about ourselves before he is ready for it, before he has proven himself to be our friend. He might think, *I didn't ask for that. I didn't want to know that.* We cannot just tell our business to everybody, even if he says he likes us. Just because a person acts as if he is interested in us doesn't mean that he means us well. Often, the next thing he does is turn around and tell somebody else about what we've shared with him. Then when our confidences are broken, we wonder why. Suddenly, we have a difficult time trusting anyone.

Sadly, many people find it hard to trust because they have made this mistake. They have not taken their relationships through the necessary stages.

While we should not disclose excessive information about ourselves, we do need to tell our acquaintances some things about ourselves and learn some things about them. Then based on what we know about each other, we make decisions whether or not to take these relationships to the next level.

I would like to give one word of caution about taking this step from acquaintanceship into casual friendship. Sometimes an acquaintance will meet you and like you and try to override your right to choose whether to extend or deny your friendship. Just because a person wants to be your friend does not mean that you have to be his friend. Do not let people put pressure on you.

The most important thing to do concerning an acquaintance is to ask God, "What is my assignment for this person in my life?" I do not believe that anybody comes across our path accidentally. I believe there is a reason for every introduction. For example, you may introduce your acquaintance to someone else who will receive and accept Christ because of the way that only your acquaintance can minister to that person. Therefore, we need to pray about each acquaintance. We need to ask God what He wants us to do about each relationship *before* taking it to the next level.

Stage Two: Casual *Friendship*

The next level is *casual friendship*, which is based on common interests and concerns. Casual friendship offers each individual the freedom to ask specific questions about the other's opinions, ideals, and goals.

Please note that casual friendship is based on common interests, not common *experiences*. Many people mistakenly believe that just because other people have had experiences like theirs, they can enter into casual friendships with them. However, *especially if their common experiences are negative ones*, entering into friendships based only on those common grounds would be a mistake.

Even if the common experiences are positive ones, they are not a basis for even casual friendships. I am not saying that you should just "throw people away" when they do not share your interests. Nevertheless, you do not have to take them to the next level of friendship. If you cannot afford to have certain people in your life as casual friends, then you must choose to remain in the acquaintanceship stage with them. What that means is that when you see them, you speak to them. You treat them politely and walk in love with them. You tell them, "It's nice to see you; I love you in Jesus' Name," and you keep going.

If, on the other hand, you do want to develop a closer friendship with a person you meet, you converse about each other's opinions, ideals, and goals. If your opinions are compatible, you become casual friends. You are no longer just acquaintances.

It is important that each person in a friendship share equally. Many people make enemies because they ask people's opinions about things without sharing their own. Then when the other people's opinions are contrary to theirs, they get mad at those people.

If you ask for someone's opinion and it does not coincide with yours, do not get mad at that person. Just know that you cannot take that person to the next level of friendship.

Many times we are scared to ask people's opinions because we like them. We are worried that they will think differently than we do and that we will have to stay in the acquaintanceship stage with them. We cannot let this fear restrict our relationships' healthy assessment. We cannot bypass this step and try to push through into intimacy. If we want to move on, even if it means having to leave a relationship in the acquaintanceship stage, we need to face our fears and ask about one another's opinions.

I have observed many marriages in which the couples have not faced this fear. For example, I have met women who have been married for years but do not know their husband's favorite color or the kinds of clothes he really likes. They should have discovered this in the casual friendship stage, before they married (but, remember, it's never too late!).

This is just one seemingly insignificant opinion, but consider how it could affect a marriage. If a husband's favorite color on his wife is a color that she can't stand, she is going to have to wear it, because a wife's interests are to please her husband. She was made for him, to please him. She can't fulfill her God-ordained role as his helper if he does not want to look at her or if he is looking at somebody else who is wearing his favorite color.

As adverse as it may seem to a "love-stricken" dating couple, it takes time to go through the stages of friendship. It takes time to learn about one another's opinions, ideals, and goals. That is why we have fewer relationships at each progressing level of friendship. In other words, we have more acquaintances than casual friends, and we have more casual friends than close friends, and we have more close friends than intimate friends.

Stage Three: *Close Friendship*

After two people have learned that they have similar opinions, ideals, and goals and are involved in the casual friendship stage, they progress to the next level: *close friendship*. Close friendship is based on mutual life goals.

Now a Christian may have an acquaintance who is a sinner. He may even have a casual friend who is a sinner. However, there is no way a Christian can have a *close* friendship with a sinner, because he will not ascribe to the sinner's "life goal" to go to hell. A sinner's natural spiritual tendency is to work hard every day to see how much he can sin, how much he can get away with. Conversely, the believer's goal is to be pleasing to God and to be a good and faithful servant to whom He will say, "Well done" (Matt. 25:21).

We need to evaluate our relationships. Do we have friends who are sinners? What do we have in common with them? When a Christian is a close friend of a sinner, it is evident that the believer has not taken the time to be a friend of God.

We have to decide that we will do things God's way and that we will not play around with the world's enticements. When we stop and think about what God gives us, the world has nothing to offer. According to God's Word, there is no comparison between what the world offers and what God has already offered and provided for us.

What agreement [can there be between] a
temple of God and idols? For we are the temple of the living God; even as God said, I will
dwell in and with and among them and will
walk in and with and among them, and I will
be their God, and they shall be My people.

So, come out from among [unbelievers],
and separate (sever) yourselves from them,
says the Lord, and touch not [any] unclean
thing; then I will receive you kindly and treat
you with favor,

And I will be a Father to you, and you shall
be My sons and daughters, says the Lord
Almighty.

2 CORINTHIANS 6:16-18 (Amplified)

Through this passage, God is saying that because we are
His children, and because we have committed our lives to
Him, we must let go of the things of this world. The enticements of this world are not of God, and we cannot please the
world and God at the same time.

Many born-again believers do not experience the victory
and the promises of God in their lives because they are still
trying to please the world. God said that we cannot have fellowship with Him *and* with the world. We have to cut off all
ties with the world if we want to be friends of God.

Now that does not negate our responsibility to pray for
sinners or to witness to them. However, the choices we make
about our relationships will determine what happens in the
rest of our lives. Our choices determine whether we walk in
victory or defeat.

We cannot go to church on Sunday, praise God, and then go home and live like the devil all week long because we do not want the world to know that we are different than them. They already know we're different! If we do not allow God's light in us to shine outward, people in the world may not know *why* we are different; but they will still know we are different.

There is no way we can fit in with unbelievers. We will be unable to develop genuinely close relationships with them because, again, close friendship is based on mutual life goals. That means Christians can only share close friendships with Christians, because the optimal mutual goal for believers is serving God and being what God wants them to be.

Close friends share goals and suggest to each other how they can reach their goals together. They talk about what is important in their lives. A Christian cannot talk to a non-Christian about such things. For example, if what is important in your life is God, a non-Christian will not understand what you're talking about when you share your values with him or her.

In so many relationships, two people become acquainted, then become casual friends, and then jump into intimate friendship, trying to bypass the close friendship stage in which they are to discover each other's goals. Often people discover only after their wedding that their husband or wife does not have any goals. A man may be just walking along blindly, wherever the wind takes him, but his wife has jumped into an intimate relationship with him before even asking him about it. She has offered her covenant "I do's" and now she is upset because her husband does not have any goals. That was something she was supposed to have found out before they even entered into an intimate friendship.

Therefore, it is essential that we take this and all of our relational responsibilities seriously. At every stage of friendship there are certain responsibilities, and they become greater at each progressing stage. The closer two people become, the more they must seek God about the relationship, especially when they are deciding whether or not they want to marry one another.

The purpose of dating is to find someone with whom you can develop a oneness of spirit. When you decide to date somebody, it should be with the end result of marriage in mind. If you are not ready to get married, you should not date. It is too dangerous to be out there one-on-one dating if you are not ready for marriage. You can go out in groups, but you should not pair off. You should not put yourself in that position, because either you or the other person will become emotionally attached. Then you will have a serious problem.

When you are ready for marriage, you and someone of the opposite sex can enter into the close friendship stage properly. Again, this is a person who seems to share your goals, someone with whom you can develop a oneness of spirit. This is a person with whom you are compatible, someone you can help and who can help you.

Men need to realize that if they don't think they need help, they are not ready for marriage; therefore, they are not ready to enter into a close friendship with a woman. They are not ready to date.

If you think, *Hey! I'm cool. I don't need anybody else. I can live life on my own*, then you need to pray! God said that you as a man needed help, so what you're really saying is that God doesn't know what He is talking about. (Why would a woman want a man like that, anyway? Single woman, do not settle for a man who thinks he knows more than God does about the matter.)

A single man needs to discover where he needs the most help. He should ask himself, *What are my areas of weakness?* And he needs to be honest with himself. Then he will have a list of discoveries to make about the woman in whom he is interested. He can find out whether or not she can and will be supportive in his areas of weakness.

We can't simply say, "Whatever will be, will be" about our relationships. It doesn't work like that. If that is the way we approach our relationships, we are just asking for trouble. We have to pray and trust God to bring the right people into our lives and to teach us how to respond to and interact with them.

Once you have found someone with whom you can develop a oneness of spirit, you spend time talking and learning the more intimate details about what is happening in each other's life. You begin to learn how to help and correct one another. This is an important part of a close friendship, because in the next stage of friendship both parties are responsible to correct one another.

If you as a man do not want anybody correcting you, then you had better go pray and ask God to make you a eunuch! The Bible says that a eunuch is the only man who does not need a woman (Matt. 19:10-12).

Now if you're questioning whether or not you are a eunuch, let me answer your question quickly. If you think you need a woman for companionship, then you are not a eunuch! If you just want to talk to a woman, if you just want to be a woman's friend and go out together, then you are not a eunuch. If you have these feelings concerning the need for companionship, then you need a woman!

Many people refuse to grow up, and that's why they fail in relationships and in other areas of their life. They want things their own way. Well, we can have things our own way, but things are supposed to be *God's* way.

Furthermore, if we know Him well enough, we know that His way is the only way we really want. His way always works out better for us than we could ever make happen for ourselves by doing things our own way. The Bible says, *"Trust in the Lord with all thine heart; and lean not unto thine own understanding"* (Prov. 3:5). A lack of trust is where people miss it when they're trying to go their own way, and we'll talk more about that in another chapter.

Stage Four: *Intimate Friendship*

In God's design, the ultimate stage of friendship is *intimate friendship*. This stage is based upon a commitment to help develop the character of God within each other. When I say "intimate," I am not talking about sex. There is an emotional intimacy that you need to have before you get married. The physical part comes after marriage, after you say "I do" — and, then, it should be only with the person to whom you said, "I do."

Sometimes we think we are doing fine in our character and Christian walk until somebody else comes along. This is when we realize we have some work to do. This is when two people have the opportunity to lovingly correct one another, to build up one another in faith.

Now if you have followed the steps in order, this stage of emotional intimacy will not be difficult at all. If you have spent your time with God, caring about the things of God, you will have a pure heart. You will already have learned to renew your mind on a daily basis. You will already have practiced getting your life in line according to what God says every time you see something in the Bible that speaks to you.

If this is how you have lived, then when you enter into intimate friendship, you have already been developing within yourself the character traits of God. It will be easy, then, to continue developing them as they apply to dealing with another person.

This is why God made women adaptable — so she can adapt to the man God has sent her. If you are a married woman and are having problems adapting, it is probably because you married before you went through all the stages of friendship with your husband. Now you have to realize that God made you for your husband. He wants you to adapt to him and to be suitable for him. If that does not come naturally for you, then you need to spend time on your knees praying for God to show you how.

Men and women speak different languages. That is why it is so important that a couple go through the casual friendship stage, in which they learn to translate each other's "language." One such way to do this is when one person says something, the other should repeat it in his or her own words to make sure he or she understands the communication before responding.

Unless a couple goes through the casual friendship stage, they will not understand one another. They will have no idea what each other is saying.

This is one reason why Keith and I encourage men not to give their girlfriend an engagement ring until after they have been through premarital counseling. If a man puts a ring on a woman's finger, she looks at that ring and says, "Okay. Let's get married!" Then when the two of them go to premarital counseling, they may try to hide some things from one another because their hearts are set on getting married. If they do get some things out in the open, and let's say it's something unfavorable about the man, either the woman will marry him anyway, or she will dump him and keep the ring.

Either way, he will have to do a whole lot of praying. If she dumps him, he will have to pay for that ring regardless of whether he still has possession of it, so he might have to pray for money. And if she decides to marry him, he'll have to pray for their relationship every day.

If you married someone with whom you did not go through the four stages of friendship, it is not too late to start now. Talk to each other about your common interests. Talk about what you thought you wanted to do back when you just met one another and about what you want to do now.

You know, we humans change. When I was in high school, I remember just wanting to get married and be a housewife. God gave me what I wanted, but now that my kids are grown, I do not want to be at the house all day every day. When I was sixteen, I did not think decades ahead. When I prayed for the opportunity to be a housewife, I wasn't thinking that my desire would change as my children grew up and became adults.

As my circumstances and desire began to change, God helped me adjust and realize that I am a help meet for my husband. Wherever he needs help, whether at home or at church, that is where I am. When the Word says to me that I am a help meet for my husband, it says that I have the ability to adapt and be suitable for whatever he needs me to do.

Until a woman can comfortably say that about her life, she does not need to be with a man. If it is too late and she is already married, she needs to spend time praying. She needs to realize that God made her to be a blessing to His man.

Only if a couple has been through the stages of friendship can they effectively resolve their differences. Couples who take the time to go through each stage of friendship together go into marriage already having learned to be patient with each other. They have already made a commitment to adapt to one another and to correct each other when it is necessary. Each one has made a commitment to see each other through things and not "jump ship" when storms come into the other's life. Each one knows that he or she has married the right person.

Both the husband and the wife have made God the center of their lives because they know He is their source. They have spent time with God, and they have prayed for one another and for themselves. They talk to God about their relationship all the time. In fact, they talk to God about *everything* all the time.

If we choose to do things God's way, we will find ourselves in beautiful friendships and blessed marriages. We will help one another get the most out of this life on earth, as He intended from the very beginning.

[1]For an in-depth study on the subject, *see* Minister Deborah Butler's book *Establishing Godly Relationships Through Marriage and Family*.

'Likewise, Ye Wives'

Keith A. Butler Sr.

LIKEWISE, ye wives be in subjection to your own husbands....

— 1 Peter 3:1

So often when we study the Word to find God's perspective on marriage, we run into this verse. However, there is something I think we've overlooked. Isn't it interesting that this sentence begins with a transition? It begins, *"Likewise...."* Now most people I know do not start a conversations by saying, "Likewise," and then begin speaking. If they did, people would wonder what was the matter with them.

Of course, Peter does not begin this discussion with a transition, either. He had actually already begun to discuss this topic — how to relate to other people in a godly way — so we really need to go back to chapter 2 to find the context of "likewise." Only then can we really see what he is talking about.

How To Relate to People in a Godly Way

Let's take a detailed look First Peter chapter 2 to find out what God is saying.

> **Submit yourselves to every ordinance of man for the Lord's sake: whether it be to the king, as supreme;**
>
> **Or unto governors, as unto them that are sent by him for the punishment of evildoers** [the purpose of government is, in part, to punish those who do evil], **and for the praise of them that do well.**
>
> **For so is the will of God, that with well doing ye may put to silence the ignorance of foolish men:**
>
> **As free, and not using your liberty for a cloke of maliciousness, but as the servants of God.**
>
> *1 PETER 2:13-16*

Peter was addressing believers or "servants of God." How does a servant of God put to silence the ignorance of foolish men (v. 15)? This passage says that he quiets them with well-doing or by doing right. Then, God continues, showing us what kind of attitude we should have toward other people.

> **Honour all men. Love the brotherhood. Fear God. Honour the king.**
>
> **Servants, be subject to your masters with all fear; not only to the good and gentle, but also to the froward.**

> **For this is thankworthy** [good, acceptable,
> pleasing], **if a man for conscience toward**
> **God endure grief, suffering wrongfully.**
>
> *1 PETER 2:17-19*

We need to honor all people and love our brothers and sisters in Christ. We should even be willing to suffer wrongfully, instead of taking matters into our own hands, because we want to be pleasing to God.

When we recognize that our true enemy is not other people but the devil, with "conscience toward God" we can endure what is coming against us from other people and not try to vindicate ourselves.

Verse 20 shows us how God sees us when we respond to wrongdoing.

> **For what glory is it, if, when ye be buffet-**
> **ed for your faults, ye shall take it patiently?**
> **but if, when ye do well, and suffer for it, ye**
> **take it patiently, this is acceptable with God.**
>
> *1 PETER 2:20*

In other words, if some bad things happen to us because we mess up, and we take "buffeting" for it with patience, that is no big deal; it is no great accomplishment. What matters is what we do if we do good and *then* get treated badly. If we do not lose our cool and start beating people down, God says, "That's good. Now you've done something."

Follow Jesus' Example

This is the way Jesus responded when people attacked Him. Verses 21-25 show us that we are called to follow Jesus' example in our relationships.

> **For even hereunto were ye called: because Christ also suffered for us, leaving us an example, that ye should follow his steps:**
>
> **Who did no sin, neither was guile found in his mouth:**
>
> **Who, when he was reviled, reviled not again; when he suffered, he threatened not; but committed himself to him that judgeth righteously:**
>
> **Who his own self bare our sins in his own body on the tree, that we, being dead to sins, should live unto righteousness: by whose stripes ye were healed.**
>
> **For ye were as sheep going astray; but are now returned unto the Shepherd and Bishop of your souls.**
>
> *1 PETER 2:21-25*

When folks came against Jesus, He did not retaliate. He went to the righteous Judge, His Father God. He said, "Father, they're doing Me wrong, but I'm going to do right by them anyway. I'm going to do it because I love You. I'm going to suffer on this cross because I love You and because You are the One who told me to come down here to save these people."

'Likewise, Ye Wives'

These verses about following Jesus' example conclude this chapter about our godly responsibilities in relationships. However, this passage does not conclude the discussion of this topic.

The next verse, First Peter 3:1 continues the discussion, beginning with the words, *"Likewise, ye wives...."*

The word "likewise" means *in the same manner*. Well, in what same manner are wives to respond to their husbands? Just as wives as believers are to honor and love others whether or not they are treated right by them, wives are to honor and love their husbands regardless of how they are treated.

We will see later in First Peter 3 that this applies to both husbands and wives. In our marriages, just as in every other relationship mentioned in First Peter 2, we are to respond from a "conscience toward God."

To a husband this means that, even if his wife does not treat him the way she should, he does not respond with threats. He does not say, "Look, woman, I'm going to kick you if you don't do such-and-such." Neither does a wife respond with threats if her husband does not treat her the way he should. Instead, they respond with love from a conscience toward God.

God is pleased when we respond before Him in a godly way even when things do not go well for us though we are doing right. This should be our goal in our relationships with our spouse, because marriage is first played out before God. Marriage is a covenant made in front of God in which a man and a woman pledge to be there for each other and to serve each other forever.

God's Word teaches us that marriage is not about receiving; it is about *giving*. With God, everything is about *giving* first before we receive. This passage of Scripture in First Peter 2 and 3 teaches that we are to give even when we do not receive back properly. We are to respond as Christians, not as people of the world.

Respect Your Husband

That is exactly what God is talking about in First Peter 3:1 and 2 when He addresses wives.

> **Likewise, ye wives, be in subjection to your own husbands; that, if any obey not the word, they also may without the word be won by the conversation [lifestyle] of the wives;**
>
> **While they behold [look upon] your chaste conversation coupled with fear** [reverential respect].
>
> *1 PETER 3:1,2*

Whenever I minister from this verse over the course of my ministry, I've heard women say, "Now wait just a minute. I would respect my husband — *if* he were somebody I could respect."

But did you see anything in this passage about the husband's being something so that the wife can respect him? No, just as the previous verses said that believers are to love and honor others when they are mistreated, wives are to give their husband respect even when he may not deserve it.

(This is one reason that going through the four stages of friendship properly with someone before you marry him or her is very important. You want to be sure you do not attach yourself to someone whom you will later have difficulty respecting. It is better to get married later in life, having gone through the proper stages of friendship with your spouse, than to marry a mere acquaintance while you are young and live in "hell on earth.")

Even if a husband does not obey the Word, God is very clear about how his wife's attitude must be toward him. He says, "He can be won by your lifestyle when he sees your reverential respect toward him, despite what he does."

Verse 3 of First Peter chapter 3 continues to show us how a wife should relate to her husband.

> **Whose adorning let it not be that outward adorning of plaiting the hair, and of wearing of gold, or of putting on of apparel.**
>
> *1 PETER 3:3*

Notice God did not say here, "Women should not wear gold or fix their hair." We cannot interpret only part of this verse to mean that without interpreting the other part of the verse in the same way. If we did, we would have to conclude that women shouldn't wear clothes, either, because the last part says, "...*or of putting on of apparel* [clothes]"!

If women cannot wear gold, then neither can they wear any clothes, because of the phrase, "...*OR of putting on of apparel.*"

Now most husbands wouldn't mind if their wife didn't wear any clothes, but that is not what God had in mind! We have to look at this verse in its context.

The next verse says, *"But let it be the hidden man of the heart, in that which is not corruptible, even the ornament of a meek and quiet spirit, which is in the sight of God of great price"*

(v. 4). What God is saying here is that inward beauty is more important than outward beauty.

Outward Beauty Is Not Completely Unimportant

However, this does not mean that outward beauty is completely unimportant. It is not giving women license to say, "Well, I don't have to comb my hair anymore. I don't have to put on any makeup. I don't have to brush my teeth, and I don't have to gargle. All I have to do is work on my spirit, and that will be good enough for my husband."

That is not what God is saying, either. The purpose of this passage of Scripture is to improve upon what is already happening in our relationships. God wants to keep things going up higher, not have them fall apart! What a woman did to get her husband, she needs to keep doing. For example, if she fought to keep her weight down before she married him, now that she has him she shouldn't just let herself go.

However, the following scenario is much too common. When she was dating him, he never saw her eat. She eats everything now!

You see, she was lying to him before he married her. The fact that she never ate much when he was around in their courtship was a lie, and it was deliberate! It was deceitful!

When they were dating, he would ask her, "How about this dessert?" She would say, "No, I don't eat sweets. I have to watch my figure." He thought, *Yeah! That's the woman I want! She's going to be looking good all the time because she doesn't pile it in.*

But then, as soon as he gets out his "I do" — *bingo* — she asks, "Where's the dessert tray? Give me some apple pie!" She puts on thirty-five pounds, jumps four or five dress sizes and then wonders why he does not see her as sexy anymore.

Then she comes in for counseling and asks, "What's the matter with him? I don't understand what's wrong with my marriage. I come to church. I pray. I don't know why God has let this happen."

I know why. Her husband loves her, but she has let herself go. They may have dated for four years, but he never saw her in rollers or without makeup. Now that they are married, though, he sees her like that all the time.

That is not what God wants. In fact, a woman's failure to take care of herself just puts her husband in a difficult position. Every day he goes to work he notices all kinds of women "dressed to the nines." These women are primping and preening — just as you used to do — and they're getting attention.

You see, a man who is saved, sober, stable, and steady is not crazy! He's not on drugs; he's as sober as he can be. So he can't help but notice the difference between a woman who spends time making herself look nice and a woman who doesn't wear makeup or fix her hair.

Now I'm not saying a woman has to be a beauty queen to keep her husband, but she *should* continue to be the best she can be spirit, soul, and body after she gets married. Some women think they're doing the right thing by not taking care of themselves. But they didn't get that notion from God. God never said to do that!

Outward Beauty Is Important, But Inward Beauty *More* Important

What God is saying in First Peter 3 is that there is something even more important than outward beauty, and that is *"... the hidden man of the heart, in that which is not corruptible, EVEN THE ORNAMENT OF A MEEK AND QUIET SPIRIT, which is in the sight of God of great price"* (v. 4).

In God's sight, a woman's attitude — her "meek and quiet spirit" — is extremely valuable.

Single man, here is the most important thing you need to evaluate in a woman. It's not the curvature of her legs, her hair style, her eye or skin color, her scent, her walk, or how she dresses. *It's her attitude that really matters.*

One reason it's so important to look at a woman's attitude, or her inward character, is that her outward characteristics will change.

She can work hard to make herself look as good as she can, but she *will* get older. She will accumulate some weight, because that comes with age for both men and women.

In other words, her figure will change somewhere down the road. And though she probably didn't have a single line in her face when you met her, when she gets older, she will have a few. Therefore, there has to be more to your attraction than just her physicality, and her most important attribute — what should most attract you to her — is her attitude. God said that the woman with the right attitude is great in His sight.

Two Types of Women

Now there are two kinds of women spoken of in the Bible. We already read about the first type in First Peter 3:4. She is meek and has a quiet spirit; in other words, she has a good attitude.

The second type has a bad attitude. She is described in the Book of Proverbs as a "brawling woman" who could drive a person to the rooftop! I call her the "rooftop woman."

It is better to dwell in a corner of the housetop, THAN WITH A BRAWLING WOMAN in a wide house.

PROVERBS 21:9

Proverbs also calls such a woman a "dripping faucet." She is always talking, nagging, dripping. After awhile, her husband says, "Ohhh, *please*, stop that dripping!"

The rooftop woman and the dripping faucet woman are women with bad attitudes. What are their attitudes? I can tell you they are not meek and of a quiet spirit! I can also tell a single man that he needs to get to know the woman he is interested in so that he does not marry a woman like this!

You see, a guy can get caught up in the external qualities of a girl and forget to evaluate her inward character, because men are physically oriented. Men are physical, *period*. They are born that way. Just watch boys, and you will see they are that way.

It doesn't matter what some social psychologists and psychiatrists say, trying to teach people that the sexes are the same. They are ruining families. The sexes are *not* the same!

Little boys are physical. Then when boys grow up, they are *still* physical, and one way this quality manifests is in the way they view women. The first thing they notice about a woman is what she looks like. You know, the first thing Adam did when he saw Eve was to say, "*Whoa*, man!"

Just let a supermodel come walking down the aisle at your church while your pastor is preaching, and you will find out how physical men are! Single and married alike, every man in that church will be looking at her — or trying hard *not* to! Now the single men will be saying, "Praise God!" and the married guys will be saying, "Help me, God!" because they cannot let their heads move!

Of course, a third thing would be happening: The wives will look to see what their husbands are doing. Then, depending upon the wives' attitudes, something else may follow, such as a thump on the arm!

Now none of those men may know anything about that super model. She may or may not be a nice person. Those guys have no idea. They've probably never met her; they don't know a thing about her. But they would immediately be interested the moment as they saw her. The single men would be saying, "Yes, sir! God must be in the house!"

However, men need to be careful with this natural tendency, because the prettiest woman you've ever seen is sometimes the ugliest. In other words, she might be exactly your type on the outside. She might be the right height and weight; she might have the right curves and dimensions; she might have the right eye and skin color; she might walk and dress right. She may be this, that, and the other thing. When you see her, your tongue just drags on the carpet! But she may have the ugliest attitude lying beneath that ideal exterior, and if you do not take the time to find that out, she could make your life hell on earth.

Obey Your Husband

First Peter 3:5 and 6 continues to instruct wives.

> **For after this manner in the old time the holy women also, who trusted in God, adorned themselves, being in subjection unto their own husbands:**

EVEN AS SARA OBEYED Abraham, calling him lord: whose daughters ye are, as long as ye do well, and are not afraid with any amazement.

1 PETER 3:5,6

Even as Sara *obeyed... Ouch!* That word "obey" is a bad one these days. However, if a husband knows how to treat his wife, she naturally wants to respond by following him, obeying him. Do you think Deborah Butler does not obey me? Yes, she does. However, I understand how that is supposed to happen. I am to give her such honor that it is easy for her to do. Yes, I am the boss, but I am not the dictator. There is a big difference in that. Yes, I am the leader, but I lead with love.

When a person leads with love, everybody will go with him. When a father leads with love, his kids will follow, and at the end of the day, they will say, "I don't hate God. I love God, because my daddy is filled with love. My mama is filled with love. They got it from God, and I want what they've got. In fact, I want to be just like them!"

Trust God

Notice, verse 5 of First Peter 3 said, *"For after this manner in the old time the holy women also, WHO TRUSTED IN GOD, adorned themselves, being in subjection unto their own husbands."*

This is the bottom line — trusting in God. The bottom line in dealing with a woman is trusting in God. The bottom line in dealing with a man is trusting in God. The bottom line in dealing with children is trusting God. Success in *all* our relationships comes down to trusting in God.

Trusting God is the only way we can do what we're supposed to do, because our flesh does not want to obey God's way. Our flesh does not want to be dependent. Our flesh does not want to yield. Our flesh wants to have its way. Our flesh thinks it is right all the time. Without trust in God, our flesh will dominate and run rampant over our spirit to the point we cannot do the right thing even though we want to (Rom. 7:15-20; Gal. 5:17).

You know yourself that you think you are right most of the time. Now you may *say*, "I'm wrong sometimes," but what you mean by "sometimes" is no more than ten percent of the time! You see, most of the time, we believe we are right, but the Word of God has told us here in First Peter that even if we believe we're right, we are to honor others above ourselves.

We can stand on the "I'm right" platform all we want to, but if we do, we will blow up our relationships with others. We will blow our spouse away, our kids away, our family structures away, and our friends away with our "I know I'm right" selves!

When we trust God, we can adorn ourselves in the meekness and quietness that God values. Again, First Peter 3:5 says, *"For after this manner in the old time the holy women also, who trusted in God, adorned themselves...."* These women adorned themselves with an attitude of respect for other people.

God wants us to trust Him so much that we can have an attitude that says, "My life is going to be such a light to you that even if you are wrong, you will look at me and decide, 'I'm going to follow Christ, because you have shown me what He is like.'" That is what this is about.

Now this is how we believers get to the place where we are acting with a conscience toward God — by trusting in Him. The reason we will be able to respond in a godly way in all of our relationships is that we trust in God to fix our situations.

Therefore, our eyes should be on God and not on the way people treat us.

Women who trust in God and adorn themselves with His attributes have found something much more valuable than jewels. They have discovered the key to pleasing God and to being His example to others in the earth, including their husbands.

'Likewise, Ye Husbands'

Keith A Butler Sr.

We have studied passages from First Peter 2 and 3 that teach believers how to relate to people in a godly way. We took a close look at First Peter 3:1 through 6, which specifically addresses believing wives. Now let's look at verse 7, which addresses believing husbands.

> **Likewise, ye husbands, dwell with them according to knowledge, giving honour unto the wife, as unto the weaker vessel, and as being heirs together of the grace of life; that your prayers be not hindered.**
>
> *1 PETER 3:7*

Just as we found in the passage to wives, here again is the word "likewise," which means *in the same manner*. That means that everything God said in chapters 2 and 3 of First

Peter also applies to men. Everything we read about suffering wrongfully applies to husbands as well as to wives.

Even the things that God talked about in the previous verses, addressing women, do not just apply to women. Christian character knows no gender. Men and women alike are to have meek and quiet spirits, not hostile ones. The woman is not the enemy. The man is not the enemy. This is how we need to see things in dealing with male-female relationships.

First Peter 2:19 through 23 says that if someone mistreats a believer, he should not deal with it by getting in the person's face, so to speak, and fighting with him or her. In the same manner, a godly husband does not respond to his wife's mistreatment by saying, "I'm standing for my rights, and I ain't taking nothing from you!"

The Word of God says that if he will do it God's way, have God's attitude, and walk in love toward her, his way of walking with God will cause her to eventually look to God.

Submit to Others

Because verse 7 begins with, "Likewise, ye husbands," every single thing that God said to wives in the first six verses also applies to husbands! We could go through those verses and change the genders and still have an accurate interpretation. Let's paraphrase it this way, starting with verse 1: *"Likewise, ye husbands, be in subjection to your own wives...."*

You may be asking, "You mean men are to submit too?" Yes, men submit too. Husbands are to submit to their wives. (Now, single man, if you are unwilling to submit yourself to a woman, you are not yet ready for marriage.)

Have a Listening Ear

What I mean by "submission" in this sense, is, first, *to listen to another*. The first thing you have to do in order to submit to anybody is to listen to him or her. You have to find out what the other person wants in order to submit to that person. The lost art of communication begins with a listening ear.

Fathers even have to learn to submit to their children. The Word says in Ephesians 6:4, *"And, ye fathers, provoke not your children to wrath...."* Children need discipline, and they do want to be disciplined because with it they get a sense of love and caring. But discipline should be done in a way that provokes them not to wrath, but to respect and love. It starts with fathers learning how to submit to their children, learning how to listen to them.

A six-year-old daughter, a sixteen-year-old son, and a thirty-six-year-old wife will tell a man what is in their heart if he will pay attention and give full weight to what each one is saying. If he will give a listening ear first without thinking of how he can respond when they're finished talked, they will respect and love him.

Regard Their Words as Their Beliefs

Husband and father, when wife or children tell you something, you need to first listen and count whatever they tell you as what they believe. This does not necessarily mean it is a right belief, but that is not the issue. You have to give respect to a person and acknowledge what he believes, even if what he believes is wrong.

If you are going to submit yourself to your wife, what should you do if she starts telling you, "Honey, you don't spend enough time with me"? I understand that you may want to say, "Well, look, I was here last Wednesday. I didn't go out with the guys on Thursday. I didn't do such-and-such on Friday." I realize that the thing you will probably want to think about is your response, about coming to your own defense. Nevertheless, you must first give credit to what she is telling you as her belief, even if you disagree.

According to the Word of God, we are to live in subjection to one another, submitting to one another. Being in subjection means placing somebody else's opinion higher than one's own.

Submitting ourselves to one another will improve the quality of our lives at home. This is home improvement at work! It will help make our families work. (Single person, do not count yourself out. You need to learn this skill before you start your family.)

Find Out Why They Feel the Way They Do

We cannot just dismiss what is in somebody's heart. When people tell us what they feel, we need to lay down our defenses and find out *why* they feel that way. We need to ask, for example, "Honey, why do you believe that?"

Then we need to allow that individual to respond. In other words, we need to keep our mouth shut for a while and listen! We are often in such a hurry to respond that we do not even hear what is said. We may be disciplined enough to listen to just a piece or two of what is said, but then we respond on half-information and frustrate the other person. Then, depending on that individual's personality, he may respond in one of the two following ways.

He may say, "Well I'm not saying anything else to you." What he is saying is, "You are offering me no respect, so I won't give you a chance to disrespect me anymore. I'm keeping my mouth shut."

On the other hand, he may say, "I will give you some of that disrespect right back! You won't listen to me? I'm gonna give you an earful!" That's a "tit-for-tat" attitude, and when that attitude is present, the temperature in the room seems to rise, and you can be sure that a battle is about to ensue!

This can happen in any kind of relationship, not just with husband and wife. I'm also talking about relationships with children in the family and with other people inside and outside of the family. We have to learn this discipline of keeping our mouth shut and listening to others. Don't use the excuse, "It's not my personality." You had better develop a meek and quiet personality so you can keep quiet when you need to.

A Soft Answer Stops Wrath In Its Path!

Proverbs 15:1 says, *"A soft answer turneth away wrath: but grievous words stir up anger."* God wouldn't have told us that unless we had the ability to give soft answers. That means we must have the ability to keep our mouth shut long enough to hear other people's hearts. Everybody has the *ability*; the question is whether we want to do it. Regardless, it is vitally important that we hear the other person out — the whole load — not just bits and pieces.

We must offer children the same respect we give adults. This is how we will keep our kids. This is how we will help our kids follow God. This is how our kids will become saved, sanctified, and filled with the Holy Spirit, instead of backsliding, running off, getting pregnant, doing drugs, and going to jail.

I am telling you from the Word of God how you can avoid all of that stuff! Submit to one another, and you will have wonderful relationships with your family members. Put a guard over your mouth and say nothing until you have heard what they want to say from their heart.

Sometimes men say, "Well, I don't want any woman telling me what to do." Then why in the world did you want to marry one? You see, the Word of God says that there is a dual submitting in marriage. He submits, just as she submits. Now he is the head of the home. God made her for him, and he has final authority. But God tells him, "You submit to her too." God gave you a help meet because you need help! Receive the help He gives you!

Dwell With Them According to Knowledge

First Peter 3:7 says, *"Likewise* [or in the same manner], *ye husbands, dwell with them according to knowledge...."* Men are not supposed to take the position that says, "Nobody can understand a woman. Can't live with 'em; can't live without 'em." If you are a married man and that is what you've been saying, you need to change your mouth. You do not have to live with *women;* you only live with *your woman.* You do not have to understand all women; you only have to understand your wife.

Furthermore, you are supposed to understand her *before* you marry her. You can't do that within a short dating period. Nevertheless, I cannot tell you how many times I have heard something similar to the following discourse with engaged couples.

"How long have you been seeing each other?"

"Six months."

"You're in here for premarital counseling after six months?"

"Why, yes."

I'll say something to the effect, "Well, you may be thirty and, yes, by law you are free marry anybody you want to whenever you want to; there's no disputing that. But we are not talking about that. We're talking about coming together to have a *successful* marriage and then a *successful* family."

Let me tell you, it is because so many people go into marriage too quickly and end up with someone who does not understand them that so many kids are daffy. However, if you do things God's way, your kids will grow up and see how God's way works. They will not run away from God; they will run *to* God. They will be what you are. In fact, they will most likely turn out to be even more anointed than you are.

That's why it is so important to dwell with one another according to knowledge. That means spending the time before getting married not only to get to know one another but to also discover what God's Word says about marriage.

Ask Questions and Be Sincere About Your Interest in Them

After you have listened to people share from their heart, then you should ask questions about what they just said. This has several positive effects. First, it shows others that you are interested in what they have said. Second, it shows them you are *listening* to what they've said. Third, it encourages them to bring out whatever else is in their heart.

You do not want all kinds of stuff bottled up inside of other people against you. This is especially true about a woman. Remember that word "likewise" — you have to win your wife with your lifestyle as well (1 Peter 3:1,2). You can't just tell her, "Look! I'm the man of this house, and I'm going to do whatever I want! Now you shut up and sit down!" Well, she may shut up and she may sit down. But when she sits down, she will be standing up on the inside!

Therefore, you need to listen to your wife, find out what she is feeling and why. Ask her questions about what she says to you. Show interest in who she is. Get to know her, as Second Peter 3:7 says: *"...Dwell with them according to knowledge...."*

Get To Know Your Wife

I will give you an example from personal experience about how important it is to get to know your wife. I didn't have this kind of teaching when I got married. I got engaged when I was eighteen years old, which was too young. I got married when I was nineteen, which was too young. I became a parent when I was twenty, which was too young. If it were not for the Word of God, Deborah and I would not have made it.

Thank God, however, that the man can be won by the lifestyle of the wife, and the woman can be won by the lifestyle of the husband when they both trust God. God can fix it all, even if a couple has not done it right because they didn't know what to do. I thank God for that because Deborah and I did not know what we were doing when we first got married. No one had taught us how to have a successful marriage. We were like most everybody else: She thought I was the most handsome thing she had ever seen (and she was right), and I thought she was the finest thing I had ever seen (because she was).

The first time I saw Deborah, I nearly broke my neck trying to keep my eyes on her! I was a visitor at the church she attended, but after seeing her, I began attending that church regularly! I joined that church. Once we started dating, all we knew was that our relationship seemed right. So we got married. We simply didn't know any better.

We thought that after the honeymoon, everything would be grand. However, as you may already know, after the honeymoon is when the real deal begins! It is when we have to deal with real life every day that a relationship is put to the test. After awhile, Deborah and I started looking at each other's lives and finding faults. We were each thinking about the other, *What is your problem?* There was a time when we looked at each other and thought, *We may have missed God.*

What did we do about it? We got out the Bible, looking for help. I looked in the Word and began working on *me*. I had been complaining to the Lord almost since day one. Things had been great for a while, but when they started going downhill, I said, "Lord, what's the matter with this woman! She's this, that, and the other." The Lord said, "You don't understand her. Why don't you find out her background?" He was telling me, "Dwell with her according to knowledge."

This is why the four steps of friendship are so important. A man and a woman are supposed to have a working knowledge of one another *before* they stand up and say, "I do." They are supposed to know and understand one another before they marry.

After the Lord told me to look at Deborah's background, I started paying attention to her. Instead of focusing on my expectations, I started discovering answers to questions such as these: "Who is she?" "Where did she come from?" "What was she trained to do?" "How does she view things?" "What does she think?"

A Disagreement Over
The Meaning of Dinnertime

Before this time, Deborah and I had disagreed over the meaning of things as seemingly insignificant as the word dinnertime. As you read on, you will see that the root of the problem was my misunderstanding of Deborah.

My mother was a very formal housewife. Every day when my dad came through the door of our house after working outside all day, my mother had his bath water running, his clean underwear and clothes laid out for him, and his dinner on the table. He would take his bath, put on his fresh clothes, come downstairs, where he was greeted by his three kids sitting at the table. He would then pray over dinner, and we would and eat a complete meal: meat, vegetables, starches, milk, and even dessert. We ate a balanced (and full) dinner like this every day!

This is what I saw every single day, so it is what dinnertime meant to me. I didn't know everybody's house was not like that. I thought this was what a man did, and this was what a woman did. We human beings tend to like things a certain way simply because of the way we were raised. All of us are influenced in one way or another by where we come from — by our associations and our environment.

Now my wife grew up with an entirely different perspective of marriage and family. I will never forget the first time I went to dinner at her family's house. She had eight brothers and three sisters. That is quite different than three kids in a family. Just eight boys alone would be a huge contrast, but her parents took care of eight boys *and* four girls!

Of course, a household of fourteen will run a little differently than a household of five, but I was not sophisticated enough to understand that yet. The first time I went to dinner there was the first time I ever saw a commercial kettle. I walked into her mom's kitchen and saw this huge commercial kettle filled with spaghetti. I looked at it and thought, *Man, what is that?*

They all sat down to dinner, and on this particular day, they had Styrofoam cups filled with Kool-Aid, paper plates, and plastic forks. Deborah's mama brought in that big old pot of spaghetti, and everyone began dishing spaghetti out on their plates. In that situation, a person had to "fight" for his food, or at least be aggressive. In my mind, her family didn't act as if there was a guest there. In other words, if I would have sat there waiting for someone to offer me some food, I would have gone hungry! In that family, if someone did not get food, that was his problem. Deborah's father had a decent job, but a decent job with twelve kids creates an entirely different economic situation than a decent job with three kids.

As you know, where I came from, spaghetti and Kool-Aid was not dinner. I still think it's not dinner. Dinner is meat, vegetables, starches, dairy, dessert, the table set with *stainless steel* flatware and real plates! However, when Deborah and I first got married, I was in for a bit of a shock. For one thing, for the first couple of weeks, Deborah cooked so much food, it was as if her eight brothers were there.

One day, I came home from work and asked, "Honey, would you run some bath water for me?"

She said, "Run your own bath water."

What! I grumbled under my breath as I headed toward the bathroom. Then when I came out after my bath, I asked, "Where is my underwear?"

"It's in the drawer. Get it yourself."

By then, I was starting to get steamed. I was thinking, *Here I am out working, just like my daddy. I'm bringing a paycheck home like my daddy. I deserve to be treated the way my mama treats my daddy, and this woman isn't doing it. She's disrespecting me.*

Then I went down to dinner and saw — you guessed it — Styrofoam cups filled with Kool-Aid, paper plates, and plastic forks, I was infuriated. "What is this! This is no dinner!" I demanded.

"What are you talking about?" Deborah said, genuinely bewildered by my hostility. Then we had intense "fellowship," and it went on for days! As I said, I didn't know the Word then as I know it today. Nobody had taught me or her what we know today about marriage and family. Therefore, we acted like people who did not know. We followed the flesh. We got with it — I mean, we had a *big* argument! (If you think Sister Deborah is too meek and can't get with it, you are big-time wrong!) Well, one thing led to another, and our relationship just began to go downhill.

I was thinking, *I am a young preacher man, and I married the wrong woman! I messed up! My career is all shot before I'm getting started good!* I was going through all this, and the devil was going, *Yeah, you blew it! You're right; you messed up. She doesn't take care of you. She doesn't respect you. You're a man, but she's not treating you like a man — she's treating you like some chump!*

I'm sure you know what I'm talking about. I'm sure you've experienced the devil getting on your shoulder, so to speak, and talking to you about your wife or husband. If you listened to him instead of to God, he probably filled your mind with all kinds of critical and accusatory thoughts, just as he did to me.

As I continued to roll these thoughts over in my mind, I was getting angrier by the day. I just *knew* I had married the wrong woman. And neither of us was doing anything to patch things up — that is, until I decided to start praying. I had been in the ministry about a year, ordained at nineteen, and I thought that as a minister, that's what I was supposed to do.

So I started praying, and that is when the Lord said to me, *You don't understand her. Why don't you go back and learn more of her history?* He was talking about dwelling with Deborah "according to knowledge."

The Lord started leading me back into who Deborah was, where she came from, and what her life experience was. Then her actions became very clear. She was not disrespecting me. She did not even understand that I felt disrespected. She honestly didn't understand why I was reacting the way I was. She thought I was being totally unreasonable, so she reacted the way she did! That's why we couldn't go forward and, in fact, were going backward in our relationship.

People Generally Respond To the Stimulus You Give Them

God made human beings to respond. Just as men respond to stimulus from others, women respond to what stimulus you give them. I am not talking about the "rooftop woman." She is completely different. She responds negatively to every stimulus. However, the average woman will respond in kind, or in a like manner, to whatever stimulus you give her. For example, if you give her praise, she will respond with praise. If you give her love, she will respond with love.

Even if you need to give her some constructive criticism, if you do it in a positive way, she will respond positively. For example, I had to learn to say things, such as, "This spaghetti is good! Some salad might be nice with this."

A Small Lesson Worth Passing On

I also learned another valuable lesson early in my marriage: Keep "Mama" out of it! I quickly learned not to say, "My mama used to fix this or that for me." There is a way to express your expectations and desires without bringing Mama into it. So avoid comparing your wife to your mother, leaving your wife in an unfavorable light. Doing that is humiliating to her, and she will react on the defensive if you make this dreaded mistake.

The Bible says that a sound marriage starts, first of all, with the man's responsibility to dwell with his wife according to knowledge. He has to take the time to ask, "Who is she?"

After I started paying attention to who Deborah was, where she was coming from when she said and did (or didn't do) things I didn't understand, and what she was really saying when she talked, I came to understand what she was about. That was when I changed my approach, and it was amazing how she warmed up! She went from being the iceberg that sunk Titanic to being the equator with the rumble! She completely turned around!

Things didn't have to get off to the rocky start that they did in our marriage. We could have gone through the four stages of friendship before we ever said, "I do." But, thank God, we got things turned around. All I did was to find out that the Bible says, *"Likewise, ye husbands, dwell with them according to knowledge..."* (1 Peter 3:7). And I acted on the wisdom of God.

Preparation Is Better Than Trying To Catch Up Along the Way

The best time to discover who a person is and where he or she is coming from is *before* you marry that person. If you marry a person after only knowing him for a short time, you will jump past all of the lessons you are supposed to learn — lessons you *need* to learn to be successful and happy.

If you push the mental and spiritual lessons to the background, what will come to the forefront instead is your physicality. This is especially true for the single man, but once he gets a woman heated up, she, too, will be in trouble. It will be hard for her to keep her perspective and remain steady in progressing through the stages of friendship one step at a time. They will both want to hurry things along. This is dangerous because they didn't take the time to build on a proper foundation. Therefore, the relationship they're building is not secure.

When the physical aspect is at the forefront of a dating relationship, the couple skips all the steps toward an emotionally intimate relationship. Then is it any wonder when they find problems afterward? They skip premarital counseling because they're afraid the counselor might find something out that's amiss in the relationship. But most counselors aren't looking to "police" relationships — in many cases, they're just trying to save two people's behinds! The counselor's job is to try to help people spare themselves unnecessary pain and unhappiness.

An unmarried couple who have pushed past the necessary stages of friendship might each be thinking, *Well, I might not get another chance to marry someone, so I'd better take this one.* They are in such doubt and disbelief and are so focused on themselves that they are not in any shape to marry anyway. That is why they are afraid of premarital counseling: It would probably reveal the underlying problems in their relationship that they really don't want, or aren't equipped, to deal with.

Give Her Your Time

It takes time for a man to get to know a woman. And it takes time for a husband to know his wife's heart on different issues. A husband should take the time to let his wife lay out what is on her heart. He should be a good listener and show her that he genuinely cares.

If you as a husband have taken the time to do this, then when a decision has to be made and, finally, you have to be the one to make it, at least your wife feels she's been heard out and that she and her opinions are respected. The decision-making process goes smoothly when the husband doesn't take a dictatorial stand. If he takes the stand of a true leader, obeying the Word of God and dwelling with his wife according to knowledge, she will not be looking for a fight. She will be saying, "I love you, Baby," even if he makes a mistake.

There Are No Shortcuts

However, you cannot get to know your wife in this way without time. You cannot do this while you are watching a football game. And you can't ask her a few questions and think you've gotten to know her once and for all. No, you have to give her some time, and you have to do it consistently, throughout your lives together.

Now some men argue that they don't have enough time and that between their career and their family, they feel "spread a little thin." But it's important to note that when you *give* time to something, you find you *have* time. You see, the Kingdom way is always, "Give, and it shall be given unto you" (*see* Luke 6:38). And it works! When you are giving proper time to your wife, she won't mind when you go out and do some of the things you've been practically fighting with her for years to be able to do. There's a big difference between a wife saying, "Sure, Honey, go on a do such-and-such; you have my blessing" and, "Well, go on and do it — you always do what you want to do, anyway"! The difference is in how much time you've given her, showing her that you love and care for her and her needs.

Go Along To *Get* Along

Usually husbands and wives each have their leisure activities of choice and often disagree on what activities they will participate in together. For example, some guys like hunting, while their wives are not interested in it. On the other hand, some women love to go to malls, while their husbands are completely disinterested in shopping.

However, if you want to *get* along, you have to *go* along! Deborah participates in things that I like to do because she has a revelation of this important truth. That is why she is a hunter: Her husband is a hunter. So when I go hunting, she slips out in the fields with me early in the morning with a rifle slung over her back and wearing camouflage from head-to-toe. She tracks that game, just as I do! Why? She wants to nurture and maintain the intimate relationship that we've developed over the years, and she is "going along" with something that I enjoy doing.

Now that truth goes both ways. Deborah's idea of a vacation is four days in New York. And let me tell you, she is going hunting too! That girl can track that "game," and when she's spotted what she wants, she brings out the big gun — me! I have learned the proper posture for a husband who is shopping with his wife: It's two steps behind, head down, and hand prepared to draw the wallet at any time! I am well trained!

The same truth applies to a parent's relationship with his kids. We all have to *go* along to *get* along. There are things kids love to do too. I had to learn how to sit down in front of a television and play Nintendo and other similar types of games with my children. My brain may have been saying, *I need to be working on a message right now*, but my spirit was saying, *I'm going to have to do it after I finish the Nintendo with the kids.*

Listen, Observe, Ask Questions, And Listen Some More!

Everybody requires time. The only way we ever get knowledge about people is by studying them. I know what Deborah likes! I know the stores where she likes to shop. I know what brands she likes. I know her tastes in clothing, and I know her sizes.

I even know what turns her off and what turns her on. I did not always know that! That did not come automatically. Hollywood lied when it said that if a man's a man he just knows what to do. Men do *not* automatically know anything about women! The only women they know anything about are their mamas, but a mama is not like a wife. Those are two completely different "entities."

The only way we as husbands can find out about our wife is by spending enough time with her. We need to listen to her, observe her, ask her questions, and then listen some more!

Everyone Is Different, and Every Relationship Takes Time

Every woman is different. We cannot say, "All women are this..." *Baloney!* Neither can we say, "All men are this..." That's nonsense. Everybody is unique. There are some bad women; there are some bad men. There are some excellent women; there are some excellent men. We cannot lump anyone into any group and judge or assess him or her based on the entire group. It is lazy to stereotype people. Stereotyping people before we've gotten to know them individually means we are unwilling to dig to find out the particulars about this case.

That kind of laziness is what kills families and marriages. You have to work at anything that you want to be good. Everything worth having in life requires work. That means that it also takes *time*.

We All See Things Differently

No two people see the same thing exactly the same way. Therefore, a man and a woman will see things differently. Nevertheless, God tells husbands, "Dwell with them according to knowledge." I learned a long time ago, Deborah does not see things as I do.

For example, my wardrobe consists of just so many suits: spring suits, summer suits, fall suits, and winter suits. I have a few pairs of shoes: black, brown, and blue. I have some matching shirts. However, clothing is not very important to me. I want to look sharp, but it doesn't matter to me how many times people see me in the same suit.

However, if your wife thinks clothing is important, she might look into an overflowing closet and say, "I don't have anything to wear." But you'd better not say, "What! Are you crazy!" A man who says that has no knowledge of his wife.

I used to be like that. I would take Deborah to the closet and say, "What? Nothing to wear? Look at all these dresses. What's the matter with this one, this one, this one, and this one?" I did not know any better. I had to learn. Nobody taught me. Most men never learn this stuff anywhere. Some learn the hard way, and, unfortunately, some go through life and never learn. That is why we wrote this book.

Recognize Your Differences And Respect Them

Originality is very important to many women. They are often looking for something that nobody else has. That is why if a woman sees another woman at an event wearing the same thing she is wearing, she might have to check her attitude or she will get upset! Originality matters to her.

That is why one way to get next to your woman's heart is to come up with original gifts every so often, at unexpected times. You need to show up "out of the blue" with an original card, written by you, with just a couple of lines of what you can come up with on your own, from your heart. It doesn't have to be long, and it may not rhyme or sound like flowing speech that you might read from a book. But that doesn't matter to her. To her it would be the sweetest thing she's ever seen.

You see, this "dwelling according to knowledge" will only come when you as a husband spend time listening to and paying attention to your wife.

Honor Her

First Peter 3:7 says husbands are to dwell with their wives according to knowledge. The next part of that verse says, "... *GIVING HONOUR UNTO THE WIFE....*"

God says, "Honor your wife." What does it mean to honor your wife? Well, for one, it means you never make fun of her. Furthermore, you never correct her or argue with her in front of other people, including your children. You may not agree on something, but you go behind closed doors to resolve your differences in an honorable, respectful, and rational way.

The Way You Honor Your Wife Can Affect The Outcome of Your Children

A man will ultimately lose the respect of his children if he fails to honor their mother properly. It may not show when they are very young, but children will not forget it if you were unkind, disrespectful, and dishonorable toward their mother. A man who fails to honor his wife not only loses her affection, but risks losing his children to wrong influences that could potentially cost them their futures.

For example, a teenager who has lived in a home where the father mistreats the mother will become resentful toward his father and will even begin to resent his father's good values. This is especially true of young boys who grow up in this kind of environment. As a young boy, he might obey his father, but it won't be from a heart of love, respect, and devotion. Then as a teen, that testosterone begins to kick in, and along with a little facial hair, muscle form, and a voice that is deepening, he will want to challenge his father.

Now it is completely natural for a boy to want to challenge his father, for example, to a game of basketball. A son wants to get out there on the court and "slam" his daddy, because boys and young men will test their manhood by their daddies. That's fine. It's normal and natural for boys to do that when it's not coming from a heart attitude of, "I can't respect you because of what you've been doing."

But it's trouble when a son grows up resenting what his father stands for because of the man's behavior in family relationships. That father has no weight or influence with his son. He's lost it, and when the man tries to talk to his son, the son won't listen to him because of what he has done to the boy's mother. This is dangerous, because if that son becomes wayward, it could deter him for years from doing what God had in mind for him to do on the earth. And in many cases, that young man may *never* do the will of God. He may miss it altogether.

A father wants his words to have "weight" with his son even when his son is grown. My son still listens to me and values what I say to him. He's grown and married, but he still talks things over with me and asks me questions. The reason so many grown men don't talk this way with their father anymore is diminished respect — or worse, the respect is gone altogether. A son will remember the wrong way his father treated their mother.

Now this works both ways. In other words, if a woman disrespects her husband and makes his life "hell on earth," it will affect the children's attitudes and behavior, especially in the teen years. If she has been arguing with those kids' father in front of them, calling him names, and putting him through the wringer, so to speak, she will lose any positive influence she might have otherwise had with her children. They won't listen to her, either. So it works both ways, but it is particularly true with men.

Honoring Her Shouldn't Be Something New — It Should Be a Continuation of the Honor You Showed Her in Courtship

Husband, honoring your wife is nothing new. You honored her before you married her. Even guys who never clean up their place, clean up for the girls they are interested in. Those who never shave, shave. Those who never shine their shoes, shine their shoes. Those who never wear suits, go out and buy suits if they think that's what she likes. A man will do everything he can to impress some particular woman. All of a sudden, he gets as sophisticated as he knows how to get! He opens doors for her, buys things for her, protects her, says nice things to her, compliments her.

But, sadly, often when a man wins a woman and marries her, he never even cleans up after himself, he doesn't shine his shoes or take care of himself like he did to get her. He won't wear a suit or the kinds of clothes she likes, and his chivalry goes out the window! He never opens doors for her anymore or says anything nice to her. She might be standing there waiting for the door to be opened, and he says, "What's your problem? Get in the car." Although he used to do things for her all the time, now, all he says is, "Get me this; get me that." He just puts his feet up on the coffee table and stares at the game. He doesn't pay attention to her at all.

But then when the game is over, he wants to crawl in bed with her, saying, "Feeling frisky tonight?" And she's saying, "Don't come near me."

Then he's upset and says something to the effect, "Honey, I bring the paycheck home, don't I? Don't be like that. Come here." About all he's going to get is a cold body while she's thinking, *Hurry up and get this over with.* Two and a half minutes later, he's sleeping.

Over time, he's wondering, *What's wrong with her? What's wrong with my marriage?*

I can tell him what is wrong: He does not honor his wife! If he does not give the woman honor, she will be like a refrigerator. He will have to work hard to warm her up.

Brother, your wife needs a little romance! Every so often, you need to go do something different than the norm — and not just on her birthday. (Speaking of which, here is a little piece of advice: Do not buy a woman a washing machine on her birthday! You might say, "But it's an expensive washing machine — the *best* — the top of the line." Are you crazy?

She does not see that washing machine as a gift! She sees it as a "slave instrument.")

Unfortunately, if no one teaches a man these things, he will probably not know any better. His wife may tell him if he's in a position to hear her and really listen to her. His buddies are certainly not going to tell him. They want to see him get "busted" so they can laugh at him!

So the responsibilities of a husband include dwelling with his wife according to knowledge. That means listening to her. Observe her and give her your time and attention. Get to know your wife! And honor her. Give honor to her, and you will find that she, as well as your relationship together, increases in value and worth in your eyes. This is pleasing to the Father God, and it is always a good thing to please the Lord and to walk in His favor.

Treat Her Right, and God Will Listen

The last part of First Peter 3:7 says, "...*giving honour unto the wife, as unto the weaker vessel, and as being heirs together of the grace of life; THAT YOUR PRAYERS BE NOT HINDERED.*"

God says, "Now you honor your wife so that your prayers won't be hindered." In other words, God is saying to us as husbands, "Listen, if you don't treat that woman right, then I don't have any time to listen to you." If we husbands will take the time to learn about our wives, to honor them "as the weaker vessels, as heirs together with us of the grace of life," God will hear our prayers and answer them. If we all will follow His instructions about dealing with one another, our marriages will be blessed, our families will be blessed, and our relationships with God will be blessed!

The Responsibilities of Godly Parenting Part 1

Deborah L. Butler

And Adam knew Eve his wife; and she conceived, and bare Cain, and said, I have gotten a man from the Lord.

— Genesis 4:1

Generally speaking, a woman cannot conceive a child if her husband does not "know" her, referring to a sexual act. He has to know her, and as we have seen in the previous chapters of this book, it should not be just a sexual knowing. He should know her totally, so when she does conceive, the couple can be confident about raising the child they've "gotten from the Lord."

Even though the word of a doctor says that some women can't conceive, we can count on the Word of Doctor Jesus! It is not the doctor who gives us children; it is the Lord who gives us children. With Him on our side, we can conceive and bear children and know they are from the Lord.

Notice that Eve said, "I have gotten a man from the Lord." She did not say she received a man from Dr. Spock or any other so-called child specialist. She knew he was from God. Likewise, you as a parent have gotten a child from God. That means your Instruction Book for rearing your child is God's Word. God has all the answers, not man. The good answers that man has come up with concerning parenting have their basis in the Word of God.

In this chapter, we will spend some time in the Instruction Book written by the One who has given us children to begin with.

We need to realize that even when a child is conceived under less than the best of circumstances, that child is still from God. We know this is true, for God is the only One who can give life. We also know that everything God does is good, so He will take the ugly circumstances — the ugly things that happen in our lives — and turn them around and bless us with them.

Our children are blessings, no matter how they got here. We must stop calling children accidents or mistakes. I believe that if we say that about our children's births, we speak accidents and mistakes into their lives.

God gave our children life. Furthermore, God has given each child a special call, which his parents are supposed to help nurture and develop within him.

Parents Are God's Vessels To Nurture Children

Matthew 6:33 in *The Amplified Bible* tells us, "Seek for (aim at and strive after) first of all His kingdom, and His righteousness [His way of doing and being right], and then all these things taken together will be given you besides." That means that as parents, we have to seek God's way of raising our children. Parents are God's vessels through which He promotes His purpose in our children's lives.

In this chapter and the following chapter, I'm going to share with you from God's Word some of the responsibilities we as parents have for our children. We need to teach, train, provide for, nurture, set boundaries for, and love our children. If we do not do these things for our children, they will be lost. We are the ones who are supposed to guide and lead our children in the way that they should go. They cannot lead themselves. They need us, their parents.

As I address the topic of parenting children according to God's Word, I want you to realize that though our society hands most of the responsibilities of parenting to the woman, God requires the man to be involved in disciplining, teaching, and training children. The woman is supposed to be a *help* meet for her husband, not a *do-it-all*. She is supposed to help the man with what he is supposed to be doing. Some of those things he is responsible for as a parent are teaching, training, providing for, nurturing, setting boundaries for, and loving his children.

Parents Are To *Teach* Their Children

The *first* parental responsibility I want to focus on is teaching our children. Let's find out what the Bible tells us about this responsibility.

> **And thou shalt teach them** [the commandments, the Word of God] **diligently unto thy children, and shalt talk of them when thou sittest in thine house, and when thou walkest by the way, and when thou liest down, and when thou risest up.**
>
> *DEUTERONOMY 6:7*

First, it says we are supposed to teach our children God's Word when we are sitting in our houses. In other words, when we are relaxing and spending time together, we are supposed to teach them about the things that God has said and what He requires of us as His people.

When We 'Walk By the Way'

Second, it says we are supposed to teach them God's Word when we "walk by the way." That is when we take them to school, to the playground, to catch the bus, to go shopping, or on a family trip. While our children are growing up, we might have to be taxi cab drivers. Everywhere our children go, we go. And when we are going somewhere together, we're supposed to be talking to our children about God. That means we do not have to have the radio, the cassette player, or the CD player on all the time. Unless we are listening to something that teaches them about God, we need to turn off the noisemakers and just spend that time talking to our children.

When We Lie Down

Third, we are supposed to teach our children God's ways when we "lie down." When our children get ready to go to bed, we should be sharing God's Word with them, helping them apply it to their lives.

When We Rise in the Morning

Fourth, God wants us to talk to our children about Him when we rise in the morning. When we get up, we are supposed to talk to our kids about the Word of God. In other

words, we're to talk to our kids about God *all the time* —
when we're relaxing in our house, walking by the way, lying
down, and getting up! Now I'm not saying we should constantly quote scriptures to them. But we should demonstrate
the Word to them and talk to them about the Word, sharing
scriptures with them and relating those scriptures to their
everyday lives so that they, too, may demonstrate the Word of
God.

God does not want us to just leave our children to themselves, because they cannot become independent and handle
what life throws at them by themselves. They need us to parent them. They need us to teach them from the Word how
they are supposed to act and behave. It is our responsibility
as parents to do that, and only godly parents who are in the
Word can do it the right way.

God says that when we are relaxing, when we are going
someplace, when we are going to bed, and when we are getting up, we should be teaching the Word to our children.
More than anything else, that is what we should be doing.

Parents Are To *Train* Their Children

It is not good enough just to tell our children something
one time. We have to *train* them by repetition and by example, and that is the *second* responsibility of godly parenting.
We have to consistently tell them what to do and then live it
before them. We always have to be explaining to them why
they shouldn't do things the wrong way and why they should
do things the right way, and we have to be doing things the
right way in front of them or the message will be lost to
them.

Proverbs 22:6 says, *"Train up a child in the way he should
go: and when he is old, he will not depart from it."* According to

this scripture, though it may look at some point as if a child will depart from his godly upbringing, when it really counts, if you have brought him up right, his training and the Word of God in his spirit will rise to the top. The Word of God is like cream: it will always rise to the top. If you give them the cream of the Word, it will always rise to the top.

Again, Proverbs 22:6 says, *"...when he is old, he will not depart from it."* Some of us are older, and others are really old, but nothing could make us *not* do the Word! Why? Simply because our parents trained us that way when we were children. We have been taught and trained in the Word. We are conditioned to respond to and obey the Word of God. Obedience to the Word is ingrained in us. It has become a part of us over the years, and we cannot and will not separate ourselves from that Word.

There are some things that are wrong that I simply cannot do. Even if nobody is looking, I cannot do them! I was trained in the Word of God, and I know He sees everything I do. I realize that not everybody understands that, but I know it's true that He sees everything we do. He even sees the thoughts and intents — the attitudes and motives — of our heart. Obedience to the Word is not for show — for the purpose of just pleasing man. We obey the Word because we love God and understand that He is always with us, and that everything is laid bare before Him.

I thank God for my parents, because what they taught me when I was a child always rises to the top. No matter what happens, no matter how crazy those around me might act, I respond according to the training I received as a child. Even if someone wants to cuss me out, I know from my parents' training that I do not have to sink to his level.

Why? Because I know that I can walk with God on His level — on the level of His way of being and doing right. Even if some Christians choose to get off of God's level, I do not have to choose to do the same. I have been trained that way all my life, so I know that it is my choice.

Some children learn at a very young age that there is no better way than God's way. However, some children decide, *Well, I think there is a better way, so I am going to go out there and find it.* Do you know where that attitude came from? It came from their parents! It came from watching them trying to do things their own way. If your children see you trying to do things your own way, they will say, "Well, if Mama and Daddy can do it their own way, then maybe I can find my own way."

Some parents spank their children because those children are doing what they see their parents doing instead of following God's Word. We can make it so much easier on our children if we just do things right and live right before them. And according to Matthew 6:33, we can always be right if we do things God's way. Contrarily, we will always be wrong if we do *not* do things His way. As parents we must be an example to our children of how to do things God's way.

Our lifestyle is one way we train our children. Training is being an example. While teaching is *telling* our children how to walk in God's ways, training is *showing* them how to do it. We show them how to do something when we do it ourselves. When they see us growing in God's way of doing and being right because we have chosen to do so, we are training them to make the choices in life too.

When we train our children to do things God's way, we do not have to be concerned about what they will do when they get to be teenagers. We do not have to be concerned about peer pressure, because God is their peer — their friend and the one they look to as an example to follow — and He doesn't pressure anybody!

I remember telling my children numerous times over the years, "If you choose to disobey me, it had better be because you decided you wanted to and not because somebody said they wanted you to do it."

That made them think, *If I'm going to get spanked, it will be because I decided to get into this mess and not because my friend wanted to or told me to.*

The only way our children can learn to take responsibility for their actions in this way is to observe us, their parents, being godly examples before them and not succumbing to peer pressure ourselves.

We are to aid in developing godly character and maturity in our children. If we never matured and developed godly character ourselves, then our children are in trouble. They have nothing to look up to. We have to make the adjustments necessary in our lives in order to live out the character of God before our children.

We are responsible to bring our children to the knowledge of God so that they can experience true fellowship with God. If they see us having true fellowship with God on a daily basis, and they see us succeeding and linking our success to God, they, too, will want to follow God and succeed.

We can't just make our children go to church, while we go somewhere else. Neither can we live like believers in front of other adults and then live like sinners in front of our kids. If we can't live for God in front of our children, then who are we living for? If they see that *we* are not living for God, *they* will not want to live for God. *We are our children's biggest role models, whether for good or for bad!* And if God is not that important to us, then why should He be important to them?

Do Not Give the Devil Your Marriage — He Will Not Stop There!

One thing we can and should explain to our children is God's forgiveness plan. However, we do not explain it so they can just go out and premeditatedly make a mistake. We cannot make excuses for them, saying, "Well, if you decide to sin, God will forgive you." We have to teach them that they will reap what they sow and that there are consequences to our actions. If they sin, that wrong choice will come back and affect them at some point (Gal. 6:7).

This is a problem among some adults Keith and I counsel. They want to divorce their spouse, so they reason it out, saying, "Well, God will forgive me if I get a divorce." What they do not understand is that if they let the devil take their spouse from them, he will not stop there. He will come after their kids, their house, their health. He does not just want one thing from them. He wants to totally destroy them (John 10:10). That is why we have to learn and to teach our children to stop the devil in his tracks and to give him no place. We must not let him get into our lives through our choices to sin.

Don't Let the Devil Ravage Your Children Because of Your Selfishness

I would not give anything up to the devil. I would never give up my marriage to him! It does not belong to him. God gave it to me! Why would people allow Satan to take something that God gave them? It is because they are *selfish*. They do not want to do what it takes to keep him out of their lives. They do not want to get on their knees and pray. They do not want to apologize or admit they were wrong.

You know, nobody wants to be wrong. Everybody wants to be right. However, no one can be right all the time unless he is always doing things God's way.

If we are doing things God's way, we will not divorce our spouse, because that is not God's way. We cannot pick and choose from God's Word what commands we will and will not do. We can't say, "Well, I'll do *this* thing God's way, but *this* one I won't." It doesn't work that way! If we want God's peace that passes understanding and His blessing on our lives, we have to do everything His way.

Stand Up for Your Family!

I encourage you to stand up and be an adult and fight for what is yours! You may be thinking, *Well, my husband* [or wife] *has his* [or her] *own will.* Your spouse proclaimed his or her will when he or she walked up to the altar and said, "I do." Anything contrary to that will is a result of satanic influence, and you do have control over that — over what you allow to influence you. Do not give up what God gave you!

We cannot ask God for things when every time He gives us something, we give it up! We have to prove we can hold on to something. We cannot give it up. We have to get a bulldog attitude. A bulldog says, "This is my bone, and you ain't getting it!" Well, sir, remember, that woman of yours is bone of your bone (Gen. 2:23). *Why would you give up your bone?*

I strongly advise unmarried women not to marry a man who has been divorced, unless the two of you have gone through a lot of counseling together. If he did not fight for his first, second, or third wife, what evidence do you have that he will fight for you?

Truly, divorce is one major reason a lot of children have problems. When their parents' marriages break apart and the parents are talking negatively about each other and then pointing out that the kids look or act like the other parent, is it any wonder that children are having problems?

Divorce is selfish. It is all about "me." But when you have children, life cannot be about "me" anymore. Bishop and I are just now getting to the point at which life is about just the two of us again, because our kids are grown. However, the day we decided to have children, it ceased to be about me and him. It was about the kids.

Even if we had split up, our lives would have been about the kids. If it had ever come to the point that we couldn't stand each other, that would have had nothing to do with them. They would not have seen us fighting. That would have been between us. What they would have seen is our being the best of friends for their sakes.

I could never get angry with Keith and attack one of my kids because he or she acts like him. I would be speaking against something God has put in them. I would be tearing down what God has given me. I cannot do that. The Bible says in Proverbs 14:1, that the wise woman *builds* her house, but a foolish woman tears hers down with her own hands. Speaking against my child would not be building my house; it would be tearing it down!

We must not speak negatively about our children's traits that we do not like. If we attack their personalities, we are attacking them. Even adults become hurt and ill-affected when somebody says something negative about them, so how can we expect our children to take it?

Parents *Provide* for Their Children

First Timothy 5:8 talks about parents' *third* responsibility, which is providing for their children.

> **But if any provide not for his own, and especially for those of his own house, he hath denied the faith, and is worse than an infidel.**
>
> *1 TIMOTHY 5:8*

A person could go to church, lift his hands and praise God, and even shout up and down all over the church, but that is not a mark of his spirituality or his obedience to the Word of God. Those things are good and right, but if he is not taking care of his own family, the Bible says he might as well not even be telling people he's saved, because he's not acting like it!

You have to take care of your own. Your family should not leave the house looking as if they just came out of the gutter. We need to show pride in the children with whom God has blessed us.

Now providing for your own covers the whole gamut from providing food, clothing, and shelter to providing a positive, healthy home life and a good education. But it goes even further than that. Providing for your children is more than just material provision. It's been said, and it's true, children don't want your money as much as they want *you*. In other words, you are to provide *yourself* to your children.

My dad had a really good job. Even by today's standards, he made good money. However, he had twelve kids living in his house, and eight of those kids were boys (and you know how boys eat)! We did not know we were poor financially, because we had our parents, who not only provided clothes and food for us but also provided *themselves* for us.

My folks were always there to talk to each of us and teach us the Word of God. In the morning, they were there to send us off to school. When we came home and had time for relaxation, they talked to us and spent time communicating with us and giving of themselves. They did not try to keep up with the Joneses; they tried to keep up with us! That meant something to us. We were rich because we had a family who loved us.

So often we talk about teenagers facing peer pressure, but I believe the peer pressure for adults to "keep up with the Joneses" is just as big a problem. But we parents need to focus on keeping up with God and forget about the Joneses; otherwise our kids will be going to hell with the Joneses! (Now, if your name is "Jones," I am not talking about you. I am talking about people who have an abundance of things, people with whom you may be tempted to compete.)

We cannot side with the world. The world boasts about what it has. But a person's life, who he is, is not based on what he has — his possessions. Who we are is determined by our walk with God and how closely we adhere to the principles in His Word. We have to show our children how important the things of God are to us. We have to allow our children to see God's promises come forth in our lives so that they, too, will developed a personal, trusting relationship with Him.

The world does not have anything to offer. The things the world offers do not remain; they are temporary. Our lives are to be all about pleasing God, doing the work of the Kingdom.

In our society today, our emphasis is on the wrong things; our priorities are all messed up. If we would just love our children, be there for them, teach them the Word of God by living it and being a godly example, our families would be truly rich.

Not having a family you can count on is what will make you poor in life. If you cannot trust your family, even if your parents are billionaires, then you are poor. Money does not buy everything.

Parents Take Care of Their Blessings Even if It Means Enduring Sacrifices Themselves

While material goods are not the most important things we can give our children, the Bible does tell us to provide for our children. Remember, First Timothy 5:8 tells us that if we do not take care of our own, we are worse than infidels or heathens.

I'm not talking about keeping up with the Joneses or trying to provide material blessings to your children that are beyond your present means. But there are heathen folks who take better care of their families than some Christian folks of comparable means. That doesn't make any sense to me. And what's worse is, some Christian parents come to church looking like a million dollars, while their children are wearing clothes that are dirty and torn! That is simply not right. It doesn't line up with what the Word of God teaches.

We Should Be Examples to Our Children In Cleanliness and Order

We need to take pride in the material things with which God has blessed us. Maybe you don't own a big house, a newer-model car, or the best clothes, but you can take care of what you do have. You can clean your house — sweep and mop the floor, dust the furniture, and so forth. And you can wash your car and make sure it's not full of trash and clutter. You can wash your clothes and keep them looking neat even if they aren't brand new.

We need to set a good example for our children in this area as well. They need to grow up in a home where there's peace, order, and cleanliness.

There is no excuse for dirtiness. I realize that some people have different definitions of "dirty," but we all know what dirty is: If it's not clean, it's dirty; if it stinks, it's dirty! So we should take pride in the things God has given us, and we should keep them clean. He cannot give us more if we do not appreciate what we already have (Matt. 25:21).

Parents Provide Stability

When we think about providing for our children, we must remember that children need stability, and we as parents need to provide that for them too. Children need to know that they have a home to go to. They need to be assured that they will not be moving from house to house every month.

We parents need to provide our children with the stability of knowing that they have a home.

That means if we cannot afford a big house, we should not move into one. Doing so would only cause our children problems. We need to get into what we can afford and spare our children the unnecessary stress of our financial irresponsibility.

Parents Provide Security

Furthermore, we need to provide our children security. That means that if a parent has three kids and can only afford a one-bedroom house in a safe area, so be it. That is much better than being on the street. To the best of our ability, we need to house our families in safe, secure areas, where they won't have to be concerned about crime all the time.

I realize that some people have to deal with making a decision whether or not to move from an unsafe neighborhood. But sometimes they wrestle with the decision because their priorities are wrong or because they haven't set their priorities to begin with. If you are living in an unsafe area, I urge you to check out your priorities. Make sure they are right and that you are doing all that you can to provide your children with a home in a secure environment.

Security Inside the Home

Even more important than providing a secure environment outside the home is providing a secure environment within. Now the Bible does tell us to spank our children (Prov. 13:24), but it does not say to beat them! Nowhere does the Word of God say we should abuse our children. But it does talk about spanking our children in the place that God designed for that purpose: their padded bottoms.

We should discipline our children out of love and concern, not out of anger. The purpose of discipline is to alter the course of a person's life. If we see our children going the wrong way, we discipline them to bring them back to the correct way.

We should never spank our children when we are angry. If a person spanks his child in anger, he we will lose control and abuse the child. However, when we spank our children out of love and concern, we will not be abusing them. We will be unable to abuse them because we love them too much. There is no room for abuse where there is genuine, loving concern for the welfare of the children.

We need to provide our children with stable, secure homes in which they know they are loved. We cannot just think, *Well, I bought such-and-such for them. That should tell them I love them.* That does not tell anybody that he is loved! Receiving material gifts may only communicate to a child that his parents have some money.

No, we have to *tell* people we love them, and we have to demonstrate it by providing more than just material blessings. As I said, we must provide *ourselves*.

Real Love Has a Voice That Can Be Heard Loud and Clear

So often I hear people explaining away their reasoning for not communicating love to their children. They'll say it's just not their style or that they find it difficult to express love or to show affection. They'll always say, "But my children know I love them."

That's just plain assumption on the part of a parent who feels that way. There are thousands of people who say they honestly did not feel love in the home as children growing up.

We cannot leave something so important to assumption. Love does not work by assumption. Love needs a voice and action. That is what we parents are called to provide for our children. Read on, and you will find more ways to fulfill your God-given role as a parent.

The Responsibilities of Godly Parenting Part 2

Deborah L. Butler

We have seen that parents need to teach, train, and provide for their children. Now I want to show you a *fourth* responsibility of godly parenting: *nurturing*. It is found in Ephesians 6:4, which says: *"And, ye fathers, provoke not your children to wrath: but bring them up in the nurture and admonition of the Lord."*

As parents we are responsible for bringing up our children in the nurture and admonition of the Lord. We are to bring them up and nurture them in God's way of doing and being right. As we have seen, this means we are to not only tell them what to do but to be living examples before them.

Notice this verse is specifically addressed to fathers. It says, "Fathers, provoke not your children to wrath." There are many ways in which one person can provoke another to wrath, but I want to address a few things that fathers may do, even inadvertently, that illicit anger from their children.

Fathers, Do Not Pick on Your Children

A father can provoke his children to wrath by constantly picking on them and talking negatively about them. For example, some dads call their boys "sissies" and "chumps" because the boys do not want to play football, basketball, or some sport that the fathers wanted them to participate in. But just because a young boy doesn't want to participate in a certain sport doesn't mean that he is a sissy! It just means he doesn't like the sport.

Just because I don't like fish, would someone be justified in going around saying, "Mrs. Butler is afraid of fish"? No! Well, it would be just as absurd to say that your son is afraid of football or basketball just because he doesn't like it. Perhaps he simply is not an athlete. Maybe he just wants to be an artist, and maybe that is exactly what God has called him to do. If you are a father, I urge you to take care not to speak against the gifts God has put within your children.

No two children are alike. Each one is totally different than the next. That means we cannot parent all of them in exactly the same way. We have to approach each of them in a specific way that we receive from God.

This is why it is so important that we pray for our children. We have to know what to speak into their lives, what to do when various circumstances arise, and how to handle the wisdom God gives us for them. Just because God tells us something about our children does not mean we are supposed to push it on them. It means we are to help them and guide them in that direction.

If you're a father, do not provoke your children to wrath by trying to make them participate in sports or other activities things that they do not enjoy. Do not let the world define your child to you. Find out what *God* wants them to be and let them be that. God has a special calling on each person's life, and He has a right through the divine covenant of Calvary to call and equip each one as He so chooses. Therefore, encourage your children to be who God called them to be, not who *you* called them to be.

Fathers, Do Not Ignore Your Children

There are other ways in which fathers can provoke their children to wrath. For example, a father can provoke his children to wrath by ignoring them.

If you're a dad, don't come home from work and tell your children, "Leave me alone. I worked hard, and I want to be alone." Your children are not a bother. If they are a bother to you, then you are a bother to yourself, because they are part of you.

Do not put your children off. Talk to them. Spend time with them while you have a chance, because they grow up so quickly. And if you spend time with then when they are young, you will not have to be concerned about them when they get to be teenagers.

Unfortunately, many fathers leave the raising of kids to their moms. Then they get angry when their teenagers won't listen to either parent. This problem is especially common with fathers and their sons, because boys usually get taller than their moms and begin to think, *Okay, now what's she going to do?* What leads children to this rebellious point? Often it is the fact that their fathers have provoked them to anger by not doing anything with them when they were young children.

Fathers, Show Your Children You Love Them

Do not allow the world to make you afraid to be with your family or to show them you love them. For example, just because your daughter has developed into a young woman does not mean that you cannot still be her father. You most certainly can still hug her.

To this day my adult daughter still sits in her daddy's lap. She has him wrapped around her finger, so to speak, and he is proud of it! She is her "daddy's daughter," and they are close. Their relationship has steered her away from some potentially damaging situations in life and has kept her on the path of God's design.

Now this relationship did not just suddenly appear. It *developed* over the years as Keith showed his children he was interested in them. He was the kind of father who would be concerned if his children came into the house and ignored him. That was when he would get upset. He would go looking for them to make things right between them and himself.

However, many fathers have upset daughters because they cannot talk to their dads. They cannot get hugs or kisses from their father, and they know they had better never sit on his lap.

One day just recently, one of my daughters had me sitting on *her* lap! We were just sitting there talking, and I looked at her and said, "Why am I sitting on your lap?" That is a result of Keith and I having developed true relationships with our children.

We have to have relationships with our children. Family members may be related to one another, but spending time together is what develops true relationships.

Our family members should be our best friends. Personally, I do not have best friends outside of my family, because my family understands me better than anybody else does. Because I don't have time to cultivate other relationships as a minister, I hang on to the people who understand me the most: my precious family with whom God has blessed me.

Parents *Set Boundaries* for Their Children

The *fifth* responsibility of a parent is *setting boundaries* for our children. Children need and want guidelines. Guidelines make life easier for them. Children just want to have fun, but if one day we tell them they're not allowed to do something, and the next day we tell them they're permitted to do it, life becomes complicated for them. They won't know how to articulate their feelings, but inside, they're begging, *Just give me a solid guideline. If I can do this today, then I should be able to do it tomorrow, next week, and next month. And if I'm not supposed to do it today, then I shouldn't be able to do it tomorrow, next week, and next month.*

Children need specific guidelines. They need to know how far they can go, and we need to be consistent about it. We cannot change the rules from day to day. Do you know why we change? It is because we do not know ourselves. We have not taken the time to get into the Word of God to find out what He has said about being godly parents.

First Timothy 3:4 and 5 tells us we must have boundaries in our homes.

> **One that ruleth well his own house, having
> his children in subjection with all gravity;**

(For if a man know not how to rule his own house, how shall he take care of the church of God?)

1 TIMOTHY 3:4,5

In this passage, God is saying, "If a man doesn't know how to take care of his own house, then how can he be a pastor and take care of the house of God?"

If your pastor walked into a church service and said, "Look, I've worked hard this week, so I'm not preaching today. Just go on home," would you not be upset? Well, that is what some fathers do with their kids. They say, "I worked hard today. Don't come in here bothering me. Don't talk to me. Go find your mama. Go bother somebody else."

However, God says, "You can't do that. You have to be a leader and an example. You have to provide for and nurture your family. And you have to set boundaries. You have to rule your house well — you have to be a father."

Keith and I were not afraid to set boundaries for our children. For example, we would not let our children go to certain parts of the city. There were times they could not go to different events and house parties because of where the activities were held.

To this day, they know they cannot go to some places, not because Mama or Daddy says so, but because they understand it is not safe to be there. Just as Proverbs 22:6 says, when you train children in the way they should go, when they get old, they will not depart from it. That means that when they get old, they will begin to understand the training they received and the messages you were endeavored to convey to them as you trained them.

When our children were young, they did not understand our decision in setting this particular boundary. But as they grew older, they understood. And, now, they won't depart from it and find themselves in trouble because they were in the wrong place at the wrong time.

I used to read newspaper articles to my kids about tragedies that happened at house parties. Almost every time those tragedies happened, the victim was an innocent bystander. I told my kids, "You will never be in the position where somebody can say you were the innocent bystander whose life was taken."

We viewed our children's safety and well-being as our responsibility. We saw it as our job to make sure they were not put in certain compromising situations that could endanger them. And we were consistent about the rules. We didn't say, "Well, I guess you can go this time, but not next time." No, if there was an activity in the wrong part of town, they simply were not allowed to go — ever, *period*. We made it simple for them. They could ask, and we would listen to all of their reasoning as to why we should make an exception, but where that boundary was concerned, our answer was always the same: "You're not going."

Parental Involvement During The School Years

Another rule that we made for our children was that they would attend Christian school. That was a commitment that we made to God before we even had our children, because we wanted them to be brought up in God's way of doing things and being right. Therefore, all of them went to private, Christian schools for their entire education.

I remember when my daughter wanted to go to a public high school. We listened to everything she had to say, but then we said, "Okay, we hear you, but you're still not going. We know all your reasons; we know it's important to you, but you are not going to a public school."

Now that decision was a sacrifice, because we paid tuition for our children's schooling all those years. I realize that not all parents can send their kids to private schools and that there are some good public schools out there. But it is still their responsibility as parents to make sure that their children get everything they need in the way of an education and at the same time to ensure that their schools — Christian or public — are not taking out of them everything that they are putting into them.

We have to pay attention to what is going on with our children. That takes time and effort and energy, but we have to do it. We have to go down to the schools with them, look at their textbooks, find out how their teachers talk to them and interact with them, how they are treated, and how they act in class. We cannot just send our kids to school and say, "Wow! They're gone! I've got eight hours of free time!" If we take this kind of disinterested attitude, when they come home, we will wish they had never gone, because they will be acting like different children.

If we do not find out what the schools are teaching our children, we cannot tell our children whether something they're learning is right or wrong. If they are in a public school, we need to make sure that the curriculum or the teachers personally are not teaching them that they are different because they're Christians, implying that they are *wrong*. Of course, they're *different* because they have a different God, a different Father, a different life. They do things God's way. Yes, they are *different*, but that does not make them worse; it actually makes them better. They are better off because they know they belong to the Lord and that they are of their Father God.

If we do not want somebody in the world talking our children out of serving God, we cannot just take them to children's church and never give them any Word ourselves. They are supposed to receive the Word from us every day. When they get up, when they get ready for school, when they come home and relax, and when they go to bed, they are supposed to get the Word of God from their parents. Furthermore, depending on what is happening in their lives, we may have to double up on the Word we give them!

Children do not just pop out of their mamas into a world in which everything is dandy. That is not how it works. Neither can we stuff them back in! Once they are born, we really have to grow up ourselves. We have now taken on the responsibility to be parents.

Parents *Love* Their Children

Our *sixth*, and most important, responsibility as parents is to love our children. First Corinthians 13:8 shows us one attribute of true love that we must display to our children: *constancy*. In *The Amplified Bible*, it says, "Love never fails — never fades out or becomes obsolete or comes to an end...."

Our children need love that does not end. No matter what they have or haven't done, we need to love our children. They need to know that we love them all the time. If they know that they have our love, they will not tend to get into trouble. It is the child who does not know he is loved who will most likely cause problems, because he will go out there trying to find somebody to love him. He will take risks and step outside the boundaries of what he knows is right in order to receive that so-called love.

Often that is what is wrong some young women. A girl's father is not being the loving male figure in her life that he ought to be, so she is out there looking for another one. But even if you as a father are divorced or were never even married, there is no reason for you to turn your back on your child.

Some single moms have good jobs and are able to financially take care of the children. But that is no reason to refuse child support, as some women do. That's selfishness. That is your children's money, not yours. If you do nothing but put that money away in the bank to give to the children when they're eighteen, do it. Say, "This is from your daddy." Accept his support.

Furthermore, as a single parent, do not say negative things about the other parent. When you do, you are talking about your own children. As parents, we are called to love our children. We need to be a support to them and always be there for them. We should never speak negatively to them, period. For example, do not call your children stupid! Why would anyone ever do that! Why would anyone call his own child stupid?

God did not make any stupid children. Even if you do think they are stupid, Romans 4:17 says, "Call those things that be not as though they were." Call it the way you want it to be. Tell them they are intelligent and that they can make it and go far in life.

Do not speak negative words over your children! Those children are blessings of God! Do not turn your back on them. Do not just toss them to the side. Love them! Get your priorities right. If you are married and have children, your priorities are first to God, then to your husband, then to your children, *then* to your job.

A Word to Single Parents

If you are not married and you have children, your priorities are first to God, then to your children, not to whomever you are dating.

If you are a single mom, you do not *need* a man in your life. But your children do need *you* in their lives. You need to spend your time with your children. Actually, some single moms don't qualify scripturally to be "found" and married by a man, because Proverbs 18:22 says, *"Whoso findeth a wife findeth a GOOD THING...."* Well, if you're not being a good mother, you are not being a "good thing." Don't make the mistake of treating your children as if something is missing in their lives because you're not married. Get involved in their lives, because all they are missing is *you*!

If you're doing the right thing, teaching your kids that they have a Father — God — in their lives, they will grow up confident that God loves them and that He is on their side. They will know they are not missing anything, because God can be better to them than any father they could ever imagine.

With God on our side and on our kids' side, we do not have any more excuses. We have the Word of God, and we can read. Even if we cannot read, we can buy Bible on cassette tape and listen to its wisdom. When we continually make excuses for not doing the right thing, we are selfish and we become more and more lazy. If we want things to be right in our lives and in the lives of our family, we need to stop making excuses and align ourselves with God's Word and His way of doing things no matter what the world around us may be doing or telling us.

Even if your husband did act like a jerk and leave you, that has nothing to do with how you treat your children. That has nothing to do with your responsibility now as a mother to your children. You are to be a parent to those children in your home, and you are not supposed to move them down on your list of priorities. Your children are to be second only to God. Do not let anyone or anything take their position away from them.

Take This Job Seriously

As parents, we have to take our job seriously. We have to get our own lives together and stop wasting time while our children are growing up before our eyes. God wants us to train up our children in His way of doing and being right. He wants godly seed. If seed is not godly, it is because the ones who planted it and nurtured it are not godly. Godly parents bring up their children in the way they should go, and those children do not depart from it when they are older.

If we make mistakes with our children, we have to make it right. We can't live in denial about it. We have to go to our children and say, "Look, I've talked to God. I did some things wrong. I went the wrong way. Let's fix this. Let's go to God together and let's fix it."

We do not have time to be fighting with our children. We need to be the ones our children look up to and listen to. We do not need them to be trusting other people more than they trust us. They don't need to be sharing their heart with others, because we don't know what the other people are saying, what their motives are, or if they really love our children.

However, we do know that we love them, so we need to keep the lines of communication wide open with them.

It is important to realize that when you have children, it's not about you anymore. You will have time for "me" after your kids are grown and out the house, but right now you have to give your all for them. That is what it will take to successfully bring up children today. They face too many challenges out there, and they need us as parents to be there for them to support them and give them loving guidance.

In order to have godly children, we have to teach them the Word of God. If we follow His instruction for being godly parents, we will have children who live right all the time because they do things God's way. They acknowledge God in all their ways, and God directs them in everything they do.

But this will not happen just because you want it to happen. You have to do the things it takes to achieve this goal: *teaching, training, providing, nurturing, setting boundaries,* and *loving.* When we take our parental responsibilities seriously, our children will be a blessing to us, to God, and to His Kingdom. They will be, as Psalm 112:2 says, "...*mighty upon earth: the generation of the upright shall be blessed.*"

Divorce and Remarriage

Keith A. Butler Sr.

D o you know what God thinks about divorce? Is divorce acceptable? If two people simply do not get along, if he does not like her cooking, or if she is no longer happy with his physique, does God mind if they get a divorce?

If we look in the Word, we can find God's thoughts about the subject. Not only does God tell us how He feels about divorce, He tells us *why* He feels the way He does. In this chapter, we will look to God's Word to find His wisdom on the subject of divorce and remarriage.

The Pharisees once asked Jesus about this topic, as recorded in the Book of Matthew.

> **The Pharisees also came unto him, tempting him, and saying unto him, Is it lawful for a man to put away his wife for every cause?**
>
> *MATTHEW 19:3*

The phrase "put away" is talking about divorce. "Is it lawful for a man to divorce his wife?" they asked Jesus. In the following verses, we find His response.

> **And he answered and said unto them, Have ye not read, that he which made them at the beginning made them male and female,**
>
> **And said, For this cause shall a man leave father and mother, and shall cleave to his wife: and they twain shall be one flesh?**
>
> **Wherefore they are no more twain, but one flesh. What therefore God hath joined together, let not man put asunder.**
>
> *MATTHEW 19:4-6*

In response to the Pharisees' question, Jesus quoted God's command to the first couple, Adam and Eve, that a man shall "cleave to his wife." As we saw previously, the word "cleave" means *to run after, pursue,* and *stick to like super glue*! God commanded a man to stick to his wife!

God Makes the Two *One*

The day a Christian man and a woman stand up and say, "I will take this person to be my lawfully wedded spouse," God joins the two and makes them one. Even if they are making a mistake by marrying one another, God unites them. In marrying one another, they are using their God-given right to choose what they want to do. But whether they realize it or not, they are making a vow before God. They are saying, "God, this is my partner for the rest of my life," so God joins them together.

Abortion: An Attempt
To Escape Consequences

Now, of course, when we choose what we want to do rather than pursuing what God wants us to do, we suffer the consequences. Everything in life has consequences. There is a result for whatever we do, good or bad. But if we do not like something that came about as a result of our wrong behavior, God does not condone our just getting rid of the result if it means sinning some more.

We cannot escape the consequences of our actions. That fact alone is one thing that makes abortion wrong. Individuals attempt to abort children in order to rid themselves of the results of their actions.

Sex has consequences. If we are going to have the fun of sex, we also have to pay the price of sex. Man reaps what he sows — especially if he is sowing sperm!

What About Moses' Command?

After Jesus said that man was not to divide what God had joined, the Pharisees responded with the following argument.

> **They say unto him, Why did Moses then command to give a writing of divorcement, and to put her away?**
>
> *MATTHEW 19:7*

They were referring to what Moses said in Deuteronomy 24:1 and 2: *"1 When a man hath taken a wife, and married her, and it come to pass that she find no favour in his eyes, because he hath found some uncleanness in her: then let him write her a bill of divorcement, and give it in her hand, and send her out of his house. And when she is departed out of his house, she may go and be another man's wife."*

According to the Law of Moses, if a man found "uncleanness" in his wife, he could divorce her and send her out of his house. Then she was free to marry someone else. What did he mean by "uncleanness"? He meant *unfaithfulness* or *fornication.*

Then Deuteronomy 24:5 gives specific instructions to the man who has divorced his unclean wife and then remarries.

> **When a man hath taken a new wife, he shall not go out to war, neither shall he be charged with any business: but he shall be free at home one year, and shall cheer up his wife which he hath taken.**
>
> *DEUTERONOMY 24:5*

God said the husband was to stay home with his bride for the first year of their marriage. Though we do not live by this Old Covenant law, it is still a good idea in principle, and we need to follow it to a certain degree. We need to get to know our spouses in that first year we are married. Even if a bride and a groom were friends for twenty years before they took their vows, they would still need to learn about each other within their new context of marriage.

At least for the first year, a bride and a groom need to focus on nothing but "me and you." They don't need to run all over the place with their friends. Instead, they need to be stuck like super glue to each other!

Brother, the first year of marriage is not the time for basketball with your guy friends. No, that is the time to spend with your bride. It is the time to find out who she is so you can dwell with her according to knowledge (1 Peter 3:7). You and your bride even need to get into job situations that allow you to spend as much time as possible with one another. You need to understand that you are no longer two singles. You are one.

'Except It Be for Fornication'

Now in Matthew 19:8 and 9, we find what Jesus said to the Pharisees about Moses' law regarding divorce.

> He saith unto them, Moses BECAUSE OF THE HARDNESS OF YOUR HEARTS suffered you to put away your wives: but from the beginning it was not so.
> And I say unto you, Whosoever shall put away his wife, except it be for fornication, and shall marry another, committeth adultery....
>
> *MATTHEW 19:8,9*

A man who divorces his wife, for reasons other than her unfaithfulness, and then marries somebody else *commits adultery*. For example, if a man divorces his wife because he does not like her cooking, and marries another woman whose cooking is better, Jesus said he was committing adultery. (Note that this passage is addressed to followers of God.)

Do Not Marry an Adulteress

The last part of verse 9 continues, saying, "... *Whosoever shall put away his wife, except it be for fornication, and shall marry another, committeth adultery: AND WHOSO MARRIETH HER WHICH IS PUT AWAY DOTH COMMIT ADULTERY."*

There has been a lot of misunderstanding about this statement. At first glance, it seems as if Jesus is saying that no divorced woman can ever remarry because doing so would be causing her new husband to sin. However, we need to look at this verse in context.

Remember, according to Jesus' previous statements, a man could only divorce his wife for *fornication*. Therefore, the woman the Lord is talking about in this context is the one who is "put away" or divorced because she was unfaithful to her husband. God is saying that if someone else marries *that* woman, he is also contributing to the defilement of her original marriage.

This is a different case than if the woman who is innocent has been put away or divorced. That woman, being innocent, is free. God will not hold an innocent person responsible for someone else's actions. If she is innocent, God will not penalize her for the rest of her life because her husband was stupid.

However, if she is not innocent and she gets put away, then anyone who marries her also enters into adultery. Now, Brother, that tells me that before you think about marrying a divorced woman, you had better know why she got that divorce. You do not want to inadvertently take part in such an offense as adultery.

The Disciples' Response

In verse 10 we find the disciples' response to Jesus' teaching against divorce for any other reason than fornication: *"His disciples say unto him, If the case of the man be so with his wife, it is not good to marry."*

They were having a fit! They said, "We ought to be able to get rid of a woman just because we want to! If we can't, then we shouldn't get married!"

However, Jesus had said, "No, God puts a husband and a wife together. What God puts together, you cannot break apart."

The Sanctity of Home and Family

Family is a sacred thing. Now we live in a society that does not esteem it that way. They have what they call "no-fault divorces." *There is no such thing!* Divorce is always somebody's fault, and it is usually *both people's* fault.

First Corinthians 13:8 tells us that love never fails. Therefore, no matter how hard it is for two people to get along, if they will walk in love, things can be worked out.

If She Leaves Her Husband

In First Corinthians 7:10 and 11 God gives wives guidelines about divorce.

> **And unto the married I command, yet not I, but the Lord, Let not the wife depart from her husband:**
>
> **But and if she depart, let her remain unmarried, or be reconciled to her husband: and let not the husband put away his wife.**
>
> *1 CORINTHIANS 7:10,11*

First, He says, "Women, do not leave your husbands" (v. 10). However, He then says, "*If* you depart...." It is not God's desire for the union of a marriage to be severed.

However, in certain situations, it is in a wife's best interest to depart. For example, God does not expect a woman to be a "whipping post" and to be beaten by some man. She is not required to remain in a violent or dangerous situation. She is not required to live in a house with a husband who is dealing drugs and who may be shot at in that home. There are all types of scenarios that permit a woman to leave her husband.

However, that does not mean she can just run off and marry somebody else. Verse 11 continues, *"But and if she depart, let her remain unmarried, or be reconciled to her husband: and let not the husband put away his wife."*

In other words, if a woman leaves her husband, she can either go back to her husband and work things out or she can remain unmarried. That is what the Scripture says.

Now, remember, this book of First Corinthians was written to believers. Some people get married fourteen times before they get saved. Nevertheless, thank God that when we accept Jesus Christ as our Lord and Savior, we get a clean slate. Now that we are born again, our days of foolishness are over.

If She Is an Unbeliever

Then in verse 12 of First Corinthians 7, God tells believing husbands what to do when their wives are not saved.

> **But to the rest speak I, not the Lord: If any brother hath a wife that believeth not and she be pleased to dwell with him, let him not put her away.**
>
> *1 CORINTHIANS 7:12*

Just because the husband gets saved but his wife hasn't, he cannot divorce her. He cannot put her away simply because she did not decide to join him in the faith. She is still his wife.

If He Is an Unbeliever

In verse 13, God tells believing wives what to do when their husbands do not believe.

> **And the woman which hath an husband that believeth not, and if he be pleased to dwell with her, let her not leave him.**
>
> *1 CORINTHIANS 7:13*

A believing woman is to stay with her unsaved husband if he still wants to live with her. If he does not kick her out because she got saved, the Word of God says she is to stay with that husband.

The Unbeliever Is Sanctified By the Believer

Verse 14 tells us *why* God wants believers to stay with their unbelieving spouses.

> **For the unbelieving husband is sanctified by the wife, and the unbelieving wife is sanctified by the husband: else were your children unclean; but now are they holy.**
>
> *1 CORINTHIANS 7:14*

There is an anointing on the believer. Even if you are saved and your spouse is an unbeliever, you are still anointed! You have the Word, and blessings can still come to your house and to your children because of your stand for the Lord.

If the Unbeliever Leaves

Now in verse 15, God tells the believer what to do if the unbelieving spouse leaves.

> But if the unbelieving depart, let him depart. A brother or a sister is not under bondage in such cases....
>
> *1 CORINTHIANS 7:15*

This scenario is about a couple who marry when they are unsaved and one of them later gets saved. Then the other one responds by saying, "What? You don't smoke anymore? You don't drink anymore? You don't wife-swap anymore? We either go back living the way we were and you stop with this 'Jesus' thing, or I'm out of here!" Of course, Jesus is that other person's Lord, and he will live holy from then on, so he runs the risk of losing his spouse. But if the unbelieving spouse leaves because of this, the believer "is not under bondage in such cases" (v. 15).

In other words, the believer is not held responsible for that divorce. If the unbeliever leaves the believer because of the believer's testimony of Christ, then the believer is not held responsible. The believer is not charged for the divorce. That person is free to remarry.

Win Your Spouse by Your Lifestyle

Remember, however, that the believer is not to leave the unbelieving spouse simply because he or she is not a believer. Verses 16 and 17 address this important truth again.

> **For what knowest thou, O wife, whether
> thou shalt save thy husband? or how know-
> est thou, O man, whether thou shalt save thy
> wife?**
>
> *1 CORINTHIANS 7:16*

To the married believer, God says, "Don't leave your unsaved spouse. Stay right there if your spouse still wants to be married to you. You may be the very one who will lead that person to Me."

As you might recall, this same truth is found in First Peter 3:1.

> **Likewise, ye wives, be in subjection to your
> own husbands; that, if any obey not the
> word, they also may without the word be
> won by the conversation** [manner of life] **of
> the wives.**
>
> *1 PETER 3:1*

Though this passage is addressed to wives, we discovered previously that it also applies to husbands. In other words, whether you are a believing husband or a wife, you are called to stay with your unbelieving spouse to win that person to the Lord by your lifestyle. You cannot win a person if you leave.

Now if the lifestyle of the unbelieving spouse produces the type of situation that makes it impossible for the believer to remain in the home, the believer is free to leave. However, the believer is not free to remarry. Why? Because God still wants that family held together. He wants it held together for the sake of the seed, the children, and for the sake of the oath that they made. Family is important, and marriage is sacred.

Marriage Is a Covenant

In Malachi 2:14, God speaks about the sacredness of marriage.

> **Yet ye say, Wherefore? Because the Lord hath been witness between thee and the wife of thy youth, against whom thou hast dealt treacherously: yet is she thy companion, and the wife of thy covenant.**
>
> *MALACHI 2:14*

God says to the divorced man, "You entered into a contract, a covenant, with her when you said, 'I do.' Now you have dealt treacherously against her by divorcing her."

This is why, single person, you should not be in a hurry to jump into marriage. You need to do some research and understand what it means to say, "I do." Marriage is a commitment for life.

Marriage is not something that you can just try and see if it works. It is not something you can skip out on if it does not work. That is the world's way, not God's, of doing things. God doesn't say, "Taste it and see if you like it, and move on if you don't." God intends for a man and woman to be joined together throughout their lifetime.

Furthermore, God intends for men and women to be virgins before they are married. He wants us to save ourselves to be gifts unspoiled for our spouses. We are gifts! God created the woman and the man to be gifts for one another in marriage. That is why we are to save ourselves: God wants us to be able to present our gifts properly. And when we make our vows, He wants us to take them seriously. He wants us to remember that we are making a covenant before Him.

God Wants Godly Seed

While we are making those vows, God is at work. He is making us one. Malachi 2:15 tells us why.

> **And did not he make one? Yet had he the residue of the spirit. And wherefore one? That he might seek a godly seed....**
>
> *MALACHI 2:15*

God wants a godly seed from this union. He wants children who are unspoiled, children who have the benefits of both father and mother, children who have the financial resources they ought to receive. He wants children who, because of their parents' example, will be able to fulfill their roles in God's structural design for their families. He wants children who will have the integrity and the resources to help their parents when they get older.

God set up this system called the family to help us take care of one another. He did not want us to be independent of one another but to be dependent on one another. Therefore, God wants the husband and the wife to stick together. He wants godly seed who will honor Him and fulfill His will on the earth.

God Hates Divorce

This is why God is so opposed to divorce. In the following verses we can see again that God says that it's treacherous to divorce one's spouse.

> **And did not he make one? Yet had he the
> residue of the spirit. And wherefore one?
> That he might seek a godly seed. Therefore
> take heed to your spirit, and let none deal
> TREACHEROUSLY against the wife of his
> youth.**
>
> **For the Lord, the God of Israel, saith that
> he hateth putting away: for one covereth vio-
> lence with his garment, saith the Lord of
> hosts: therefore take heed to your spirit, that
> ye deal not TREACHEROUSLY.**
>
> *MALACHI 2:15,16*

God said, "I hate divorce." He hates it because it robs
multiple people of His blessings. It robs wives; it robs husbands; it robs children; it robs seniors. It is a killer!

God said, "Divorce is dealing treacherously. Take heed to
yourself that you do not deal treacherously, that you do not
divorce." Obviously, then, divorce is sin. However, it is not
unpardonable. It is like any other sin except the unpardonable sin of refusing God's saving grace. God can forgive a person of the sin of divorce *if* the person will truly repent.

True repentance is not saying, "Well, I know God will forgive me, so I'm going to do this," and then doing it again.
The word "repent" means *to turn and to go in the opposite
direction*. True repentance says, "This is not the way I'm going
to go anymore."

Now if you have been divorced for any reason other than
the ones God clearly gave us in His Word, you can repent of
that and God will cleanse you of all sin. However, you must
understand that now that you are saved and have attained

this knowledge before God, you cannot go and act like you did before.

Stay Put!

God hates divorce, so why would believers whose spouses are being faithful and are not harming them even think about doing it? I cannot divorce Deborah Lorraine Butler. I am not even thinking about doing it. I will not do it, *period*.

(My wife is not twenty-five anymore. Now I'm sure there are twenty-five-year olds who would love to have me because I am handsome and rich! But I will not leave Deborah for any twenty-five-year-old! First, God said that would be treacherous and that I would have to pay the penalty for it and be under the curse. Second, I love my wife with all my heart. We have built a beautiful life together, and I will not forsake the wife of my youth!)

Divorce is a robber and it destroys families. In the next chapter, we will address in greater detail people in second marriages as well as people in blended families. However, we need to first understand that we have to stay put wherever we are now. Unless we have the Bible reasons for divorce, then we should just stay put.

Even if you and your spouse are having a lot of difficulty getting along, you cannot just walk out and be right about it in the eyes of God. You are held by your vows to stick together like glue. Nobody put a gun to your head and made you make your marriage vows. No, you made a decision and you yourself said, "I do."

If your marriage situation is not a blessing, it can be turned around to be one. You can make it work through the power of the Holy Ghost if you decide to take God's route. Now if you try to force your spouse to be something he or she is not, that will not work. If you fight with your spouse every day, that will not work.

However, if you do it God's way and allow Him to be the Lord of your marriage, He can turn any situation around. He will make it possible for you to function successfully and happily in marriage in Jesus' Name.

Thank God I Obeyed the Word in My Marriage

I know from experience that succeeding in marriage starts with a decision. I could have bailed out on Deborah after our first year of marriage. That first year was tough! We did not understand each other. We were nineteen years old. We had no money and no teaching. All we knew was that we both thought each other was fine! Then *bam*! We hit the wall, just as most newlyweds do. We found that we didn't "mesh"; we didn't jibe. Our marriage just didn't seem to be working properly. We both thought, *Oh, Lord, what did we do?*

What turned things around so that we have a marriage that's "heaven on earth" today? The man of the house made a decision. I decided first. I said, "God's Word said this deal can work, so, Lord, show me what I'm doing wrong." I did *not* say, "Lord, show me what *she* is doing wrong." I asked Him to show me what *I* was doing wrong.

He did. Then I began to act on the Word of God concerning her, and it started to affect her. Then she started acting on the Word of God concerning me and what had been unhappiness started turning into happiness. What had been a mess started turning into a blessing. It did not happen overnight, but it was one decision that started the process.

I just decided that I was not going to walk away. I admit that jumping ship would have been easy to do. It would not have taken much effort to say, as many folks do, "Well, it just didn't work. We have irreconcilable differences. We just don't get along. I'm leaving." I could have gone out and found another woman, but I would have been messed up if I had done that.

Why? Because no other woman is the one called for me. *Deborah* is the one called for me. I would have been in my second or third marriage by now had I run from my marriage to Deborah. My ministry would not have been where it is today. My children would not have had the benefit of having their father with them. Yes, they would have gotten my money, but that is not enough. They needed *me*!

And they got me. Thank God I made the decision to do what God said. Because my children got me, they turned out all right. Because there was leadership at the helm of the ship, Satan was not able to steal our lives together. God was able to raise us up and bless us.

Because I have obeyed God, our family is in a blessed position. If my mother or Deborah's mother becomes a widow, or if people in our family who are living for God honestly run into difficult situations, we can help them! And we will. That is the way God intended family to operate. He wants us to be blessed and to be a blessing. That is why He says, "What I have joined together, let no man or woman break apart." If we will follow His way in our marriages, He will help us stay together forever.

Blended Families: Preparations and Pitfalls

Keith and Deborah Butler

Statistics tell us that the so-called "nuclear family" — husband, wife, and children — is no longer the norm in America. Family researchers tell us that the blended family has rapidly become the norm. Whether by death, divorce, or incarceration, many parents are finding themselves single and responsible for rearing their children alone. Often those single parents remarry. In those second marriages, entire families may come together.

Such blending of families has resulted in all types of problems. Indeed, we have found that the divorce rate for second-time marriages and blended family marriages is fifteen percent higher than for first-time marriages.

When multiple kids from multiple parents and multiple backgrounds join together as a family unit, the two adults have to deal with many more issues than just those relating to their own marriage. Not only are the two adults' lives affected, but their children's lives are affected as well. Therefore, the two adults must handle some particular issues with far more dispatch and care than would ever be required in their relationship otherwise.

This is why we have devoted this chapter to a discussion of blended families in light of the Word of God. If you are considering becoming involved in a blended family, we strongly recommend that you and every party involved in the transition first invest your time in extensive, specific, godly counseling.

Even if you are not in a blended family or considering becoming part of one yourself, we encourage you to read on about this important subject. Then you may be able to take God's wisdom and be a blessing and a help to somebody else who is in this situation.

Children Are Important to God

When two families blend together, what happens with the children is critical to the well-being of each child's spirit, soul, and body, and of the entire family. Have you ever looked into the Word of God and noticed the importance God places on children? For example, look at Psalm 127:3.

> **Lo, children are an heritage of the Lord:**
> **and the fruit of the womb is his reward.**
>
> *PSALM 127:3*

God says that children are our heritage and reward from Him. He wants us to know they are a priceless gift from Himself, so we should treat them as such.

Furthermore, God makes it a point to bless our seed, our children, as we can see in the following Psalm, talking about the seed of a righteous man.

> He is ever merciful, and lendeth; and his
> seed is blessed.
>
> *PSALM 37:26*

Indeed, the Bible tells us that the very reason God put man and woman together as husband and wife was for the unique purpose of creating "godly seed" or righteous children.

> Yet ye say, Wherefore? Because the Lord
> hath been witness between thee and the wife
> of thy youth, against whom thou hast dealt
> treacherously: yet is she thy companion, and
> the wife of thy covenant.
> And did not he make one? Yet had he the
> residue of the spirit. And wherefore one?
> THAT HE MIGHT SEEK A GODLY SEED.
>
> *MALACHI 2:14,15*

God's attitude toward His little ones, His children, is serious. One prominent example of this truth is found in Jesus' statement in the Gospel according to Matthew.

> But whoso shall offend one of these little
> ones which believe in me, it were better for
> him that a millstone were hanged about his
> neck, and that he were drowned in the depth
> of the sea.
>
> *MATTHEW 18:6:*

Jesus essentially said, "It would be better for you to have to deal with having a stone tied around your neck, being thrown into the river, and drowning than to mess with My Father's kids."

The Child's Best Interest

We can see from these strong statements in God's Word that a very important issue for any parent should be discovering what is in the best interest of his or her child. In fact, for single parents, securing the welfare of their children should be the second highest priority, next to loving God.

This is in stark contrast to what is the focal point of many single parents today, and that is, "What is in *my* best interest?"

The first thing some single parents think about is their own need. They may say things like, "I need a husband," "I need a wife," or "I'm so lonely; I need somebody to go to bed with tonight." Of course, they usually do not say it, but what they really mean is, "My kids will just have to adjust."

However, Scripture teaches that the responsibility of a single parent is first to the child, even ahead of himself. Caring for the child's need, instead of one's own, is to be of utmost concern.

Communicate With Your Child

How do we know what our children need? We cannot look out for our children's best interest if we do not allow them to speak to us. We have to communicate with them. We have to be up-front with our children, and we must also allow our children to freely express to us thoughts and concerns.

For example, if you are a single parent considering marriage, you need to tell your child about it. Then you need to give your child the opportunity to respond with his or her honest thoughts and feelings about the matter.

Differing Ages, Different Responses

You will find that children of differing ages will respond differently. For example, a younger child — if he is even old enough to have an opinion about it — may be more open to the idea of a parent marrying than a teenager might be. An older child will most likely resist such a change.

If, for instance, a child has grown up without one of his parents in the home, he will have grown accustomed to relating only to the single parent who has taken the responsibility to rear and nurture him. If, then, that single parent suddenly wants to introduce a new parental figure into the home — and possibly even other children — that child will probably have some concerns that need to be heard and worked out between himself and his parent.

Regardless what age a child may be, he needs to be in support of the restructuring of his family. Otherwise, the new family will not be a happy, peaceful one. This is why a single parent who wants to marry simply must consult with his child before making such a decision — a decision that will affect more than just himself.

As a matter of fact, we strongly recommend that single parents of teenagers simply wait to think about marrying until their children are out on their own. If you are in this situation, this may sound difficult. But remember, you only have a couple more years to wait, and a happy, peaceful home is worth the wait.

Do Not Invite Trouble

If you are a parent of a teenager and, in marrying, you think you are just inviting a *spouse* into your home, you may actually be inviting *trouble*. The older your child is, the more problems you could have introducing another person into your family.

For example, think about what might happen if a mother introduces a stepfather into her teenaged son's life. If her son does not like the way that man talks to his mama, and if he is bigger than that man, he might beat up on that man! Then, in retaliation, that man may just beat up on her! It has happened.

Older Children Require More Attention

One reason we recommend waiting to marry until a teenaged child is out on his own is that the older a child is, the more attention that child needs. When a child of any age has spent much of his life with only one parent, receiving all of that parent's time, attention, and money, then becoming part of a blended family will be a difficult transition for that child to make. However, when a much older child, a young adult, loses time, attention, and money, he is certain to get upset!

A parent of a teenager must take the time to have a serious discussion with the child about whether or not to pursue marriage at all while that teenager is still at home. The parent must ask questions and listen to the child's responses about what marriage would really mean to the child. The child's view will certainly be different than the parent's, and the parent needs to hear what the child is really saying.

Ask Yourself Why, And Be Honest With Your Answer

If you are a single parent seeking marriage, not only must you ask your child what he or she thinks about the topic; you must also ask yourself. You need to ask yourself, *Why am I getting married? What's the real reason?*

There are reasons *not* to get married. For example, you should not get married because you think your child needs a daddy or a mama. Now, of course, it is good to have both a man and a woman in the home caring for the children, providing they are the *right* man and the *right* woman! Yet finding that other parental figure should not be the number-one reason for marrying anyone.

If a man with three kids and a woman with two kids come together, there had better be some serious depth to their reasons for doing so.

Biblical Reasons for Marrying

First of all, before the issue of children is involved, a man and a woman must decide what the Word of God tells us to consider in a mate. They must find out what steps to follow before entering the covenant of marriage. In previous chapters, we discussed these issues, but we will briefly reiterate them here.

First, a Christian considering marriage must be certain that the other person is born again and shares the same beliefs as he or she does.

Next, the two people must be going in the same direction. The Bible says, *"Can two walk together, except they be agreed?"* (Amos 3:3).

Then the two people must do all the necessary "research" about one another and be certain that they are compatible.

These are some of the steps a single parent must take in a relationship *before* introducing the other person to the children. It is crucial that a single parent *never* introduce to a child a boyfriend or girlfriend who may later have to be removed from the child's life because that person did not fit.

Let us put it in plain language: Sally should not start dating Joe and then introduce Joe to her children after three weeks. After six weeks, Sally may find that Joe has some serious problems that make him incompatible as a potential marriage partner. She may have to cut him loose, so she should do it before her children have even met him.

But if Sally *does* introduce Joe to her children after only three weeks of dating this man, the kids will be damaged, especially if they have begun to love Joe, when she has to cut him loose. If they've fallen in love with Joe, and Joe is gone, they will be crushed, and Joe will be gone to them like their daddy is gone. It will be like re-wounding your children even if Sally had nothing to do with the fact that their biological father left in the first place.

This is why we say not to introduce a potential spouse to your children until you are convinced that he or she is the right one for you.

There's More Besides That!

However, as a parent, discovering that you and that other person are compatible is not all there is to the pre-marriage screening process. Once you accept that person as the right one for you, you may still have to reject that person if he or she is incompatible with your children.

When someone decides to marry a single parent, that person is not only choosing a spouse but also his or her children. That needs to be clear to all parties involved. There can be no separating of a parent from his or her children.

Some potential spouses of single parents don't even understand what it means to be a parent. So talking about parenthood on a surface level won't suffice. Both parties have to dig deep into this topic so that the one who is planning to take on this new parental role will know exactly what it will entail to be the mother or the father of these particular children. This new parent needs to know in detail the responsibilities he or she will be taking on.

A single parent shouldn't jump into marriage just because he or she shares a mutual love with another person. She may love him, and he may love her; but what if the children hate the new spouse? Marriage in this case would not lead toward a happy marriage, and it certainly would not lead toward a peaceful home life.

If you are a single parent who is interested in pursuing marriage, something you need to determine before introducing someone to your children is whether he or she even likes children! That seems like an obvious determination to make, but we've actually seen blended families in which the new parent didn't even like kids, yet wanted to be married to the children's parent.

Everyone ends up hurt in a situation like that in which selfishness abounds. The children are ignored, and when they *aren't* being ignored by their parent, the spouse is jealous and, perhaps, infuriated at the little bit of extra attention the children are getting. The parent feels pulled in two different directions and finds himself or herself in the position of having to attend to the children in secret so as not to upset the spouse.

Observe Your Intended One With Other Children Before Allowing Him or Her to Meet Yours

If you are a single parent considering marriage, before you introduce your intended one to your children, put him or her in a situation in which he or she is around other children. Observe how that person relates to them.

For example, notice what happens if you go to the park with that person. If some kids kick a ball in your path and he or she shouts, "Get that ball away from here!" you know right then that you have a problem. If that person picks up the ball and throws it hard in the opposite direction, *that* is evidence of a problem!

If, by word or deed, that other person shows you that he or she does not want children around, you know right then that you're going to have to say good-bye to that person.

Again, do not test this issue by introducing your boyfriend or girlfriend to *your* children. If you do, he or she is going to act appropriately to keep things going smoothly between the two of you. Instead, you need to see that person in his true light, when he's not trying to "put his best foot forward," so to speak.

Exercise Self-Control

Because you may discover that a person is incompatible with children and you, therefore, have to end the relationship, you will need to be able to control your emotions from the very beginning of a relationship. You will have to exercise some self-control.

If you allow yourself to become emotionally attached to another person too soon, it will be much more difficult to walk away from that relationship if it becomes necessary to do so.

This is why you must not make the decision to pursue marriage in a hurry. You need to take *twice* the amount of time in the dating phase of the relationship that you would take if it were just two adults being joined without any children involved in the equation.

We believe that a couple should not even consider the question of marriage unless they have been dating for a minimum of one year. Then, if they have kids, they need to double that period of time. As we said, even if the potential spouse is compatible with your children, the children must have "pre-marriage" counseling as well and be allowed to disclose all of their thoughts and feelings about the change. They did not ask to come into this world. Their parents brought them here. Now their parents have a responsibility to make sure they are not harmed.

Children Are Intuitive By Nature

One of the best ways to discover whether a person will get along well with your kids is to check your children's initial reaction to that person. Children are very intuitive people; they can read what kind of person one is, and they can tell whether or not that person likes them.

We have actually seen instances in which people have sworn up and down to children: "I like you! I really do!" However, the truth was that they did *not* like those children, and the children picked up on that. *They knew it!*

Sometimes, the truth of the matter is, if a parent will just pay attention to his or her child before saying, "I do," that parent will not say, "I do" to begin with. *Children know things intuitively that adults are not as perceptive about.*

If a parent continues in a relationship with someone who does not like his or her children, the kids will become resentful. What's worse is when a single parent has habitually ignored his or her child and is now introducing someone new to the child's life. Not only does that child resent never having been able to communicate with his parent beforehand, but now he resents the fact that someone has walked in and completely stolen all hope of his ever being able to do so. This ministers rejection to a child and can wound him deeply, perhaps even for life.

A healthy home life for a blended family requires the cooperation of every party involved. A signal that the marriage of a single parent will result in happiness for the children involved can be seen in the parent's courtship. Once involved in the new relationship, if a child's parent continues to relate well to him, spend time with him, and nurture their parent-child relationship, the child will likely feel better about the addition of a spouse to the family.

On the other hand, if the child sees the new person as someone who is wielding influence over his parent in an unfavorable way, coming between him and his parent, he will resent it, and he will not cooperate with the new arrangement.

For example, if the parent's relationship with a new person changes the way the parent looks at his child or communicates with him, the child will not view his parent's relationship as something that's going to add happiness to his life. In fact, he's probably going to become fearful of losing the sense of love and nurturing and stability that he's known from the most meaningful relationship in his young life — the relationship between him and his parent.

Parents who find themselves caught in the middle between new spouses and children have not done their job.

They have not followed the proper steps toward marriage, putting God first and their children second. God will hold Christian parents responsible for their children turning away from Him and the Church if the parents refused to put the children's needs ahead of their own. A parent's selfishness in meeting his needs above those of his children is why problems occur so many times in blended families in the first place.

'Dating' the Children

What happens when a couple has taken all the steps toward marriage, prayerfully considering each step, and they have determined that they are right for one another and for the children? The person who will be filling the new parental role will need to initiate spending some quality time with the children.

At first, this time should also be spent with the parent. Then, after the children become comfortable with the new person, he or she should start "dating" the children, spending time getting to know who they are, what they believe, what direction they are heading in life, and so forth.

Then the children will know that not only is their parent important to this new person, but they are valued as well.

Compatible Parenting Styles

Not only must you decide whether the person you are considering marrying is right for your children, but you must ask yourself, *What is this person's philosophy on rearing children?* It should at least be similar to yours.

When two individuals get married, they already have enough to argue about. There is enough to deal with just as a man and a woman learn how to live and flow together as a married couple. They do not need anything new to argue about! However, and this is especially true in blended families, child-discipline may become a source of debate if it is not discussed before marriage.

We have seen instances in which two people have gotten married, and the new spouse believes the child needs a spanking, but the parent doesn't believe in using spanking as a form of discipline. Then the newlyweds became divided on the vitally important issue of how to discipline the child.

The family is not about division; it is about oneness. It is not "my children," "your children," "her children," "his children," "my car," "my money," and so forth. No, family is *oneness*; it's *unity*. It is not independence, but interdependence.

If you are a single parent, you must understand that if you bring a new man or woman into your home, your child also belongs to that person. Your child is no longer just your child. And when two parents decide how to enforce the rules in their household, both parents — the parent and the stepparent — must follow through on that decision. So if you are unwilling to allow the person you are considering marrying to discipline your child, then you should not marry him or her.

Child-Discipline Is a Requirement, Not an Option

Proverbs 22:6 says, *"Train up a child in the way he should go: and when he is old, he will not depart from it."* The word "train" connotes *disciplining by repetition*. In other words, you cannot train a child by telling him once what to do. (You can't even expect adults to comply with a new set of instructions if you only tell them once. It often takes people several times of hearing something new before they can fully understand and apply it.) Therefore, parents must continuously and consistently instruct their children. That is child-training, and God says many times in His Word that it must be part of every child's life.

For example, in Proverbs 22:15, God says, *"Foolishness is bound in the heart of a child; but the rod of correction shall drive it far from him."* In other words, without discipline, foolishness will be bound in a child's heart.

Furthermore, Proverbs 23:13 and 14 says, *"Withhold not correction from the child: for if thou beatest him with the rod, he shall not die. Thou shalt beat him with the rod, and shalt deliver his soul from hell."* God is saying here that godly discipline will save a child from hell. You see, disciplining our children is not an option; it is a mandate from God.

Every Child Needs Discipline

Unfortunately, however, some Christian single parents whom we have counseled have told us that they have difficulty controlling their children because they admittedly do not discipline them. Why? It is because they feel sorry for them. Feeling as though their children are deprived of a second parent, they let them do whatever they want.

However, such parents need to know that their children are not necessarily deprived because they don't have two parents in the household. They *are*, however, deprived if their parents treat the issue of discipline like that. Their parents' negative reaction to having only one parent in the home deprives the children of fully enjoying life.

Nobody said life was fair. We have to adjust to whatever comes and make the most of our present situations. We have to do what it takes to win, and we need to teach that mentality to our children.

Children of single parents can be very well-adjusted. They will be happy, emotionally healthy, and productive if they receive love, peace, discipline, and sound teaching from one parent.

The Importance of Maintaining Respect In Child-Discipline

As we said, when a single parent does decide to bring a new parent into the home, he or she must realize that this person will contribute to the discipline of the children. If the children do not respect that person before the two are married, then after the wedding, that stepparent will not be able to discipline those children, and there will be war in that house.

Therefore, even if a single parent is in love, if his or her children do not respect the other person, then the two of them simply should not pursue marriage. Why do we say that? Because we have seen people in this situation get married, anyway, and then completely lose their children. The children say, "I can't wait till I turn eighteen so I can get out of here and never come back again." Children should never be put in a position that provokes that kind of thinking.

When our children were eighteen, they did not want to leave home. They went to school, and, afterward, they came back home. Why? Because they did not see "hell" happening at our house.

If you want your children to love being at home, then before you get married, you need to think: *Once I marry this person, we will be one. Will I be able to watch this person discipline my child, who will be "our" child once we say, "I do"?*

Don't Fall Prey to Manipulation By Your Children

If you can answer yes to that question, then once you do marry that person, you must never allow your child to pit you and your spouse against each other. If children try this once and it works, they will keep doing it. Children are not stupid. Sometimes we make them that way with our poor training, but they do not come to this earth that way. They know exactly what to do to get what they want, and they will try it and keep trying it until a parent wises up to them!

Therefore, if a child sees that he can make his parent mad by saying, for example, that his stepparent did something to hurt him, he will continue to do that to avoid being disciplined by the stepparent.

Unfortunately, this tactic is especially effective against mothers. If mothers hear that anyone hurts their children, they want to say, "Where is this person? Let me deal him!" When children see this reaction, they take full advantage of it.

Never Side With Anyone Against Your Spouse

This is why we must be careful that we never publicly agree with anyone's negative words, even our children's, about our spouse. If your children have complaints about your spouse, you first need to privately talk things over with your husband or wife and then go to the children and talk to them. You should never side with your children against your spouse. Doing so teaches them that you do not respect your spouse, so they will not respect him or her, either.

Never publicly agree with *anyone* who speaks against your spouse, whether it be your mama, your daddy, your friends, your children — whoever. What they say might be right, but you should not agree with them; you should be calling those things that be not as though they were (Rom. 4:17). If you are just "calling those things that be" as though they *are*, then things will not change. If you just agree with the negatives, you will only become more frustrated, get further from the Word, and have to deal more with circumstances than with God's promises.

Changes in the Household

When a couple decides to marry, a few things will change in the household. We have already discussed how discipline will change. In addition, priorities and money management will be different. These are things that every member of the new family should discuss before the marriage vows are exchanged.

Priority Changes

When single parents get married, their priorities will change, affecting their relationships with their children. Before marriage, single parents' priorities are first to love God, then to secure the welfare of their children, then to do their jobs, and then to spend time with their extended families.

When they get married, this list changes. A new priority is added. Now their priorities are first to love God, *then to love their spouses*, then to secure the welfare of their children, and so forth.

A clear change of priority takes place. Before a single parent gets married, the child gets the parent's time, attention, and energy. However, priorities change when his parent marries someone. That spouse is now the one who wants the first cut on the parent's time, attention, and energy.

You can imagine that this would cause quite a paradigm shift for a child. He is used to coming home and saying, "Mama, Mama, Mama..." or "Daddy, Daddy, Daddy..." "I need this. I need that. Do this. Do that. Drive me here. Drive me there." Though the child does not understand it because he has perpetual energy, all that takes a toll on the parent's body.

Therefore, when a new person comes into the family, the child sees that person as one who wants to cut off the limited energy that the parent has always given to him. Then the stepparent thinks, *Well, that kid ought to be able to understand that.* They don't. In fact, nobody understands that! Everyone wants time, attention, and energy from loved ones. If you have been a single parent and are now married, your child expects to get the same thing from you that he got before. Yet your new spouse expects to have your attention and energy too. That person did not marry you just to look at you from afar as you spend all your time with the children.

That is why we say that before blending a family, every individual involved must receive a whole lot of counsel and ministry. That is also why we encourage single parents to make sure that the people they intend to marry take the time out to "date" the children.

The perfect situation is that in which a new person in the family has become so involved in the parent's life and the child's life that he or she is just as concerned as the parent is that the child's needs are fulfilled. In marriages where this is the case, if the parent is too tired to meet the child's needs, then the child can comfortably go to the stepparent to have his needs met. In this scenario, the child will not miss anything.

What the child cares about is getting what he wants. If he has not had that opportunity to get to know this new parent, he will say, "I don't want you. I want my mama [or my daddy]."

If you are a single parent, you have to let the person you may potentially marry spend time with your child, taking the child out, finding out what the child is interested in. It is not good enough for you just to tell that person what your child is interested in.

You can see that this takes time, and the more children you have, the more time it will take. However, you need to make sure that time is taken, because if you do not, you will pay for it later. If you do not allow your children to get to know this new person and then rush into marriage, you will have a messed-up child and a messed-up marriage.

Furthermore, if you are a parent planning to marry another parent, you *each* need to take the time to date the other's children. And you have to do this *before* you even make the final decision to be married.

You do not want those children fighting among themselves, saying, "He did such-and-such for *his* kids, but not for *us*." Children already fight enough among themselves. However, if they fight about unequal treatment from the parents, it is your fault. You put them in that situation.

Money

Another topic you must consider before blending a family is money. You need to ask yourself, *How will this transition affect the money in this household?*

The number-one reason that couples divorce is money — how it is handled, how it is managed, what happens to it, who gets it, and so forth. This is the case in blended families as well.

For example, a man who has been supporting two kids and decides to marry a woman with three kids must now support six people in addition to himself. Thus, the living standard for the people in that home will certainly change — and, more often than not, it will be for the worse. The children of the woman he marries may be used to having their own rooms, taking vacations, getting allowances, and so forth. Now things may be different. Furthermore, perhaps one of the parents set aside money for the children to go to college. Now that there are five children, will the parents be able to provide higher education for all of them?

Now the parents' monetary priorities will have changed. They may need to pay for a bigger house, another car, more medical insurance, more food, more clothes, and so forth.

The two parents considering marriage may say, "Oh, we'll make it somehow." However, they need to be asking, "Will this change the children's lifestyle?" If it will, then the children need to know about it beforehand. If they are not prepared for the shift, then they will resent the fact that the money has been removed from them to be used on the other kids, the other person, or whatever needs may arise.

Many people do not think about these nitty-gritty issues until after they get married. They never think about it. That is why we so strongly recommend pre-marriage counseling and getting all these things out in the open.

A single mom entering marriage especially needs to be aware that, though her parents may be used to buying things for her children, now that responsibility needs to be on her husband. He will want to take care of them. He will not want anybody else supporting them because the grandparents' support says to him, "You can't take care of them, and you need help." Therefore, in order to avoid insulting him, her parents should wait until birthdays or special occasions to buy things for the children.

Blind Love?

These are the types of things that need to be out in the open long before a couple even make the decision to go to the altar to enter the covenant of marriage together. Once a couple are married, they cannot write each other off — they have to put each other on their prayer lists!

We like to say, "Love is blind, but marriage is an eye-opener!" A blended family marriage opens *both* eyes — before the honeymoon is even over. In fact, there probably will not be a real honeymoon because the children will want to come along!

Do not go into marriage blind. There are some things you can do to keep yourself from making a mistake at the altar. You and the person you are intending to marry need to do some research about one another so that your eyes will be opened and you can see things more clearly while you still have the option to change your minds.

Other Children Not Living in the Home

One area of research and discussion is the sometimes subtle issue of children who don't live with the parent. Some people actually try to hide this information from a potential marriage partner. But when a person is evasive in answering questions and tries to hide things from the other party, it is a clear sign that something is not right with that relationship, and the other person should put the brakes on it immediately.

We have actually heard of people getting married, and, afterward, saying something to their spouse, such as, "Oh, I forgot to tell you; I have a son in California" or "I have a daughter in such-and-such place." First, being evasive or untruthful is an indicator that a relationship is on shaky ground. So you want to tell your prospective spouse the truth. Second, he or she needs to know about all your off-spring because you both need to discuss what would happen should it become necessary for any one of those children to make his or her home with the two of you.

For example, imagine that a woman with children and a man with children are considering marriage. Let's say that the man has two kids who live with their mother. However, when the children are old enough, they will have the right to say, "I want to go be with Daddy." The woman marrying this man, then, needs to ask herself, *Am I willing to let her kids be in my house with my man and my kids?*

There are many issues attached to marrying a parent, even if the children do not live with that person. For example, the other person even needs to ask, *Am I willing to let my spouse go pick up the kids at the ex-spouse's house?*

Furthermore, you need to observe how that parent you intend to marry takes care of his or her children who don't live with him or her. We have counseled people who were dating parents who neither lived with their children *nor* paid child support. If you were a parent and discovered that about your "intended," why would you want to pursue entering into a covenant relationship with him or her? *If a person is not responsible enough to take care of his own flesh-and-blood, then he will certainly not take care of yours!*

A person like that has no sense of responsibility. What you need to say to him or her is, "Bye! You were a nice acquaintance, but that's it! I can't have anything to do with you!" *Before* you marry anyone like that, you need to just write that person off.

Credit Reports

Not only do you need to find out whether or not the person you want to marry has children and is taking care of them, but you also need to see that person's credit report.

So often people get married and do not find out until after the wedding that their spouse has terrible credit. Then theirs is ruined as well. We have seen so many people ruined by spouses who could not handle money.

Creditors do not care who causes financial problems. Once you say, "I do," they do not care that you are not the one who accumulated all this debt. But once you are married to a poor money-manager, you're married, and now in addition to having to adjust to married life, you're going to have to plow through trying to organize and repay debt that you didn't even incur.

Then in the unfortunate event the spouse leaves you and continues to mismanage money, guess who the creditors are going to come after? They're going to come after you, the unfortunate spouse who didn't do his homework before heading to the altar.

As a single woman, do not allow yourself to get caught up in a man's muscles or his physique or how big and strong he looks and how safe he makes you feel. And as a single man, do not allow yourself to become entangled by a woman's curves, how nice she smells, or how adoringly she looks at you. If you are looking only superficially at a prospective mate, you may end up with a good-looking mate, messed-up children, bad credit, no money, and "hell on earth" in your house!

It sounds cold, but you might have to require looking at your intended's credit. You might be thinking, *Well, that's not romantic.* But you will not live on romance. You will live on dollars, and you need to know how that other person manages his dollars *before* you say, "I do."

Medical Records

The next thing you need to see is medical information. You want to know before you get married if the person you intend to marry has a venereal disease, high blood pressure, anemia, impotence, or some other medical problem or concern.

Many people will not disclose that kind of sensitive information, even to the ones they intend to marry. Many people will not tell the truth because they are afraid the truth will drive others away.

If you are planning to marry someone, you need to learn to be honest with that person before you get married. If that person walks away from you because of a truth that you disclose, then you do not need to marry that person, anyway.

When you intend to marry someone, make sure both of you get a physical even if you both a healthy medical history. So often people get lulled into believing that bad things only happen to other people. We must take the time and effort to do things right so that we can ensure God's best in our marriages.

'An Ounce of Prevention...'

As you can see, there are many topics to discuss and to be worked out before families blend. We just scratched the surface of all of the challenges that come when families are broken apart and rejoined as new families. This is why God is against sin: *Sin hurts people.* This is why God is against pre-marital sex: *Children born out of wedlock start life with a challenge.*

This is why God is against divorce: *There's more to divorce than just getting rid of one person.* Any children involved must deal with the loss of a parent, the loss of self-esteem, and the loss of finances. They often blame themselves for the divorce. Then they often have to deal with a new mother or father in the home, new siblings, new surroundings, and so forth. Their future is now compromised. All kinds of destructive things happen when a family breaks up.

This is why you must learn to make things work with your husband or wife. This is why we firmly say, "Keep your family together! Work it out!" In most cases, it is better to work out what you already have than to start all over again.

Keep your family together. If you desire to honor God in your family, pray the following prayer from your heart.

"Heavenly Father, give me wisdom so that I may conduct myself in a way that pleases You and that does not harm other people. Give me patience to make the right decisions. Help me not to be in a hurry. Help me to be more responsible and to govern my body. You have given me victory in every area as I obey Your Word. So in Jesus' Name, I thank and praise You for giving me the Bible, Your Word, so that I can walk in Your best. In Jesus' Name I pray. Amen."

The Importance of Wisdom And Understanding in The Marriage Relationship

Deborah L. Butler

God wants us to walk in His best in every area of our lives. If anything in our lives — including our marriage and family — is not full of life, God's Word tells us why: *"Let thine heart retain my words: keep my commandments, and live. Get wisdom, get understanding: forget it not; neither decline from the words of my mouth"* (Prov. 4:4,5).

I like to read this passage like this: "If you want to live, keep God's commandments and walk in His wisdom and understanding. If you *don't* want to live, then *don't* keep the commandments of the Lord or walk in His wisdom and understanding."

If something is not going right in our marriages, our families, or any area of our lives, we need to ask ourselves these questions: "Am I keeping God's commandments? Am I walking in His wisdom and understanding?"

Proverbs 4:7 says, *"Wisdom is the principal thing; therefore get wisdom: and with all thy getting get understanding."* In order to walk in God's best for our life, we have to have wisdom.

We Can Ask for Wisdom

What do we do if we need wisdom? God tells us in James 1:5: *"If any of you lack wisdom, let him ask of God...."*

Notice God did *not* say, "Ask your girlfriend." He didn't even say, "Ask your preacher." He said, "Ask *Me.*" He is the only One who can give us wisdom. He is the only One who has it to give.

When we ask God to give us wisdom, James 1:5 says that God will give it to us. "Why do I have to ask? Why doesn't He just give it?" someone may ask. Because God's Word says that we must ask Him for it.

God is waiting for us to ask. Of course, when we ask God for something, we have to expect to receive it. The next verses say, *"BUT LET HIM ASK IN FAITH, nothing wavering. For he that wavereth is like a wave of the sea driven with the wind and tossed. For let not that man think that he shall receive any thing of the Lord."* Of course, when we ask God for wisdom with an expectation and faith to receive it, He gives us more than we ask for.

Solomon Asked for Wisdom

God gave Solomon more than he asked for. From an early age, Solomon offered sacrifices to God and did what he knew to do to please God. In response, according to First Kings 3:5, *"The Lord appeared to Solomon in a dream by night: and God said, Ask what I shall give thee."*

Solomon's reply is found in verse 9.

> **Give therefore thy servant an understanding heart to judge thy people, that I may discern between good and bad: for who is able to judge this thy so great a people?**
>
> *1 KINGS 3:9*

In other words, Solomon asked God for wisdom, an understanding heart so that he could rule the people of God. He said, "I want to be able to lead these people whom You have given into my care. I want to be able to understand them and tell them the right thing to do. I can't do that on my own. In order to do it, I know I will need Your input."

Solomon's prayer pleased the Lord. And true to His Word and nature, God gave Solomon more than he asked for.

> **And God said unto him, Because thou hast asked this thing, and hast not asked for thyself long life; neither hast asked riches for thyself, nor hast asked the life of thine enemies; but hast asked for thyself understanding to discern judgment;**
>
> **Behold, I have done according to thy words: lo, I have given thee a wise and an understanding heart; so that there was none like thee before thee, neither after thee shall any arise like unto thee.**
>
> **And I have also given thee that which thou hast not asked, both riches, and honour: so that there shall not be any among the kings like unto thee all thy days.**
>
> **And if thou wilt walk in my ways, to keep my statutes and my commandments, as thy**

father David did walk, then I will lengthen thy days.

1KINGS 3:11-14

In First Kings 4:29-31, we find that God followed through on this promise.

> **And God gave Solomon wisdom and understanding exceeding much, and large-ness of heart, even as the sand that is on the sea shore.**
>
> **And Solomon's wisdom excelled the wisdom of all the children of the east country, and all the wisdom of Egypt.**
>
> **For he was wiser than all men; than Ethan the Ezrahite, and Heman, and Chalcol, and Darda, the sons of Mahol: and his fame was in all nations round about.**
>
> *1 KINGS 4:29-31*

Why did God bless Solomon in this way? He told him why in First Kings 3:11: *"Because thou hast asked this thing, and hast not asked for thyself long life; neither hast asked riches for thyself, nor hast asked the life of thine enemies...."*

If God asked many of us, "What is it that You want me to do for you?" we might say, "Give me money so I can build a church" or "I want a new house" or "I've had my eye on this sports car..."

Solomon asked God for wisdom — and not for his own sake. He asked God for wisdom so he could help God's people. That is why God gave him everything else besides — including material things that he did not ask for.

Seek First the Kingdom

Solomon's story is a perfect example of Jesus' profound statement in Matthew 6:33. He said, *"Seek ye first the kingdom of God, and his righteousness; and all these things shall be added unto you."*

Everything that Solomon needed was added to him when he sought first what was best for God's Kingdom, not what was best for Solomon. Because he had a heart hungry for God's wisdom, Solomon became not only the wisest man on the earth until Jesus Christ Himself came, but also the richest man on earth.

Nevertheless, you can be wiser than Solomon. Solomon did not have Jesus living inside of him. We have the wisdom of God already residing inside of us. It is one of the things that Christ came to give us. In fact, it is one of the things that He *is* for us, according to First Corinthians 1:30: *"Of him are ye in Christ Jesus, who of God IS MADE UNTO US WISDOM."*

Wisdom Must Be Applied to Benefit Us

God's wisdom is available to us today in great supply. We need to start applying God's wisdom to our lives. We are so interested in finding out what other people think and what they have done that we constantly find ourselves doing things the way the world does them instead of the way God wants us to.

God's wisdom should be the only influence in our marriage and home life. We might be influenced by a great preacher or Christian writer whom we respect. But their influence is based on God's wisdom. We do not need to hear worldly opinions and advice that isn't rooted solidly in Scriptures. Ephesians 4:27 says, *"Neither give place to the devil."* We need to stop allowing the devil to get in our marriages. He has no right in there, so we just need to stop letting him interfere in what God has put together.

We need to stop listening to what the world tells us about marriage. If Hollywood knew how marriage was supposed to work, Hollywood actors would stay married. Instead, we hear of Hollywood breakups almost daily, and when one marriage lasts twenty years or longer, we are surprised and hold that marriage up as an example because it stands out so much.

So if longevity in Hollywood marriages is not the norm, why do we follow Hollywood's version of what love is as if it were our guide? Why do we become starry-eyed when we see two people fall in love on the big screen?

Do not believe all the things you see on television. Those actors are paid to do what they do, and their lines are scripted. They do not behave the same way at home! In many cases, an actor will behave recklessly on screen and come off as the hero with a girl hanging on his arm and gazing at him adoringly. But in real life, his ungodly behavior would likely result in destruction and heartache, not the happy ending that is often portrayed.

Sadly, many in the Church act as if the Bible is just a script. We read it and act it out, but we do not allow it to govern our lives day in and day out behind the scenes as well as in the presence of others. We come to church and act out God's script, and then we go home and act out the world's script.

We will not find true wisdom anywhere but in the Word of God, so we had better read the Bible as if our lives depended on it. As Proverbs 4:4 says, *"Let thine heart retain my words: keep my commandments, and live."* Proverbs 14:12 says, *"There is a way which seemeth right unto a man, but the end thereof are the ways of death"* (*see* also Proverbs 13:14 and 14:27). We need to meditate on the Bible, the words of God, or our actions will result in death.

Sometimes the reason we need physical healing because we are not obeying God's commandments. We need to make a decision to obey His commandments. We need to decide that whatever we see in the Word of God, whether we like it or not, we will do. It's a *decision*; whether we agree with it or not, totally understand it or not, or feel like doing it or not, we must *decide* that we *will* obey God's Word.

We have to learn that without wisdom, we can't receive from God or accomplish anything for Him. Wisdom is the principal thing; there is nothing more vital. If we do not have wisdom, we will not receive from God, and we will eventually lose what we have.

Wisdom Has a Beginning, But There Is No End to God's Wisdom

The opposite is true if we do possess godly wisdom.

> The wise also will hear and increase in learning, and the person of understanding will acquire skill and attain to sound counsel [so that he may be able to steer his course rightly].
>
> That people may understand a proverb and a figure of speech or an enigma with its interpretation, and the words of the wise and their dark sayings or riddles.
>
> The reverent and worshipful fear of the Lord is the beginning and the principal and choice part of knowledge [its starting point and its essence]; but fools despise skillful and godly Wisdom, instruction, and discipline.
>
> *PROVERBS 1:5-7 (Amplified)*

Verse 7 says that knowledge has a beginning: "the reverent and worshipful fear of the Lord." Now the good thing about knowledge is that it has a beginning but not an end. Therefore, no one can ever say that he knows it all. Each of us has the capacity to have knowledge and wisdom, but no one has it all. We have to act on what we have in order to flow in more wisdom. We have to use what we have and grow from there. We need to grow up in the wisdom of God.

All of God's Wisdom for All Times

As I said, in order to grow in wisdom, we have to walk in the wisdom that we have. And we have to walk in it continually. In other words, we can't walk in God's wisdom in certain situations but not in others. When we fail to walk in God's wisdom, we walk in the wisdom of the world, and God's wisdom and the world's wisdom do not mix! Remember, God's wisdom is the principal thing. There is nothing else, really.

God is an "all-or-nothing" God. And He requires that, for us to walk in His wisdom, we walk in all of His Word, not just the parts of our choosing. If we accept only part of God's wisdom, we will not reap the benefit of godly wisdom. It will not work for us, because God is an all-or-nothing God.

Of course, God is gracious, and He will often meet us where we are, especially when we are young in the Word — spiritual babies in Christ. However, if we do not *continue* to attain His wisdom from His Word, even the small part that was working for us for a while will stop working.

Some Christians experience trouble and then forsake wisdom, crying out, "Why me, Lord? Why did you let this happen?" That is foolishness, not wisdom, because God is not withholding from them. They are simply not walking in His wisdom. They are not obeying all of His Word. If they were, they would trust Him and rest assured that He would deliver them.

Being a child of God is like being married: Once you say, "I do," you have to *do* something! There's a reason why that action word "do" is in that statement. In marriage, you cannot just do what you want to do when you want to do it; you have to do what the two of you have agreed to do. Likewise, in your relationship with God, as far as God is concerned, you must do what He tells you to do at all times.

At the Heart of Wisdom Is *Trust*

That sounds like a hard statement, but it's true. To benefit fully from your relationship with the Lord, you have to obey Him explicitly. In order to do that, you have to trust Him. You have to trust and believe Him at all times, taking Him at His Word and accepting it as final authority in your life.

When you trust God, nobody can tell you that He's not going to do what He told you He would do. No circumstance will be big or bad enough to make you believe that He will not come through for you. When you trust God, you will never blame Him when things don't seem to be going the way they should. No accusation or negative word toward God will come out of your mouth when you're truly trusting Him.

Even if the devil sends you the thought that it's all God's fault, your lips will not form the words, because you are trusting God. Wisdom and knowledge are precious to you, and you will know and believe and act on the truth that God is not to blame. You will put your trust in Him.

God Gives to Us Without Fault-Finding

If, however, we admit when we have failed to follow the Word in its entirety, we can get right back into the Word and flow in God's blessings. Once we have repented, we do not have to feel condemned about our mistakes. That is what James was talking about in James 1:5

> **If any of you is deficient in wisdom, let him ask of the giving God [Who gives] to everyone liberally and ungrudgingly, without reproaching or faultfinding, and it will be given him.**
>
> *JAMES 1:5 (Amplified)*

God will give us what we ask for with no thought of our past. For example, if I did something stupid — something contrary to the wisdom of God — the Bible tells me in James 1:5 that I can go to God and ask him for wisdom to straighten out the mess my stupidity caused.

When I ask God for this wisdom, He will not give me a lecture and say, "If you had only done it this way, this would not have happened. I'm going to make you 'wallow' in your mistake for a couple of days because you were stupid. This is all your fault, you know. You fell into this on your own."

No, God will give me what I ask for. He will give me wisdom. All I have to do is ask Him in faith, trusting Him for what I need, and He will give it.

Many people will not ask God for wisdom because they find fault with themselves. But if God will not reproach us, what right do we have to reproach ourselves? Instead of spending so much time finding fault with ourselves, we should be getting back to what God said: "Ask Me."

When we ask Him, God will not only tell us what to do in a situation, but He will straighten it out for us. He will take the bad thing that happened and turn it around for good for us.

If There Was Ever a Place For Wisdom, It's in Marriage!

If something in our lives looks bad, the first thing we need to check is whether we are following God's commandments and walking in His wisdom and understanding. We are not supposed to check anyone else's life to see if he or she is doing the right thing. We are responsible for our own relationship with our Father God. *We are not called to try to change anyone else — not even our spouse!* When we walk in God's wisdom in our marriage, we will follow His commandments regardless of what our spouse does or doesn't do.

The Bible says, *"What therefore God hath joined together, let no man put asunder"* (Mark 10:9). What is so sad is that often the ones who are "putting asunder" marriages are the husbands and wives themselves. They are tearing their marriages apart because they are not walking in the wisdom of the Word.

I love my husband. Certainly, there have been times when I could have said, "You go; I'm staying." There are many unwise things that I could have done, but I would have missed out on so many good things in these twenty-five years with my husband.

What does it mean to walk in God's wisdom in marriage? Well, here are a few wise things that you can do.

Do Not Give Ungodly Counsel

First, do not give ungodly counsel to your spouse. Never let it be said of you that you advised your spouse unsoundly — in ways not based on the Word. Do not tell your husband or your wife to do a certain thing because *you* want it, whether it's right or wrong.

Proverbs 1:7 SAYS, *"Fools despise skillful and godly Wisdom, instruction, and discipline"* (*Amplified*). When I see the term "godly wisdom" in the Bible, that tells me automatically that there is such a thing as *ungodly* wisdom!

Psalm 1:1 tells us about ungodly wisdom: *"Blessed is the man that walketh not in the COUNSEL OF THE UNGODLY, nor standeth in the way of sinners, nor sitteth in the seat of the scornful."*

Ungodly counsel does not just come from people who are not born again. Unfortunately, there are many born-again people giving ungodly counsel. Ungodly counsel is anything that is contrary to the Word of God.

This is why each person needs godly wisdom for himself. If we do not have wisdom, we will be unable to distinguish between ungodly counsel and God's wisdom.

Many of us have grown up in churches in which we received ungodly "wisdom" every week. We did not bring our Bibles, so we did not know it was not God's wisdom. The *ministers* didn't even know it was ungodly wisdom. They were just preaching what somebody else told them to preach.

Therefore, in order to give godly counsel to our spouse or to anyone at all, we have to have God's wisdom for ourselves. It is time to stop making excuses, such as, "Well, I didn't know about that." We can't say that anymore, because we can ask God for wisdom and receive it. We have the Bible. We have eyes; we can read — and if we cannot, we can listen to the Bible on cassettes or compact discs. We can ask God to lead us to a church to attend that teaches the whole Bible, not just selected parts of it.

Do Not Hinder Your Spouse's Vision

Second, to walk in God's wisdom in marriage, do not hinder the vision that God has given to your spouse. You are one with your spouse. You are the only person in the flesh your spouse can count on. That is God's will and order, so get in line with that and be a support to your mate.

Let God Control Your Words and Actions

Third, let God control what you say and do — not just in the good times, but in the difficult times. For example, if your spouse is doing something wrong, do not criticize him or her. Nobody likes to be criticized, and commenting on the problem actually makes it worse.

God knows how to respond to your spouse when you do not. Seek Him, and He will show you what to say and do.

Resolve Conflicts Quickly

Fourth, to walk in God's wisdom in your marriage, *"…let not the sun go down upon your wrath"* (Eph. 4:26). That verse is not just pretty words; it is truth. So resolve any conflicts before the day is over.

Some married couples do not talk to each other for days at a time because one of them did not like something the other one said or did. Do not follow that example. Never allow conflicts to build over long periods of time, or they will become destructive forces against the life of your marriage.

Learn When To Be Quiet

Fifth, to walk in wisdom in your marriage, *learn when to be quiet*. If it seems your spouse is trying to start an argument, if you will learn not to say anything, your partner will realize he (or she) is arguing with himself (or herself) and stop.

After twenty-five years of marriage, I understand a few things about my husband. For one thing, I know that if he is bothered by something, I need to just keep my mouth shut. I know this is the way my husband works.

Often, once people have had their say and we do not try to prove them wrong, there never is any argument to begin with. If we do not challenge them or try to go toe-to-toe with them, it is over before it even starts. All we have to do is show them that we have paid attention to what they've said. Then if what they have said is wrong, we simply talk to God about it.

When we spend time with God, praying and talking to Him, God shows us our spouse the way He sees him or her. Then as we continue to go to God, seeing our mates the way He does, before we know it, we look up one day, and they are the way God sees them!

Our submission to God and to our spouse allows God to work in situations that could otherwise be tumultuous. Our praying about those things instead of verbalizing our own thoughts and opinions quiets us so we can hear from God, and it also quiets our spouse so he or she can hear from Him too.

Many times, people cannot hear what God is saying because all they can hear are their husbands or wives complaining. Nagging does not help anyone, so we need to be quiet and let God be God.

God's Wisdom Especially to Wives

Through the years I have found some nuggets of wisdom from God's Word specifically for women. For instance, God's answer to us when our husbands are doing something contrary to His Word is found in First Peter chapter 3.

> Likewise, ye wives, be in subjection to your
> own husbands; that, if any obey not the
> word, they also may without the word be
> won by the conversation of the wives;
> while they behold your chaste conversa-
> tion coupled with fear.
>
> *1 PETER 3:1,2*

That phrase "if any obey not the word" does not only refer to people who are not saved. It refers to anyone who is not walking in the whole counsel of the Word. Therefore, if your husband is not walking uprightly in a certain area of the Word, he may be won over — changed — without the Word by your "chaste conversation."

That word "conversation" does not mean talking. It does not mean nagging. It means *lifestyle* or how you live.

In other words, just because your husband is not following the Word does not give you an excuse not do what God tells you to do.

Wives, Respect Your Husbands

Verse 2 continues, saying that a wife is to couple her "chaste conversation" or her *godly lifestyle* with "fear" or *respect*. As a wife, you are to respect not only God but your husband.

Now, notice that this verse does *not* say that you only have to respect your husband if he *deserves* it. Your respecting your husband has nothing to do with what he deserves. It has everything to do with whether or not you will be obedient to God.

God's is instructions to wives continue in verses 3 and 4.

> Whose adorning let it not be that outward
> adorning of plaiting the hair, and of wearing
> of gold, or of putting on of apparel;
>
> But let it be the hidden man of the heart,
> in that which is not corruptible, even the
> ornament of a meek and quiet spirit, which
> is in the sight of God of great price.
>
> *1 PETER 3:3,4*

Now this passage is not saying that women cannot put on gold or dress themselves up. However, some women spend more time putting on makeup and making sure they have the right clothes on than they do showing their husbands respect.

What does it mean for a wife to respect her husband? Verse 2 in *The Amplified Bible* tells us.

> When they observe the pure and modest
> way in which you conduct yourselves, togeth-
> er with your reverence [for your husband;
> you are to feel for him all that reverence
> includes: to respect, defer to, revere him—to
> honor, esteem, appreciate, prize, and, in the
> human sense, to adore him, that is, to
> admire, praise, be devoted to, deeply love,
> and enjoy your husband].
>
> *1 PETER 3:2 (Amplified)*

First, this verse says that husbands should be able to see their wives being pure and modest. They should see their wives conducting themselves in a godly way, which includes a reverence for their husbands.

Then God tells us exactly how a wife is to revere her husband. She is to "respect, defer to, revere —honor, esteem, appreciate, prize, and, in the human sense, to adore him, that is, to admire, praise, be devoted to, deeply love, and enjoy her husband."

I believe this means that if my husband decides not to operate in any area in God's Word, if I follow God's Word anyway, then I obligate God and allow Him to step into the situation and set it right. Things may not change when I want them to, but it will be set right.

We have to learn how to trust God and take Him at His Word.

Wisdom for Women in Ministry

In twenty-five years of marriage, I have also had the opportunity to learn many practical ways to take God at His Word and apply His wisdom to my ministry and to my relationship with my husband, who is also my pastor.

First, I learned that if I wanted to be effective in ministry, I needed to live what I preach, because the first way people learn is by watching. People are watching me, so I need to live what I preach. I need to seek out wisdom from God's Word and apply it to every area of my life.

Second, as a minister's wife, I need to live out what my husband is preaching. *Sometimes a man's biggest obstacle to effectiveness in ministry is dealing with his wife.* God says that if she does not respect him even if he is wrong, she is being disobedient to the Word.

Third, I need to support my husband and his vision. If God has given your husband a vision, you are supposed to do everything you can to support him. Whatever your husband needs you to do — short of sinning, of course — you should do it.

Fourth, I must keep my personal relationship with my husband separate from our professional relationship. The Lord instructed me about this when I first went to work in the office with my husband.

The following is an illustration that will help you see the importance of this point. Imagine that I make a mistake while working at the office. Then my boss, who happens to be my husband, calls me into his office and says, "This is what you did, and you should not have done it." I cannot then go home and decide not to cook his dinner. That would not make any sense, because the one has nothing to do with the other.

In the office, my husband is my boss. At home, he is my husband. I have made the decision that the day I allow what happens at the ministry to affect what happens at home is the day I quit.

Accept Your Husband As Your Pastor

Let me take this a step further. Some people who are married to pastors have problems in their marriages because they have not accepted their spouses as their pastors. For example, some women cannot watch their husbands preach because all they see are their husbands. They have not accepted the anointing on their husbands' lives.

When I look at my husband, yes, I see my husband, but I also see my pastor. If I think something should happen at our church one way, and he thinks it should happen another way, I drop my case. He is the visionary. He is the one who must answer to God. If he has to answer to God for something I do wrong, it makes it difficult. Therefore, I have to get my act together and my attitude right and help him do what needs to be done.

My first calling is to be my husband's wife. I am to be a help meet for him. People ask me all the time, "What do you do at the church?" I cannot answer that question with specifics, because I do whatever my husband needs me to do. That is what I am called to do — to help him. I am called, not to hinder him or cause him more problems, but to help him.

Go With the Flow and Look for the Positive

We as ministers' wives may not always like everything our spouses ask us to do in ministry, but our own ideas have nothing to do with it. We made a vow before God to love and honor them — and that includes supporting them in ministry — and that is what we must do.

I have also learned to look for the positive in what could be seemingly negative situations. For example, my husband is a stickler for punctuality. Once, an hour and fifteen minutes before we had to leave for a ministry trip, he asked our daughter who was at home at the time, "Are you ready? Where's your suitcase? Get ready now; you're late."

Now I have learned after all these years that I cannot let the devil take this positive character trait in my husband and make it a negative thing about which I could argue with him. Regretfully, at the time of this incident, our daughter fell into the devil's trap. She explained to her dad that she had plenty of time and that she was ready whether she looked ready or not. As she was talking, I could tell he was getting a little bit more upset, and she was getting upset too. When I stepped in to try and make peace, frustrated, Keith said, "I'm talking to you too"!

Of course, my flesh wanted to start defending me, just as our daughter had done, but I had learned long ago that that was not the right response. My response was *nothing*. I didn't say a thing. I just dropped it. Our daughter followed suit and dropped it too. Everyone cooled off and not another word was said about it.

Do you know why I responded that way? I was just being obedient to the Lord.

We have to be wise enough to recognize the devil's techniques. He often tries to use petty things — anything to get a husband and wife to be at odds with each other. But to give place to it is not worth the trouble that it could cause.

For example, if I had chosen to argue with my husband about our being on time to leave for our ministry trip, I would have wasted time that I could have spent on packing. I could have said sarcastically, "My things are packed; all I need to do is pack your things," but that would not have been using wisdom.

Wisdom and Understanding Will Bear Fruit

In that situation, not only did I need to exercise wisdom from God's Word to respect and honor my husband, but I also needed to exercise understanding. I understood that punctuality was a character trait in my husband that I could not, and should not, try to change, so I knew to just let it go.

As husbands and wives, we need to understand and love each other despite what we perceive in each other to be flaws. When we practice wisdom and understanding in our marriages, we will not give the devil any place.

You Can Practice Wisdom Even When Your Understanding Is Lacking

However, sometimes we do not always understand why our spouses do the things they do. Nevertheless, God's Word says that we have a responsibility to walk in God's wisdom and submit to one another. We have to keep our attitudes right.

If I chose, instead, to have an attitude and to argue and fight with my husband every step of the way, not only will I have a problem, my husband will have a problem because the effects of my attitude will show up in our marriage.

We do not have to like or understand everything our spouses do. We do need to flow with him or her. It's so much better to talk to God about what we're feeling and let Him show us how to talk to our mate about it. When we obey God's Word, He will step in and make things right. And that's what we want: God's rightness in our marriages.

If we want God's best, we have to do things His way. We can't respond to argumentative words or bothersome behavior with our natural humanity, saying things like, "Why are you acting that way?" We have to lean on God and allow Him to respond through us with His wisdom, understanding, and love.

Follow Wisdom and Be Protected

We may not always understand *God*'s wisdom with our natural mind. Nevertheless, we need to follow it. I learned this lesson as a child learning to obey the wisdom of my parents. For example, they used to tell us, "You *can't go to the corner store because it's not safe.*" *In our childish minds, we would think, You taught us that God will protect us, so why can't we go?*

However, *as we grew older, we found out that our parents were speaking wisdom to us. It was not wise for us to go to that corner store,* and as *we followed wisdom, we were protected. We were* safe at home when that corner store got "shot up" one day.

Proverbs 4:6 tells us that protection, or preservation, is a benefit of wisdom: "Forsake her not, and she shall preserve thee: love her, and she shall keep thee." If we walk in wisdom, *God will preserve us.*

Have you ever heard about people who were at the wrong place at the wrong time, even though they had been told or impressed not to be there? They did not follow wisdom, so they did not have protection. It's only as you follow wisdom that you will have wisdom's protection.

Other Benefits of Walking in Wisdom

Wisdom is the principal thing. We have to forget what the world has said about what we should do. The world does not know right from left when it comes to walking in the wisdom of God. We have to find out for ourselves what God says and then accept and receive it and walk in the light of it.

When we flow in the wisdom of God, He will lead us and direct our paths. He will show us how to be successful. He will show us how to get and keep our lives on the right track. We need to exalt wisdom in our lives. Proverbs 4:8 tells us, *"Exalt her* [wisdom], *and she shall promote thee: she shall bring thee to honour, when thou dost embrace her."* Promotion and honor will come when we exalt the wisdom of God.

There are many benefits of wisdom listed in God's Word. Ever-increasing learning, preservation, promotion, and honor are just a few. All we have to do to acquire these things is to walk in wisdom. In order to do that, we must have wisdom, and to have wisdom, we must ask God for it. And He will give us more than we asked for. Just as He did for Solomon, He will do for us, giving us wisdom and all the benefits in His Word besides.

Wisdom is the principal thing. If we will walk in wisdom in everything — including in our marriages — if we'll do it at all costs, we will experience the full success that God has promised us in His Word.

How To Have a Satisfying Sex Life Part 1

Keith A. Butler Sr.

I want to ask you a question: If God had designed marriage without sex, would you still want to be married? I once asked the singles in my congregation this question. Out of about 1,500 singles, only four raised their hands to say that they would still get married if they could not have sex. (I'm praying for those four that they learn to be truthful! They may just be better than I am, but I know I would not have gotten married if I could not have had sex. I would have stayed single.)

That tells me that sex is a big deal in marriage. In fact, the second most common reason people divorce is over the issue of sex. That response from those singles in my church also tells me that everyone comes to the table in marriage expecting to receive, and that if they do not receive according to their expectations, there will be some disappointment.

Because of the weight we give sex in our decision to marry, we need to look into God's Word to find His perspective on this important issue. Now, single person, do not shut the book yet!

You need to find out about God's design for sexual intimacy before you get involved with someone. If you've watched any television at all, you have already seen the way sex works in the world. However, sex is God's idea, not the world's. Therefore, whether you are single or married, you need to find out how God wants sex to work so that you can have a successful sex life in God's timing — within the context of the marital relationship.

Sex Is Good

We know one reason God designed sex was that He wanted to multiply people on the earth. Genesis 4:1 says, *"And Adam knew Eve his wife; and she conceived...."* Now when the Bible says Adam "knew" Eve, it does not mean that he knew her name! It is referring specifically to his knowing her in a physical way; in other words, it is saying that he had sex with his wife. When Adam *knew* or had sex with Eve, she conceived and brought forth a son (Gen 4:1). Though there are many other reasons that sex is good, we know for this reason alone, that God designed a good thing when He created sex.

God also created sex so that a man and his wife can enjoy each other and become totally one in every way — spiritually, mentally, psychologically, and physically. Sex is God's idea; sex is God's doing. He's the One who came up with this "idea." I don't know about you, but I am thankful that He did!

Why Paul Said It Is Good Not To Marry

However, First Corinthians 7:1 seems to contradict the thought that sex is good.

> **Now concerning the things whereof ye wrote unto me: It is good for a man not to touch a woman.**
>
> *1 CORINTHIANS 7:1*

I want to clarify what Paul was talking about when he said, "It's good for a man not to touch a woman." Some people have taken that and really stretched it beyond what he was talking about. The Greek word here for "touch" means *to attach oneself*. Paul, the writer of this Book, is saying, "Don't get married if you don't have to."

Other Bible translations also interpret it this way. *The Living Bible* paraphrases it like this: "...if you do not marry, it is good." *The Amplified Bible* says it in another way: "It is well [and by that I mean advantageous, expedient, profitable, and wholesome] for a man not to touch a woman [to cohabit with her] but to remain unmarried."

So you see, Paul was talking about making the decision either to get married or to remain single. His personal opinion, as we can see throughout First Corinthians 7, is that it is better to be single, as he was.

In First Corinthians 7:32 and 33, Paul goes on to explain why.

> **But I would have you without carefulness. He that is unmarried careth for the things**

that belong to the Lord, how he may please
the Lord:

But he that is married careth for the things
that are of the world, how he may please his
wife.

1 CORINTHIANS 7:32,33

Paul says that single people are in the position to give
their lives wholly to the Lord. They do not have to be concerned with anybody or anything else. However, he writes
that individuals who are married have to be concerned about
their spouse.

It's Not a Sin To Marry

Paul is not saying that it is against God's will for two
individuals to marry. Quite the contrary, God designed marriage and blesses it.

Let's continue reading Paul's discussion on marriage.

But and if thou marry, thou hast not
sinned; and if a virgin marry, she hath not
sinned. Nevertheless such shall have trouble
in the flesh: but I spare you.

1 CORINTHIANS 7:28

Paul says, "While it is certainly not against God's will for
you to marry, I want you to know that if you get married,
you'll have to deal with some things in the natural."

Just two verses prior to this statement, in verse 26, Paul
said that this was particularly true "for the present distress."
What was the "present distress"? At that time, people were

being persecuted and killed for their testimony of Jesus Christ. Therefore, he was saying, "It is better that you be by yourself and be able to move suddenly as needed by yourself than to have to drag a whole family with you."

Not Everyone Can Remain Single

Back in verses 6 through 9 of First Corinthians 7, Paul explains that not everyone can remain single.

> **But I speak this by permission, and not of commandment.**
>
> **For I would that all men were even as I myself. But every man hath his proper gift of God, one after this manner, and another after that.**
>
> **I say therefore to the unmarried and widows, It is good for them if they abide even as I.**
>
> **But if they cannot contain, let them marry: for it is better to marry than to burn.**
>
> *1 CORINTHIANS 7:6-9*

Paul argues, "It's better to stay single so that you can attend to the things of the Lord without distraction. *But if* you cannot remain sexually pure as a single, then it is better for you to marry than to sin."

In verses 36 and 37, Paul addresses the single man who is having difficulty remaining pure with his girlfriend.

> **But if any man think that he behaveth himself uncomely toward his virgin, if she pass**

the flower of her age, AND NEED SO
REQUIRE, let him do what he will, he sinneth not: LET THEM MARRY.

Nevertheless he that standeth stedfast in
his heart, HAVING NO NECESSITY, but hath
power over his own will, and hath so decreed
in his heart that he will keep his virgin,
doeth well.

So then he that giveth her in marriage
doeth well; but he that giveth her not in marriage doeth better.

1 CORINTHIANS 7:36-38

Of course, we already discovered that Jesus said that some
folks are called to be eunuchs. They are called by God to
remain single and to serve the Kingdom of God. These are
people who "have no requirement or necessity." If you have a
need, then Paul says you should marry. One pastor said it
bluntly: "If you get 'hot,' Paul ain't talking about you!" And,
indeed, that rules out most single people. To them, Paul says,
"If you don't have power over your own flesh, or if you do so
require, then you should marry."

Requirements for Married People

To the people who do decide to marry, Paul says that
there are certain things they must do as married people.

Nevertheless, to avoid fornication, let every
man have his own wife, and let every woman
have her own husband.

> **Let the husband render unto the wife due benevolence [respect]: and likewise also the wife unto the husband.**
>
> *1 CORINTHIANS 7:2,3*

First and foremost, Paul says that the wife is to respect her husband and the husband is to respect his wife.

Their Bodies Belong to One Another

Then he goes on in the very next verse to tell us what else is due the spouse.

> **The wife hath not power of her own body, but the husband: and likewise also the husband hath not power of his own body, but the wife.**
>
> *1 CORINTHIANS 7:4*

The wife's body does not belong just to her, but also to her husband. That means she has to give her body to her husband. Likewise, the husband's body does not belong just to him, but also to his wife.

That means he must also give his body to her.

As I mentioned in the beginning of this chapter, people get married in order to be able to have that other person's body. If you do not believe that, then just let a married person be refused sex and see what happens. You will see that person getting angry in a hurry.

Now we are not a body. We are spirit beings who possess a soul and live in a physical body (1 Thess. 5:23). However, nobody will want to marry us without our body. *People do not want to get married just to pray!* They can get prayer partners without getting married.

Honestly, married person, when you thought about marrying your mate, what did you do? You looked at that person to see if you liked what you saw. You wanted to see if that person had some sex appeal for you.

Then you decided, "Oh, this would be a great blessing to me!" and you eventually married that person.

Single person, if you are honest with yourself, you know you are looking to marry someone who is sexually appealing to you. Now, of course, you are looking for somebody who is saved and filled with the Word, but those are not the only things you are looking for. You want to marry "Brother spiritual" or "Sister spiritual" as long as that person brings the body along!

In fact, if you meet a believer who is not sexually appealing to you, you say, "Let me go find someone else who's saved, sanctified, and filled with the Word of God." Even if you thought the Lord said, "I want you to marry this individual" and that person weighed 950 pounds, you would probably disobey! You would say, "That's not God talking. That's the *devil*! There's no way I'm going to date that person."

Paul understood that sex was very important to a marriage. That's why he said, by inspiration of the Holy Spirit, that a husband and wife should give their bodies to one another.

Do Not Abstain From Sex Unless Both Spouses Agree

Then in verse 5, Paul expounds on this thought.

Defraud ye not one the other, except it be with consent for a time, that ye may give your-

**selves to fasting and prayer; and come togeth-
er again, that Satan tempt you not for your
incontinency.**

1 CORINTHIANS 7:5

Paul says, "Unless you both agree to stop having sex for a
time of fasting and prayer, do not withhold sex from one
another."

There is a time for everything. A couple will not be very
spiritually minded if the only thing they do is have sex.
Therefore, it is appropriate for a couple to set sex aside at
times in order to spend more time with God. However, Paul
says they are not to stay apart for long. They are to "come
together again, that Satan tempt them not for their incontinency or *lack of self-control.*" A husband and wife should
come back together physically after their time of fasting and
praying so that Satan will be unable to tempt them to
become involved in sexual sin.

Men and Women Approach Sex Differently

Satan would love to step in to our marriages and break
them apart. He would love to divide a man and a woman in
any way he can so that they could not produce godly seed.
One thing he will try to use against a man and a woman is
the difference in their approaches to sex.

Women are quite different than men, as men are quite
different than women. It is neither gender's fault. God
designed them to approach sex in different ways.

For example, to women sex is an emotional issue. It is
first emotional, then psychological, and third physical. On
the other hand, to men sex is a physical issue. It is first physical, then psychological, and third emotional.

Notice the difference between the two. If it is first emotional with a wife and first physical with a husband, they will approach their union together in two completely different ways. If they do not know how to reconcile these two approaches, they could have some trouble. For instance, she will be turned off if sex is *only* a physical thing with She has to be talked to, loved on. She has to be told good things. She has to feel as though he is interested in *her* and not just in her curves.

However, if a husband does not understand this, he will wonder, *What's the matter with her? Why do I have to do all this romantic stuff before she gets "ready"? It doesn't take me any time to get ready. All I need is to see her walk by, and I'm ready to go!*

Differences Teach Them To Serve One Another

While it is true that men and women are quite different in their approaches and responses to each other in sexual intimacy, their differences are not meant to be a point of conflict. They are meant to bring the two together by teaching them how to serve one another.

Marriage is about interdependence. It is about two working together as one. It is about each person finding out what is important for the other and then meeting that person's needs. In marriage, each party is to put his or her own needs second.

Sex Is Not a Weapon or a Reward

If we are to put each other's needs first, then we cannot use sex as a weapon for "bad behavior" by withholding it or as a reward for "good behavior." In the twenty-six years I have been in the ministry, I have counseled countless married couples in who were using sex in these ways.

But sex is not a reward or a weapon. Sex is not a "yo-yo" that we dangle in front of our spouse, saying, "If you do this, this, and this, then you can have it. But if you don't do what I want you to do, I'm going to withhold it from you until you do what I tell you."

When people use sex either as a weapon or reward, they denigrate the wonderful thing that God designed.

Such misuse could even break apart their marriage and family.

How To Meet Her Needs

If we want to follow God's design for sexual intimacy in our marriages, then we will do things that will build one another up. We will put each other's needs first.

I want to first address men about how to meet their wives' needs. Paul says in First Corinthians 7:36, "...*if she pass the flower of her age, and need so require, let him do what he will, he sinneth not: let them marry.*" A woman has sexual needs, and her husband is to fulfill those needs.

Now women are responders. Therefore, sir, if you are interested in blessing your wife physically *tonight*, you need to understand that what you do *today* has a lot to do with what will happen tonight.

A husband and a wife may have a disagreement. They may argue with each other, slam doors, and so forth. Then what will normally happen is that four hours later, the husband will be thinking, *Well, that's old history. What happened, happened. This issue's over with.* And he will tell her, "I'm sorry."

That night, he will look at his wife and say, "Baby…" but, even though he has apologized, he is confronted with "Sister Frigidaire"! Why? Because he has not brought her along emotionally.

The Bible tells us in First Peter 3:7 that the husband is to dwell with the wife according to knowledge. We need to know our spouse's needs. Many men do not know how to satisfy their wife's needs because they were not brought up to do so. They were trained to think that a woman was something that you conquer. They were taught the "wham-bam, thank you, ma'am" theory!

When a man treats a woman this way, she thinks, *What just happened? Where did he go? He just had himself a good time, and now he's gone. He hasn't ministered to my needs at all.*

Sex Is About Giving, Not Getting

According to a survey conducted by Masters and Johnson in 1999, at least half of the sexually active female population in America have never had an orgasm. If that is true, something is wrong. Do you know what's wrong? *Men are not finding out what women need.* There is no love in the act of intercourse between couples. There is no emotional development in it. It is time for men to start ministering to the needs of their wives and not to their own needs.

According to this same survey, it only takes a man two minutes and thirty seconds to be able to ejaculate. However, it takes at least triple that amount of time for the woman to have an orgasm.

What does that tell men? It tells us we need to sow our "seed" to our woman's spirit and to her emotions. In other words, she needs to know that we care about her needs first, not about our own needs. We need to make giving to them our priority.

One of the things that God requires in everything is that we walk in love and give to others. Family life is about *giving, giving, giving.*

If you are not ready to give — if you are selfish — then you are not ready to get married.

Husband, you need to give your wife what she requires. She requires talk. She requires love. She requires time. If you want to have a blessed sexual life with her, then you need to fulfill these emotional and psychological needs.

Fulfilling Each Other's Needs Requires Teamwork

A husband and wife can work as a team to fulfill each other's needs when they know what those needs are. One thing women should know is that the average married man requires sex three to four times per week. When a woman knows that her husband is interested in physical intimacy with her, she can prepare her own mind by deciding to think good things about her husband. She can think about the things about him that give her joy, such as the good things that he has done for her. She can think about the last time that he fulfilled her needs. When she prepares herself mentally to receive her husband, she is deciding to give to her husband, and she is ready when her husband requires her.

Now, of course, he still needs to do the things I have mentioned to prepare her, but she also needs to prepare herself mentally. When a couple works as a team in this way, they will enjoy the kind of physical union that God wants them to have.

How To Have a Satisfying Sex Life Part 2

Keith A. Butler Sr.

God wants everything you do to be successful. He wants your spiritual life to be successful. He wants your finances and your career to be successful. He wants your children to be successful. He wants your sex life to be successful.

However, He never said that success in any area would come without some work. In fact, after Adam and Eve sinned, according to Genesis 3:23, the Lord sent Adam forth from the garden of Eden, to till the ground from whence he was taken.

In the Garden of Eden before man and woman sinned, their every need was met. Things were easy for them; everything was sweatless. Now everything would come by the sweat of their brow. They would have to work hard for everything they wanted.

When we make a decision to get married, we make a decision to do some work in order to be able to dwell together according to knowledge. Hollywood has sold the idea that somehow a man and woman just know instantly what to do. That is absolutely not so! That is a lie of the devil that has resulted in many families becoming dysfunctional. When people buy into this lie and then run into the need for some kind of work or effort to be put forth in their marriage, they think something is wrong and they give up.

We believers need to dispel this lie in our own families. Parents need to sit down with their children and explain how marriage is supposed to work. They even need to help them understand that their mom and dad have a sex life together. Parents need to show them the scriptures about God's design for sex and explain that this is the pattern for their mom and dad's sex life. Tell them, "This is a wonderful thing. And if you see this door closed, you don't open this door!"

This is important to a family. I taught my children about the subject of sex when they were young so that they would get it from the Word and from me rather than from the television or the locker room. Do you know how boys are at school? They have all kinds of questions by the time they are eleven , so they make up all these stories to tell others about how they did this, that, and the other. They are "educating" each other. That is not the education I wanted my children to receive.

My children have always known that Deborah and I have a successful physical relationship. They are grown now, but they still tease us today. If I come home after traveling to minister, they say, "Daddy's home. He's been gone four days preaching somewhere, and you know he's looking for Mama! See you later, Daddy! We'll come back in a couple of hours."

We believing parents need to provide a godly explanation and example to our children so that they can see marriages that are happy and that are working spiritually, emotionally, socially, physically, and financially. They must see successful married life in every realm. When children see all these things work, they do not grow up thinking, *I don't want to get married. I just want to have sex without committing to marriage. Sex seems like a good thing, but marriage doesn't sound like it's "all that."*

When children have seen a godly example of marriage, they do not grow up to create dysfunctional families. They grow up to follow God's way and to become godly parents of godly seed.

Circumstances Change the Sex Life

We need to show our children that we can have successful married lives despite the changing circumstances around us. Then when they get married, after the honeymoon is over and real life begins, they will not be looking at each other, asking, "What is your problem?" After their first child is born, they will not be scared away from marriage.

If you are a parent, you know that having a child changes the dynamics of the household completely, including the sex life. Many people, particularly men, have trouble coping with the change. The man is no longer the woman's "one and only." He is no longer the king of the household. That child has changed how she approaches things. Most of that change is legitimate for the time being, during the child's infancy. But sometimes the mother *inappropriately* excludes her husband and gives almost all of her time to the child.

Furthermore, carrying that baby for nine months in her womb, and then bringing him or her into the world has changed how her body looks and most likely how her body responds sexually.

So you see, children change things. They are a blessing of the Lord, but they require adjustment. We need to make the appropriate adjustments for any life changes that we go through as married couples so that we can remain unified with our spouse.

Plan Ahead

This is why planning ahead is so important. It can help us make the appropriate adjustments as these life changes occur. The media has tried to give us the idea that everything must be spontaneous. Well, there will be times of spontaneity, but everything should not be spontaneous. Most people who have financial trouble do so because they do not have a plan for their finances. They are spontaneous spenders; they spend almost all that they get as it comes in. Well, just as a financial plan is required, a sexual plan is required.

This is why in pre-marriage counseling, we ask each person , "How many times do you expect to have sex with your spouse every week?" We want to help remove all the mystery so that when two people get married, they have no doubt about what is expected.

I have heard men answer, "Four to ten times." Before I asked that question, their fiancé had not known he felt that way. They had never talked about it.

Then we ask the women that same question, and, usually, the difference is stark. She is thinking, *Twice a week is far sufficient!* and he is thinking, *Seven times a week — at least!* Can you see why failing to plan ahead and discuss these expectations could cause some problems?

Now, of course, at the honeymoon, both spouses are "hot to trot." However, when things calm down, and they return to reality, she may begin claiming, "Not now; I've got a headache." She may seem to have no interest in sex. She puts her husband in a bad position and is being unfair by refusing his overtures.

Conversely, he may be the one who seems disinterested. He may work six or seven days a week, twelve hours a day, and be too tired to be interested. If this is the case, his wife is most likely saying, "I don't have a man to meet my needs."

Meet Your Spouse's Need

Both the husband and the wife have to understand what the apostle Paul said in First Corinthians 7:4 and 5: *"The wife hath not power of her own body, but the husband: and likewise also the husband hath not power of his own body, but the wife. Defraud ye not one the other, except it be with consent for a time...."*

Married woman, if your husband needs to share sexual intimacy with you five times a week, then that is the need you are to meet. Likewise, married man, if your wife needs you five times a week, then that is the need you are to meet.

In other words, you "have to do what you have to do," as the saying goes. Married man, don't walk into the bedroom and tell her you are too tired. I do not care if you have to take some vitamin pills or buy some Viagra — just do something! Be a blessing to your wife. Men in certain professions, such as traveling salesmen and truck drivers and so forth, need to be there for their wife when she needs you. If your wife has not seen you for an extended period of time, when you get home, she is going to want certain things from you.

First, she will want to talk to you. Now if you want to fulfill this desire properly, you need to first realize that men and women are quite different in that women tend to be detail-oriented, while men tend to think in generalities.

For example, when a truck driver comes off the road, his wife will say, "What all did you do for the past three days?"

He will likely say, "Well, I went to such-and-such city and delivered such-and-such, and that's it. Where's dinner?"

Then she is sitting there feeling as if he did not answer her at all. She wants to know about every stop he made. She wants to know what happened on Monday, how he was feeling on Tuesday, and to whom he talked on Wednesday.

So, you see, men and women are very different. That is why you can readily notice the difference between how a group of women talk and how a group of men talk. They do not have the same kind of conversations. Men speak in generalities. Women speak in specifics — what color the dress was, how long it was, what kind of fabric it was made of.

When a guy sits at a table with five women and those girls start talking, it does not take very long before rolls his eyes, so to speak, thinking, *Oh, my God! What am I doing here?* That is because there is an apparent difference between the two genders, and that difference translates from their physical appearance and emotional makeup all the way to the bedroom.

That is why, sir, your wife asks you all those questions when you come home from your work. She has a specific need for specific communication. And if you will meet that need, you have begun the sex process.

Some men say, "Well, I just don't like to talk. She talks too much." Those men had better learn how to talk! They had better learn how to communicate to their wife if they want to have enjoyable sexual experiences with her. If those men want their wife to be satisfied and verbally responsive in the bedroom — and I know that is what men want — then they have to satisfy her communication needs first.

How do I know that men want their wives to be satisfied? I know so because after a man and a woman have sex, the first thing the man does is start asking the fifty questions! Married woman, have you ever noticed how your husband wants a "score card"? He asks, "How was it?"

A Man's Self-esteem Is Tied to Sex

Do you know why he always asks that question? It is because his self-esteem is tied to this issue. He considers himself a man if he is able to bless his woman and if she is verbally responsive to him in sexual intimacy.

If she is unresponsive, he begins to doubt himself and his ability to make his wife happy. This is one thing that Satan uses to open the door to another woman's getting to that man. Satan makes him think that this other woman will be the kind of woman who will respond to him. That is Satan's deceit works!

Married man, you will not receive the verbal responsiveness you are looking for if you do not understand that for your wife, sex starts the moment you walk in the door and she wants to talk.

Nothing Is Wrong With Your Spouse!

Because your spouse has a completely different approach to sex than you do, you may have often wondered, *What is wrong with my spouse?* The fact is that there is nothing wrong with the man or the woman you are married to. Now both of you may need some good teaching and an attitude adjustment, but the fact that your spouse sees sex differently than you do does not make that person wrong. The two of you just need to make some mental adjustments so that you can know each other's needs and work toward fulfilling them.

Married man, that means you need to begin to discuss particulars with your wife. Learn to talk to her. Single man, if you just do not like to talk, now you know an area that you can begin working on today.

Again, during your conversations is when sex starts for a woman. As her husband talks to her and listens to what she wants to talk about, he lets her know he is interested in her.

But if a man does not know how important communication is to his wife, he may unknowingly completely shut her down sexually. She might start talking about what the kids did while he was out driving his truck, and he will think, *Man, I almost got run off the road by some fool. The policeman gave me a ticket because I had too much weight on my truck. I don't want to hear about the kids breaking the toys and Johnny smacking Sally!* If he will not listen or respond, then his wife's need for emotional intimacy will be unfulfilled and she will later be unable to fulfill his need for sexual intimacy.

A man needs to understand that talking with his wife about Johnny smacking Sally is what makes her say, "I love that man. He listens to me." That will certainly be her response if, when she talks to you about Johnny smacking Sally, you go talk to Johnny and Sally rather than leaving all the responsibility of disciplining the children to her.

Some men say, "I'm too tired to mess with the kids." If that is the case, then you shouldn't have gotten married. Remember, marriage is *work*! A successful home life takes time and effort.

Marriage Is a '24/7' Job!

Now can you understand why Paul said, "Now look, you will have trouble in the flesh if you marry, and I'm wanting to spare you." He said, "If you get married, then you will have to pay attention to your spouse instead of just to God." Of course, we know that a married individual can still pay attention to God, but he cannot devote as much time to taking care of the things of God as can a single individual. What Paul was saying is that marriage is a twenty-four-hour-per-day, seven-day-per-week job.

The work of marriage will produce benefits, just as the work of a job produces a paycheck. The harder you work at your job and the more you give of what you have, the bigger the paycheck. Likewise, the harder you work at marriage and the more you give of what you have, the greater the benefits of marriage will be for you, your spouse, and your entire family. It works just as God says: "Give and it will be given unto you" (Luke 6:38).

A Husband and Wife Should Play Together

In Genesis 26 is a story about a loving married pair, Isaac and Rebekah.

> And there was a famine in the land, beside the first famine that was in the days of Abraham. And Isaac went unto Abimelech king of the Philistines unto Gerar.
>
> And the Lord appeared unto him [Isaac], and said, Go not down into Egypt; dwell in the land which I shall tell thee of:
>
> Sojourn in this land, and I will be with thee, and will bless thee; for unto thee, and unto thy seed, I will give all these countries, and I will perform the oath which I sware unto Abraham thy father;

> And I will make thy seed to multiply as the stars of heaven, and will give unto thy seed all these countries; and in thy seed shall all the nations of the earth be blessed;
>
> Because that Abraham obeyed my voice, and kept my charge, my commandments, my statutes, and my laws.
>
> And Isaac dwelt in Gerar:
>
> And the men of the place asked him of his wife; and he said, She is my sister: for he feared to say, She is my wife....
>
> GENESIS 26:1-7

Isaac was acting like his daddy, Abraham. Do you remember what Abraham did? He did almost the exact same thing in Egypt, telling the pharaoh that Sarah was his sister (Gen. 12:13). It should not surprise us that whatever our children see us do, they will replicate, even when they become adults. That is why it is so important that we give them a godly example in everything we do, even in the way we approach each other sexually.

The story continues in verse 8.

> And the men of the place asked him of his wife; and he said, She is my sister: for he feared to say, She is my wife; lest, said he, the men of the place should kill me for Rebekah; because she was fair to look upon [she was fine!].
>
> And it came to pass, when he had been there a long time, that Abimelech king of the Philistines looked out at a window, and saw,

> **and, behold, Isaac was sporting with Rebekah his wife.**
>
> *GENESIS 26:7,8*

Verse 8 says that King Abimelech looked out the window and saw Isaac sporting with Rebekah. What is "sporting"? Well, it means he was playing with his wife, running and chasing her, having fun with her, even playing in a sexually suggestive manner with her. There had to have been some suggestiveness between Isaac and Rebekah; otherwise, Abimelech would not have realized that Rebekah was Isaac's wife, not his sister. Verse 9 says, *"And Abimelech called Isaac, and said, BEHOLD, OF A SURETY SHE IS THY WIFE: and how saidst thou, She is my sister? And Isaac said unto him, Because I said, Lest I die for her."*

When Abimelech saw Isaac sporting with Rebekah, he knew she was Isaac's wife. He could tell that by the way they were acting. Married man, can people tell that you are married to your wife by the way you act with her? It is time to be "sporting" with your wife. You must set aside time in order to do that.

I point this passage out to let you know that a husband and a wife are supposed to have fun together! Families are supposed to play together! The day has to go in which people become so spiritual that they forget that play is required with their entire family. Children should see their daddy playing with their mama and having fun with her, not *slapping* her!

You may think, *But Christian men don't hit their wives. They wouldn't do that kind of awful thing.* Oh, no? I know of quite a few of them who have. And that is what their children see. Then they see their father's Bible on his lap on Sunday morning. They see him singing, "The joy of the Lord is my strength." Then they remember what happened Thursday night at the house and they think, *Yeah, right, Dad. Like I'm really going to follow your God.*

Ultimately they might say, "There is no God." They want nothing to do with God because their father would not have fun with his family but, instead, could only abuse them.

Some parents say, "I don't understand why my kids aren't following God. I mean, I take them to church. How come they're still going the wrong way?"

Well, the Bible says we are supposed to bring up our children in the nurture and admonition of the Lord. That takes a whole lot more than just words or a trip to church on Sunday. It takes *deeds*. Children have to see your words being consistently put into action or the words will become meaningless to them.

It is time to lay down the super-spiritual facades and have some fun with our families. Our spouse and children need to know we enjoy spending time with them.

'Keeping Up With the Joneses' Can Ruin Your Sex Life and Destroy Your Family

Married man, I understand that you feel a great pull toward your work and career because you want to provide financially for your family. However, it is more important for you to provide *yourself* to them than to provide material things.

Sometimes people get so involved in trying to keep up with the Joneses — to have certain houses, certain clothes made by certain designers, and certain cars — that their pursuit for things destroys their families.

Someone may say, "Well, don't we need money?"

Yes, but you do not need as much as you think you do. A person can be happy *without* a lot of money, and a person can be very unhappy *with* a lot of money. The deciding factor is how much of your time the pursuit of money takes away from your home life. You need to ask yourself, "Does my job take away all the time I have to spend with the kids? Is our lifestyle causing us to always have to use our faith to get out of debt? Is the drive for money pushing my spouse and I into a predicament in which we cannot do what the Bible really tells us to do — to sport with one another?"

The decision to buy a $200,000 house as opposed to a $150,000 house may determine whether you have time to sport with your spouse or have to work two jobs and be full of worry and care. The decision to buy that luxury car may determine whether or not the kids have money to go to youth camp. Brother, the decision to "live the high life" rather than sticking to what you can reasonably afford may determine whether your wife is verbally responsive when you make love to her or disinterested and sullen, overcome with pressures and cares.

Someone may ask, "What does money have to do with our sex life?" *It has a lot to do with it!* The most important thing to a woman is security. Therefore, if she is getting phone calls because the creditors are calling, or if she is wondering whether or not you will be able to pay the bills, then emotionally she cannot enter freely into sexual activity with you. She will be stifled because sex to her is first of all *emotional*.

Furthermore, financial pressure doesn't only affect women. It also affects men. It can even drive some to impotence.

I always lived in a lesser house than I could afford. I drove lesser cars than I could buy. I lived below what the banks would loan me. I was not thinking about what anyone else thought about it. I did it because I wanted to be sure that there was no financial pressure in my household. I wanted to be sure that I could take Deborah and sport with her any-where in the world she wanted to go. I wanted to be sure that my children had whatever they needed and that the pursuit of money did not blow us all apart.

Even today, I could live in a bigger house than I do. Yet what is most important to me still is making sure there is no financial pressure in my home.

You should not allow yourself to be in a position in which you would be homeless in two weeks if you took a financial hit. If most people didn't get a paycheck for two weeks, they would be in dire financial trouble, and that should not be. That only happens because of a lack of plan-ning. You should have a financial plan to set aside money while the going is good, while you *are* getting that paycheck. You should never live off one hundred percent of everything you make. However, most people set their standard of living above what they make.

We need to be honest with ourselves. We need to evaluate our current status. Hearing this is one thing. Deciding to act and to change if necessary is another thing altogether. We need to start getting our lives in line and our homes in divine order, and that includes financial order.

For some people, that will mean downsizing. I have heard so many people say, "Well, God would never tell me to give up my house. He'd never tell me to give up my car." A lack of finances is causing all their trouble; they are practical-ly killing each other over it. Yet they say the Lord would not have them downsize! *Certainly, He would!* Those people are operating outside the perimeters of the Word. The Word tells us to be moderate in all things, and you can know you have gone past moderation in some area when that thing becomes a constant point of conflict. At that point, you have entered into the lust of flesh.

A wife may be pushing her husband, saying, "I need you to make a certain amount of money" because she has an image in her mind that she wants to "keep up with." She may not even acknowledge or recognize it; it may be subconscious. Yet she is trying to keep up with other people. She may even utilize her physicality to manipulate that man. This is not the way marriage is supposed to work!

Do you know the axiom "Nobody's happy unless Mama's happy?" We use that saying in fun, but, in reality, that is not the way it is supposed to be. Married woman, if you are driving your man to make a certain amount of money to make you happy, then you have made money, instead of your love for him and your family, the critical issue of your household.

Married man, if you push your wife out into the work force whether she wants to go or not, and you put pressure on her so that she feels as if she has to work or you will not be able to make it, you will have trouble in your household! Do you know why? It is because internally she feels she is doing your job. She feels that because you want to live at a certain standard, she has to do your job to keep up with that standard.

Married man, your wife should never *have* to work. She certainly can if she wants to, or if the two of you agree that she will work for a certain period of time to meet some certain selected goal. However, for her to have to work means that money is driving the marriage. Instead of you being in control, "keeping up with the Joneses" is in control.

This will inevitably destroy your family. It will destroy your children. It will destroy your sexual relationship with your spouse. It will even destroy your walk with God by getting you into in fear, doubt, and worry.

Therefore, if you want to have a successful family, successful children, a successful sex life, a successful relationship with God, you will not make material things your first priority. You will make God's Word and will your priority. You will find out what He says about family, sex, marriage, children — absolutely everything that concerns you — and you will follow His way. Then you will have great success in all you do, just as He intended.

Questions and Answers

Keith and Deborah Butler

(Authors' Note: All answers are a collaboration by both Keith Butler Sr. and Deborah Butler unless segments are specifically addressed by only one author as indicated.*)*

B efore we get into the Questions and Answers on the subject of home and family, let's read First Corinthians 13:4-8 as a foundation, because all the answers we have to give come from the standpoint of God's love. In everything — every situation and circumstance — that presents itself to us in life, we need to respond by asking, "What does God's Word say?" and "What would love do?"

> Love endures long *and* is patient and kind;
> love never is envious *nor* boils over with jeal-
> ousy, is not boastful *or* vainglorious, does not
> display itself haughtily.
> It is not conceited (arrogant and inflated
> with pride); it is not rude (unmannerly) *and*
> does not act unbecomingly. Love (God's love
> in us) does not insist on its own rights *or* its
> own way, *for* it is not self-seeking; it is not
> touchy *or* fretful *or* resentful; it takes no

account of the evil done to it [it pays no attention to a suffered wrong].

It does not rejoice at injustice *and* unrighteousness, but rejoices when right *and* truth prevail.

Love bears up under anything *and* everything that comes, is ever ready to believe the best of every person, its hopes are fadeless under all circumstances, and it endures everything [without weakening].

Love never fails [never fades out or becomes obsolete or comes to an end]....

1 Corinthians 13:4-8 (Amplified)

Let us also begin by saying that there is no help for the person who disdains the Word of God or who does not consider His Word as the final arbiter or authority. The United States Supreme Court is the highest court in the land in this country, and the members of that court render decisions based on their interpretation of the law. Whatever decision they make is the final word.

Well, the Word of God is the absolute final arbiter. And the Supreme Court pales in comparison to the authority of God's Word. The point is, we should respect God's Word as holy and esteem it as precious.

A person can't be helped who will not submit himself to some authority higher than his own opinion. There will always be disagreements between people. In legal cases, we have arbiters to decide the issue — to make a decision to which both parties submit as the final word. In a marriage, there must be a mutual submission to each other and to the Arbiter of all arbiters, God and His Word. The married person who will not receive the Word for himself and be corrected is not going to be successful in marriage. He's not going to win. He may think he's winning by having the attitude, "It's my way or the highway," but he will never have the marriage God intended for him until he learns some submission.

Some spouses attend marriage counseling and marriage conferences for the sole purpose of looking for "ammunition" with which to knock their mates "upside the head"! They're seeking to use *info* as *ammo*! These people have no intention of receiving the Word for themselves or to allow themselves to be corrected in any measure. I'm always saddened to encounter such people. They will likely never know the marital bliss that could be theirs.

When you want to be helped in your marriage, or you simply want your marriage to be improved and be the best it can be, you have to put pride aside. Pride will keep you from seeking assistance and could doom you to failure. Even if you did manage to ask for help, pride will hinder you from receiving that help if you don't deal with it.

A well-publicized orator once said, in essence, "If you try, you might lose. But if you don't try, you will *surely* lose." We could add to that statement, "If you obey the Word of God, it *will* work for you."

Some of the following questions were posed to us during a teaching series on the home and family that we ministered in two of our churches. Other questions are those presented to us over the course of the last twenty-seven years of ministry. Since the Word of God says that tests and trials of life come to us all (John 16:33) and that the same "afflictions" or problems you experience are experienced by the brethren (1 Peter 5:9)— by others in the Body of Christ —

we are confident that in answering these questions, some of your own questions will be answered too!

Q: My husband is a smoker and has been for years. He also doesn't have much of a sex drive. Does smoking have something to do with the sex drive?

A: Smoking has very little to do with the sex drive. If smoking meant that people didn't have sex, many of us would not be here today!

Sex is one of the basic issues of a marriage and is one of three major categories in which married couples have the most problems. Other categories include *communication* and *finances*.

Actually, the categories of *sex* and *finances* fall under a broader category of *communication*. The marriage union should provide the availability of open and honest discussion with the ability to communicate to each other clearly and consistently in a manner that can be understood and received. Well, concerning finances, the questions to be broached and discussed are *what constitutes enough money, who works for the money, who spends it, how it's spent, when it's spent,* and so forth. The same is true concerning sex. Couples should be able to communicate regarding whether they're having enough sex, how they have it, when they have it, and all the issues that pertain to sex.

These three categories of communication, finances, and sex are huge issues to be reconciled between spouses in a marriage if that marriage is to succeed. In fact, most of the questions we will deal with in this chapter can be categorized under those three subjects.

Now concerning smoking, that is a habit that we as ministers of the Gospel teach people not to indulge. We teach against smoking as well as against drinking and illicit drugs, because these things harm the body. The Word says in First Corinthians chapter 6 and in other places that the body of the Christian is the temple of the Living God. It also says that when you're a Christian, your body does not belong to you; it belongs to God. So in any context in which you are knowingly and consistently causing harm or damage to your body, you are in error and in sin. You have made a decision not to respect the house of God, your body.

However, if you've missed it in this area, First John 1:9 says that if we confess our sins, God is faithful and just to forgive our sins and to cleanse us from all unrighteousness. If you are a person faced with the challenge of kicking a bad habit, there is a way to walk free! We have taught thousands of people how to kick smoking. You *can* be free of this and other harmful habits.

The issue of sex is more complicated. There are a number of reasons why a person loses his or her sex drive. A lack of libido could be a symptom of a medical problem or a side-effect of taking certain medications. It could also be related to financial stress or other problems or crises, and it could also be the result of marital infidelity (for example, a spouse is being sexually satisfied outside the marriage union). Without more information, we could not aptly determine the cause of your husband's lack of desire for sex. We encourage you to discuss this problem with your husband and seek counseling if necessary. We will also address a specific case later in this chapter that might shed some light on your situation.

Q: My wife and I were just recently married. I had many male and female friends before I met my wife, and I've always kept in pretty good contact with them. I've known some of these friends for almost all of my life. I want my wife to meet all of my friends, including the

females. I don't want her to have any misgivings or misunderstandings about my relationship with these women. I don't want to dismiss any of my female friends, but I am facing this dilemma because my wife refuses to meet them. I don't feel that it's right for me to have to talk to them only if my wife is not present. What should I do?

A: First, this is an issue that should have been discussed and reconciled before you said your "I dos." But since you're already, we would encourage your wife to be reasonable. For her to refuse to even meet your friends is unreasonable. She doesn't have a leg to stand on to justify her position of unwillingness. After all, she can't decide whether or not she can be friends with your friends if she never meets them.

On the other hand, if your wife met your friends and didn't feel good about any one of them, she could talk to you from a more reasonable standpoint. Then the two of you would need to make a decision that, really, you've already made, and that is the choice of each other as the person you want to be with. You have chosen each other above everyone else, and if *both* of you can't get along with your friends, then the friends will have to "disappear." They will find other friends and so will the two of you, *together.*

Remember, we talked about the responsibility of the married person to please his or her spouse. The important thing is to be reasonable. If a spouse is unreasonable at one state of the marriage, the husband or wife is not going to be as motivated to be reasonable when the spouse wants to be accommodated about something down the road.

There is a bottom line to everything, and we're just going to give you the bottom line to the problem you're facing. Genesis 2:24 says, *"Therefore shall a man leave his father and his mother, and shall cleave unto his wife: and they shall be one flesh."* Remember, we said that "to cleave" means *to stick to; to pursue hard;* and *to run after.*

When we got married more than twenty-five years ago, this was one of the verses we looked at closely. We decided together then that we were not going to allow anyone else to come between us. We decided that if our relationship faltered, it wouldn't be because we were fighting about somebody else!

You are supposed to cleave to your wife, and she is supposed to cleave to you. She should meet your friends, but if she doesn't feel good about them as her friends, too, it is your responsibility at that point to make the determination that your wife is more important that your friendship with So-and-so. You don't live with So-and-so, and you're not going to have to give an account to God about So-and-so.

If you have children, your children are not going to be affected by your friends. But your kids *will* be affected by your relationship with your wife. If it comes to the choice of cutting off those friendships or having strife between you and your wife, you need to "cut" your friends. Your responsibility is first and foremost to your spouse.

Of course, the same is true concerning relatives who often come between a husband and wife. Whether it's mamas, daddies, sisters, brothers, aunts, uncles, nieces, nephews, or cousins, your first obligation and responsibility is to your spouse.

Q: My husband wants me to wear my hair very short. I prefer my hair to be long. There is really no compromise in what we like. Should I cut my hair?

A (Deborah Butler): I like my hair short. But I don't wear it short, because my husband likes it long. I decided a long time ago that I'd rather have my husband look at my long hair than somebody else's long hair!

Keep in mind that men admire what they like. So your style should be what your husband likes. You should want to be attractive to your husband. Whatever that takes, as long as he's not asking you to do anything that's against the Word of God, you should want to make the sacrifice in order to please him. Love never fails. Remember, we said that marriage is not about *you* being pleased; it's about you pleasing your *mate*.

There is an option to consider, and that is to buy a short-haired wig. Wear it until you get used to wearing short hair, and then have your hair cut. However, your husband may decide in the meantime that he likes the variety. He may want a short-haired wife one day and a long-haired wife the next!

Keith Butler Sr.: My wife does prefer to wear her hair short. She tested out a short haircut with me once, and I didn't like it. I liked her long hair when I met her, and I like her long hair now.

When I first laid eyes on my wife, I was instantly interested, if not smitten! She had long hair then, and I liked what I saw! If I had wanted a short-haired woman, I would have pursued a short-haired woman. But I wanted a woman with locks! I mean, the woman I would marry would have to have more hair than me!

I like my wife's long hair. I like to be able to put my hands in it and play with it. I like our differences. I don't have anything against women with short hair. I'm not at all saying that it's wrong to have short hair! I'm simply saying that long hair on my wife is my preference.

Now on the other side of the coin, there are physical traits about me that Deborah is attracted to, and I owe it to her to please her with my appearance too. When my wife married me, I weighed on about 130 pounds. Now on a six-feet, two-inch frame, that is extremely thin! Deborah preferred that I be a little heavier, so I did some things to help myself gain some weight. Of course, I went too far with it! But I always say that it's her fault!

When you married your spouse, in so many words, you told him or her, "My parents don't matter, my friends don't matter. You're the one who matters to me the most." For you to say that and then do something with your appearance that you know will displease your mate is going to come across as a contradiction. If you have the attitude, "I don't care what you like; I'm going to do what *I* like," you're asking for trouble, because we're talking about something as simple as a hairstyle, but that selfish attitude will carry over into other areas of your marriage.

And with a selfish attitude, not only are you being disrespectful, you're tempting the other person. For example, if your husband likes short hair and you refuse to cut it, he is put in the unfair and unhappy predicament of trying to avoid looking at women with the kind of hairstyle he likes.

Q: I've heard that a husband and wife should be best friends and should do almost everything together. Is there such a thing as spending *too much* time together? If so, how much is too much?

A: First, too much time is when the two of you can't stand each other anymore!

Now we said that in fun, but, seriously, everybody needs a break at times. It has nothing to do with not being in love; it's just that human beings were created to need some moments of solitude.

A spouse should represent a number of things. For one, a spouse should represent *pleasure*; he or she is a companion with whom you enjoy life. A spouse also represents *work*, because marriage is like the ministry: It should be spelled w-o-r-k! But one thing a spouse will never represent is utter and full completeness and satisfaction, because nothing or no one on earth can fulfill you as God can.

God never created anything for man that would fully and completely satisfy him. Why? Because it is God's place to satisfy us completely. The Bible says that God is a jealous God (Exod. 20:5) and that you should have no other gods before you (Exod. 34:14). That means that nothing should come before God in your life.

That's why everything on this earth lacks the ability to meet your every need. Only God Himself can do that. Now with that understanding, you need to realize that your relationship with your spouse, no matter how close it is, will require some work — some effort on your part — for it to succeed. Even if Jesus Himself appeared to you and told you that the person you were seeing was the one for you, that relationship would still require work to make it what God intended.

So not only should a married person see pleasure and enjoyment in his spouse, he should also see work. Well, you realize that everyone needs a respite from work from time to time. We're not talking about set days and times, but a husband and wife should communicate about when they will each have time alone. It may mean a time of day when one spouse goes to one part of the house and the other goes to another part of the house. They may spend hours apart from each other, using those times to fellowship with the Lord and meditate on His Word, and to do things they enjoy doing whether it be reading or enjoying some other hobby or interest.

Not only does this solitude provide a respite from the effort that marriage requires of each spouse, it keeps each partner fresh for when they come together again. Their time spent apart enhances their relationship and their enjoyment of one another when they're together again.

Now we do *not* suggest taking separate vacations as a means of spending time apart! That is an extreme that more often hurts marriages than helps them.

Q: My husband and I both work full-time jobs. I have the primary responsibility for the cooking, cleaning, laundry, helping the children with homework and so forth, and for shopping, and running errands.

My job does not end at 5:00 p.m. When I come home from work, I still have a long list of things to do, and I try really hard to accomplish all of them. The problem is, it's wearing me out physically and emotionally. My husband doesn't understand why there's no energy left for him at night when he's ready for sex. We both feel resentment — he's resentful because his needs aren't getting met properly, and I'm resentful because I feel like the house maid.

I could understand his feelings if I had the luxury of staying home, but I don't. This is a sore spot between us. When I try to talk about it, it causes an argument. He says his father didn't have to do any housework, and he shouldn't have to, either.

Please address this for my sake and for the sake of others in my predicament. I know there are other men who expect their wives to earn part of the family income while at the same time take care of the home, the family, and their husbands' physical needs. These women are expected to be a career woman, a maid, a mother, and then "Linda Lovelace" in the bedroom! What are your thoughts on this?

A (Keith Butler Sr.): The Word of God says repeatedly that the male is the one who's responsible for providing the substance of the household. "Head of the home" also means *provider* of the home. If you as the head of your home send your wife out to work, there is a cost associated with the decision that she be out of her biblically assigned role. Her biblically assigned role is that she should be giving her time to you and yours — to her home and family. I'm talking about what the *Bible* teaches, not what the universities teach in the year 2001.

Anytime a married woman goes out to work, there is a cost associated with it. If she works 20 hours to help bring in some family income, then that's 20 hours worth of labor she's expended doing something other than taking care of her home and family.

God did not create the wife to bear the responsibility of both supporting the family budget and caring for the needs of her household. The Scripture says she is the weaker vessel (1 Peter 3:7). It didn't say she was *inferior*, but it did say she was weaker. That means she does not have the strength and stamina her husband has. That's how she was created.

Now I'm the "Energizer Bunny"! I mean, I run all over the country pastoring churches and performing the duties of a pastor. Then I make sure I spend time with my wife (and when my kids were young and lived at home, I always spent quality time with them, even if it meant sacrificing time for myself). Then on top of that, I love to go hunting! I can expend energy fifteen or sixteen hours in a day and then have no trouble "getting busy" when it's time to make love to my wife.

I'm stronger than my wife. I still have stamina at the end of even the busiest of days. If she tried to keep my schedule, she'd be dead. She simply can't do it. Therefore, *I should not view what she should do based on how I feel, because we're not the same!* We weren't created the same, and I'm glad about that!

Some men are trying to compare apples with oranges, so to speak. If a man's wife has to spend 20, 30, or 40 hours a week doing what is really supposed to be his area of responsibility, there is going to be a physical, emotional, and psychological toll on her mind and body. Then, if in addition to performing his role, she has to cook, clean, do laundry, and care for the children and the needs of her house, she is performing two roles — his and hers.

Then for him to say he expects her to be ready to hang out all night with him really curls my toes! She can't do it all. Her husband is asking too much of her, and he is taking her out of her role.

Now, of course, there can be compromise, but it will take some effort on the husband's part. If your wife's being fresh is important to you, husband, you have a decision to make. You can't have it both ways and expect things to be right in your house! You're going to have to carry the extra responsibilities if she's out earning income for the family.

You have to decide which is more important: having the woman who's fresh at the end of the day or the woman who's bringing in money and running your house.

Certainly, some women are stronger than others, but you can't make a woman something physically and emotionally that she is not. This is important because men are very physical. And most of them want physical women. But a man is not going to get a physical woman if she has no time to rest. If she has no respite — no time of solitude — to revive and refresh herself spirit, soul, and body, he is not going to get what he wants from his relationship with her.

What usually happens when a woman is stretched trying to take on dual roles is, he becomes upset because she's not this, that, and the other. And she's upset because she feels like the house maid and the doormat, and she feels unloved by her husband. The whole marriage begins spiraling downward. Some little thing could be said and — *poof* — get blown out of proportion when, really, the problem wasn't that little something that was said; the problem is what began to happen at the beginning when the decision was made that she take on two roles.

Some pastors' wives are so overworked that problems arise in the marriage that would never have existed otherwise. The wife is teaching, counseling, trouble-shooting, dealing with personnel, hosting ladies' fellowships and visiting speakers, organizing outreaches, and doing administrative tasks. Then the marriage begins to suffer, and the ministry ends up being hindered instead of helped because there's trouble at Pastor's house.

My wife has always been a helpmate to me in the ministry, but I said from the beginning that any responsibility of the ministry should not affect her ability to perform the duties of a wife and mother. I told her we would adjust her responsibilities at the ministry to her ability to operate. That meant that there were days she was at home all day taking care of herself and the needs of the family. I told Deborah she could help me at the ministry but that the ministry was my job, not hers.

There's another side to this altogether, and that is the situation in which the wife is pressuring her husband to maintain a certain financial lifestyle that he cannot sustain by himself.

If you are a wife whose husband makes $50,000, and you want to live like he's making $70,000, that is a problem. You're going to have to understand that the reason you're out there working is, he's not making enough for you. You also need to realize that there is going to be a cost associated with your high expectations.

Before you decide to marry, you must determine whether you can make yourself comfortable with your intended's salary. That's why the command, "Thou shall not covet" is in the Scripture. In other words, if your husband-to-be makes $50,000 a year, you need to marry him with the expectation of making yourself comfortable with $50,000 a year.

One of the reasons many women work is, they want more stuff! That's why they pay the price associated with taking on dual roles. There are days when they're too tired to get dressed up for work, and they wish they didn't have to go and put up with all the things that go on in the workplace. But the desire for that paycheck inspires them to do it anyway. The money they'll earn equals the stuff they want.

These things need to be discussed together and agreed upon if things are to remain stable and balanced at home. If the husband agrees or decides to have the wife earn some of the income, he should take on some of the responsibilities of the home. Extra money in the household should not come at the expense of the wife's well-being — or *either* spouse's well-being, for that matter. There has to be teamwork — each member must carry his or her share of the responsibility — if a family expects to win in the game of life.

Q: In some families, there is the tendency for relatives to ask to borrow money when they see their family members blessed and doing well financially. Is it disrespectful to my mate if I loan money without discussing it with him?

A (Deborah Butler): Yes. First, it's not your money; that money belongs to *both of you*. Therefore, *both of you* should be included in decisions about what to do with it. When anyone comes to me wanting to borrow money, I just send him or her to my husband, saying, "You'll have to talk to him about it." I *don't* say, "Yes, we'll loan it to you, but go talk to Keith first." That puts him in a bad light in their eyes if he doesn't want to loan them the money.

Anytime we loan people money, they have to answer a series of questions. We want to know how they came to be in the place of need that they're in. For example, if they lost money gambling, we are not going to finance someone's sin.

Also, we let them know that we are not the bank! We are not their source that they can just run to, instead of to God, every time they hit a snag or run into a problem. We are willing to help people, but we are not in the business of loaning money to people.

That may sound hard, but sometimes love is tough. And more important than loaning money to a friend or family member is walking in love and maintaining a right relationship with your spouse.

Actually, a good rule of thumb in a marriage is, "Don't mess with the money!" In other words, when it comes to loaning money to others, just don't mess with it. First, there's a risk to loaning money, because there's a chance you'll never see it again after you loan it. And it's doubly bad if you've loaned it secretly, without telling your spouse. He or she might miss that money and ask you about it. Then there's going to be trouble in your house.

You definitely need to let your spouse in on decisions about whether or not to loan money. And you need to be in agreement. In other words, don't hold it against your spouse if he or she doesn't want to loan money to someone. This goes back to refusing to allow anyone to come between you and your spouse. You should view your money as *"our"* money. It belongs to the two of you, not to your friends and relatives. You work hard for your money. If you want to help someone out, fine. But if you don't, don't let it come between the two of you.

Keith Butler Sr.: My wife and I sow money into people's lives all the time. But having the Lord speak to you about blessing somebody is different than someone asking you for money.

Deborah and I have a household budget that we've both agreed upon, and we each receive an "allowance" from our paychecks. It's our own personal money to do with what we want until we're broke! We could loan our own personal money if we wanted to, without consulting the other one. But the rest of that money is *our* money together, and it requires decisions between us. We have to be in agreement.

I have discovered that people with dishonorable intentions will "probe" the spouse they consider to be the weak link between the two of you. I have also discovered, unfortunately, that with some people, if you loan them money once, they will return and ask for money again later.

Many marriages have been ruined over money. I like the statement Deborah made: "Don't mess with the money!" Whenever we loan money, we tell people that we expect to be repaid and that we don't expect them to ask for more money for quite awhile. As Deborah said, that may sound hard, but in so doing, we are avoiding potential pitfalls in our finances *and* in our marriage.

Q: My husband and I are members of separate churches. He belongs to a certain type of church where the pastor spent several weeks teaching against speaking in tongues. My husband and I both desire to be "one" in our worship,

but I don't want to get back into the "dead, dry" traditions of men. God's Word is alive to me, and my experience with God is precious. I feel pulled because it is my heart's desire that my husband and I and our children worship together at one church. Please give me some direction in this matter.

A: The best situation, of course, would be an entire family worshipping together in the same place. But we would need more details to ascertain specifically where your family should worship or if your situation is going to work best for now as it is.

In general, if a situation allows it, we counsel wives to attend church where their husband attends, with this stipulation: Your husband is not your God, and you must give an account to God as an individual for what you did with His Word. You will also have to give an account to what teaching your children were exposed to. Therefore, in some cases, the best situation is not always possible at the moment, particularly if the church you as a wife would have to attend attacks your core beliefs.

It is very difficult for us to go back to many traditional churches. We go for funerals and other circumstances, but it is hard to listen to the preacher get up and blame God for killing a twenty-two year old because he was so wonderful that God wanted Him in His heavenly garden! It makes you want to jump out of your skin, so to speak, to hear someone talk that way about your God. Now we realize that people say those kinds of things out of spiritual ignorance — ignorance of the Word. But it's lying. God is not out killing people.

It's one thing to have to attend that kind of service here and there — every once in a while — for family matters. But it's another thing entirely having to attend a service like that week in and week out.

Marriage is about walking in love with each other and compromising. We see no reason why you can't go to a church where the Word is preached and taught. and then, perhaps, even attend a service with your husband at his church. Many churches, including ours, have multiple services on Sunday mornings. So, for example, you could attend the early service at your church and then go with your husband to church at 10:00 or 11:00 a.m.

If a husband and wife agree that they should go to church together, but can't agree on which church to attend, they could go to both churches on Sunday mornings. In other words, instead of arguing over whose church you'll attend, attend them both for the time being. Find a way to try to accomplish your mutual goals.

The bottom line is, God does not expect you to put yourself in a position where you are not receiving the Word. He holds you responsible for acting on the Word that you know, so why would He deprive you of the ability to receive the Word?

God holds people responsible for the Word they have, but it's not because He is a tyrant or taskmaster. No, He knows that the only way you're going to be able to function successfully and victoriously is with the Word. He knows that the only way you're going to stay healthy — or stay alive in some instances — is through His Word, or through His Word that you receive. So He would not require you to regularly attend a church where no Word was being taught.

Where you go to church is very important. And what your minister ministers to you is very important. They're *extremely* important. So based on the situation you described, it might be best that you attend separate churches. But you ought to know that in so doing, neither of you should come home from church and start trying to talk about what was taught in church that day! That would be breeding ground for strife. After all, your spouse is already in disagreement with you concerning a place of worship. Don't perpetuate your disagreement by your discussion of Bible doctrine.

If anything, you ought to return home from your church where the Word is ministered and just be the happiest he's ever seen you! Lavish him with love, attention, and affection. Tell him you're glad to see him. Otherwise, the fact that you're each attending a different church could drive a wedge between you. Just because you compromised and agreed to go to separate churches is no sign in itself that your relationship is going to automatically improve. The relationship could, in fact, do just the opposite if your disagreements doctrinally are accentuated. It's better to win your husband over with your conversation — your behavior and lifestyle — than with your theological discourses and debates.

Q: Why do men seemingly have difficulty admitting when they are in error?

A: That sounds like a sexist question, but we are going to comment on the question itself, anyway.

First, we said previously that you can't intelligently make broad, sweeping generalizations about the male (or female) gender, saying, "All men (or women) are this, that, and the other." There is no such thing as, "All men are this" or, "All women are that." Maybe *your* man has difficulty admitting his error. There are men who *will* admit their mistakes, and there are men who *won't* admit their mistakes; it depends on the individual man. And sometimes it depends on the woman he's with as to his willingness to admit his error.

For example, are you asking, "Why do men have trouble admitting error?" because your husband, specifically, has trouble admitting error? If so, does he have trouble because you want him to admit it so much that you nag him about it? If you are nagging him about admitting something, he will probably never do it, so don't go there. Even if he knows you're right and he's wrong, he probably will never admit it, because you're constantly nagging him.

It's very simple: If someone views his or her spouse as the opposing team instead of as a teammate, he will not likely cooperate. Some married people want to be right and to prove their point more than they want a peaceful, loving, harmonious relationship with their spouse. This puts the other person in the marriage on the defensive; he will not likely let his guard down for his spouse and admit even the slightest shortcoming or error.

As a rule, a husband won't do even what God told him to do if the wife keeps pushing him. So if you're nagging your husband about something, you need to back off. Often men feel that if they do everything their little woman tells them to do, they aren't being a man. Their ego is involved.

So if you know God wants your husband to do something that your husband doesn't seem open to, you pray for him. Do the things that you know are right to do as a wife. If it's a case of where to attend church, as in the case of the previous writer, make your husband see by your behavior that where you're attending church is making you a better wife for him. He'll probably end up going over to your "side," curious to know what's happening at that church, because it's made you such a good wife. For example, he might say, "Well, you know I don't believe in that 'speaking in tongues' stuff. But you're such a blessing. Maybe I should take another look. I might learn something."

Q: What happens when God speaks to the wife about a situation and not to the husband? He is the priest and head of the family. Could it be that he not listening?

A (Keith Butler Sr.): Yes, the husband is the head and "priest" of the family. But the Bible also says that you, the woman, are a priest as well. Male or female, we as Christians have been made as kings and priests unto God (Rev. 1:6; 5:10).

Anything that God is saying to a husband and wife, He does speak to both parties. There may be one party, such as the husband, who is not listening. Or it could be that he has heard from God, but before he got a chance to be the priest, the wife decided to interpret for him what God was saying. If that is her habit, the husband may eventually get to the point where he refuses to listen to the "little woman." Even if what she is saying is right, he may not cooperate. He may disobey God, because he gets stubborn and feels that in doing everything his wife says, he is simply obeying her every whim.

Deborah Butler: The way this question is worded implies that the wife believes that God has spoken to her first. The writer is under the assumption that God didn't speak first to her husband. It may be true that the husband has not listened to God. Or it may be that he has listened and is still weighing some things in his heart before verbalizing anything to his wife.

When I believe God is saying something to me, I won't just automatically run to Keith and tell him. Sometimes men are slower about saying, "God said such-and-such" than women are. But once they have heard from Heaven and are sure about the direction they've received, it does not take them long to make up their mind.

But just because the husband doesn't move on something that the wife believes she's heard from God about doesn't mean that He hasn't heard from God too. Sometimes I think we women mess things up because we move on things too quickly, and it looks to the husband as if we are trying to lead. To try and usurp the husband as the head of the home can be insulting to him as well as disrespectful. So we need to learn how to stay in our place. God will tell us when to speak. And He will tell us *what* to speak.

I believe that when God speaks to me, I am supposed to *confirm* to Keith what God has said to him, not *inform* him about what God is saying! Therefore, as a rule, I wait for him to say something to me.

It's really hard to say who God is speaking to first, the husband or the wife. When Keith tells me, "The Lord's been saying such-and-such to me," if I've already heard from God, too, I can say to him, "Yes, that fits." But then I'm not going to turn around and say, "Well, when did God speak to *you*? He spoke to *me* months ago"! If a wife does that, whether she intends to or not, she is telling her husband that she is more spiritual than him. And he is probably thinking, *Yeah, and now she thinks she's 'all that.'*

It's best for a wife to pray about a matter she's heard from God about, and let God deal with her husband. It is a mistake for a woman to try to coerce a man to do something. Even if she succeeds in coercing him and wins the battle, he will resent the fact that she coerced him, and that will have consequences later.

Keith Butler Sr.: One last thing about this is, who you married is who you married! You didn't know everything about your spouse before you said, "I do." You've had some revelations about that person since then! Maybe you learned something about your mate and thought, *Oh, I didn't see that one coming!* But you need to be true to the person you married and accept your spouse as he or she is.

Maybe with other men, it might be easier for a wife to just walk up to him and say, "God said we're to do such-and-such, and that's what we're going to do." But with me, that would have to be worded differently! (Sometimes it's not *what* a wife says to her husband as it is the *way* she says it.) Then I would respond, "All right. I'm going to pray about it." In other words, I wouldn't be moved by someone else giving me God's direction for my life, even if it was coming from my wife. Then I may pray three months about it before I move on it. I want to have the right sense *for myself* about what I'm to do before I run out and do it.

If Deborah were to say to me, "What's your problem!" and keep after me about it, I might have the attitude, "Oh? So you think you're going to pin my arm behind my back and make me say, 'Uncle'?" She would never do that, but the point I want to make is, that kind of approach would not work with me. And I'm sure that most husbands feel the same way. A wife should approach her husband in a respectful way.

Q: What are some steps we can take in reestablishing trust in our relationship when that trust has been violated by infidelity?

A: This is a frequently asked question because, unfortunately, it is a frequently occurring event. The Word of God tells you that you and your spouse are covenant partners. Matthew 19:3-9 says you cannot put away your spouse except for certain reasons, and one of those exceptions is infidelity. So a spouse would have scriptural grounds for divorce in that case, provided he or she didn't cause the infidelity by refusing to do what the Bible says you should do. For example, if you refuse to have sex with your spouse and then treat him or her like a dog, you shouldn't be surprised if he or she becomes unfaithful. (In that case, the person who was the offender to begin with needs to be honest with himself or herself and seek to right the relationship if possible.)

Now we are in no way justifying marital infidelity, but in such cases, the person who gets hurt by the other person's unfaithfulness may not be totally clean and in the clear, either. But assuming that a spouse is obeying the Bible and his or her mate has an affair, anyway, the spouse that gets hurt now has a choice, a decision, to make. You can make the decision to end the marriage, or you can make the decision to stay with your mate.

If you decide to stay and try to work things out, once you make the decision to stay, you must put the rest of the Scriptures into action as well, such as those dealing with forgiveness. And to forgive someone means you *put the issue behind you; you lay it to rest.* If the offending party has asked for forgiveness and wants to make your marriage work, you can't hire a private investigator and question your spouse's every move. If the offending spouse has repented, you will destroy the marriage by continuing to bring up his or her offense. If you're always asking, "Why are you ten minutes late? Where have you been? Have you been out with So-and-so again?" you are eventually going to put a wedge between you and, perhaps, drive your spouse away.

Trust cannot be rebuilt and a relationship cannot be healed where there is an atmosphere of suspicion. You cannot go forward in a relationship if you are always looking backward.

Incidentally, we have dealt with many cases in the church in which something similar happened. The couples made the decision to base their marriage and their lives on the Word, and those marriages are far better today than before the unfortunate event took place. When both parties are honest and mature enough to recognize in the case of infidelity that something is seriously wrong in their marriage, they can begin to work to fix the relationship.

So if you decide to stay with a mate who's been unfaithful, you have to make a decision also to let it go. In other words, forgive *and* forget the offense. If you don't, the pain will never heal. It will continue to be like a wound in your life that never closes. Every time it begins to close, you rip it open again and keep exposing it.

Certainly, trust is earned. And your trust in a spouse who's been wayward is an earned response. But, on the other hand, you have to give the person a chance to re-earn that trust. Yes, it will take time, but if you don't exercise forgiveness, nothing will happen to heal your relationship and make it better.

Q: How long should a person continue to stay with a spouse who knows God's will on an issue but willfully refuses to obey it? If a person has heard the Word all his life and rejects it, what recourse does the spouse have? I'm specifically talking about my husband who is in the church, yet smokes, drinks, has unidentified calls on the phone bill, and has a private bank account. He spends most of the money, shopping readily for himself, yet forces me to budget expenses for the house and for myself and our children.

My husband refuses to account for his whereabouts, refuses to do any household chores without arguing, and refuses to make any contribution to the home or marriage. He scoffs if I bring up the fact that these things are wrong.

I know a couple should discover these major differences in beliefs before they are married, but what now?

A: We will address the specific issues one at a time that you brought up, and encourage you to pray for your husband and to seek counseling.

There can be no separate bank accounts in a healthy, godly marriage. When you and your mate got married, you become one flesh (Gen. 2:24; Eph. 5:31). What does it mean to become one flesh? For one, it means you can't operate like you're single! If you married somebody, that means that the other person has a right to be informed regarding *one-hundred percent of the finances*. It means that he or she has a right to discuss the financial matters of your house. It means he or she has a right to participate in deciding how those finances will be managed and spent.

If a person makes the decision that he or she is not going to disclose certain information or that he or she is going to have a private bank account, that person has chosen to operate in opposition to the Word of God. And we know that the result of sin is death (Rom. 6:23) — in this case, the death of the marriage. The number-one reason why marriages break up is problems over money.

Keith Butler Sr.: If you're going to operate your finances scripturally, you must have financial goals. For example, I want to save a certain amount of money each year. I want our savings to go up every year by a certain amount. I know where I want to be financially every year, because I'm the one who's responsible to God for my family's long-term existence. So I set goals.

Now in order to reach that target or goal, that means there has to be some plan that we both agree on that allows every paycheck so many dollars to go toward funding that target amount. Then besides savings, we reach an agreement on roughly how much we can spend. I don't bother too much about that if my target for saving money is being met. After that, it doesn't matter to me how many dresses my wife buys. The only exception is, neither my wife nor myself can make major purchases without the other's consent. Neither of us has free license to destroy the household budget.

In other words, the wife should know through communication and full disclosure of the family's financial affairs that she cannot spend more than such-and-such amount of money each month. But more often than not, problems do not arise because a husband is too liberal; problems arise because he is not liberal enough!

What the husband should do for his wife is to be liberal with her. In general, her everyday needs are greater than his. For example, I can get my hair cut for $10 or $15. Deborah's hair cut and style can cost $60.

Then on top of that, women need manicures and pedicures. I realize some men get manicures and pedicures, too, but the point is, it is generally more expensive for the wife to take care of her "grooming" needs than it is for the husband.

A man doesn't need to buy makeup. A man doesn't usually have twenty suits and forty-five pairs of shoes. I know I could get by with five suits. But I like for Deborah to have variety. She needs to wear pink one day and red the next. She needs a pantsuit one day and a dress another day. I like it when Deborah dresses to the nines and takes care of herself. Therefore, I am more than willing to pay for it. I will not begrudge her the things she needs to feel good about herself (not to mention to make me happy!).

Have you ever noticed that when men do spend money on themselves, it's usually on a big-ticket item such as a car? He might not spend anything for a while. Then he'll buy one thing, and it costs thousands of dollars. His wife could buy several wardrobes with the money he spent! So, you see, that means that a husband and wife should set aside a budget that is basically equal, giving more to her on a daily or weekly basis.

I will discuss here the issue of budgeting, because a budget is so important, no matter what your income. Some folks want to hear the prosperity message, not so they can have more to give to the Gospel, but so they can get out of the financial trouble they're in, because they have no budget. They live week to week, "hand to mouth," so to speak. They spend everything they get and more. If they make $100, they spend $105. The extra $5 is spent on credit.

Someone asked, "What exactly does the Scripture have to say about a budget?" Well, Romans 12:11 says not to be slothful in business. That includes your personal business. God doesn't want us to be lazy or negligent in financial matters.

Proverbs 6:6 through 8 also says something about the way we should conduct our financial affairs. It says, *"Go to the ant, thou sluggard; consider her ways, and be wise"* (v. 6). Then it goes on to say about the ant, *"Which having no guide, overseer, or ruler, Provideth her meat in the summer, and gathereth her food in the harvest"* (vv. 7,8).

The ant does its work in the summer, gathers its harvest in the fall, and stores the harvest for the winter months. In other words, even the ant has a plan and provides for its own. The ant has a savings account. The ant has a budget. If it didn't, it couldn't survive. And if you run your household without a budget, you're going to run into problems too. If you start the year without a plan, as the year progresses, you're going to start having financial troubles, and you're going to fight about it. Failure to operate by a budget always leads to fighting.

Some people think that if you live by faith, you don't need to have a budget. That is nonsense, because the same Word of God that teaches faith teaches that we should have a budget and manage our affairs wisely. So if you don't know how to budget, *find out how*! There are organizations that teach families how to budget, and some of them do it for free. Community colleges also offer classes on budgeting.

It's not necessarily people with lower incomes who have problems keeping a budget. We've seen professionals earning more than half a million dollars who are in debt up to their eyeballs! For example, you could be a brilliant surgeon who knows how to expertly cut people, sew them back together again, and make them as good as new, yet not know basic budgeting principles! But you can learn.

Nothing on this earth can operate for long without a budget. Whether it's a small, medium, or large business, an organization, or a family, everything needs a budget.

Closely related to a lack of equity between husband and wife in the budgeting of money is another issue of accountability. For example, some people have the mistaken idea that when they get married, they will have to account to no one for their whereabouts. Their attitude is, "You're not my mama (or daddy). I don't have to tell you where I'm going." The truth is, your spouse is *higher* than your mama or your daddy, and you *do* have to account to him or her.

The position of your husband or wife is higher than that of your parents. Your spouse has a higher calling where you're concerned than do your parents. When you said, "I do," you swore before God that you would serve that man or woman. Therefore, that person is entitled to know of your whereabouts.

That's an attitude problem when you think your spouse is trying to be your mama or your daddy just because he or she wants to know where you're going. I'll say it again: *A spouse is entitled to that information!*

At this writing, I am forty-five years of age. I am a bishop, having founded several churches. I have held public office in my local community and have counseled Presidents of the United States. God has allowed me to accomplish a great deal over the past twenty or so years, yet I still have to report! To whom? *To my wife*, my covenant partner.

Conversely, I expect my wife to let me know of her whereabouts. We made that decision early on, and we've always abided by that. We both have telephones. At any time, I can call her and ask, "Where are you, Baby?" (And she will say, "On my way to see you, Sweetie"!)

Now on the issue of refusing to do household chores, that falls under the category of each partner playing his or her role in the family. We covered than in a previous chapter, but we will review it here briefly.

A man's primary role — the area to which most of his efforts are to be expended — is to provide financially for his wife and family, to be a father to his children, spending time with them, and ministering to his wife's physical and emotional needs.

Now we're *not* saying that men aren't supposed to do anything in the house; we're simply stating that this should not be his primary focus. Just as the wife should not be expected to do everything, neither should he. The husband has a role, which we just discussed. And the wife has a role, which is primarily to take care of the home, the children, and meeting the needs of her husband.

However, if both the husband and wife are out there working to provide income for the family, both husband and wife are going to have to share the duties at home. There's no sense in a husband thinking it's unmanly to wash dishes when the wife is doing some of his chores. If she's doing some of his job, then he should be doing some of hers.

Q (Husband): How do I make my wife feel that she second in my life only to God. I have the responsibility of helping my parents with various financial and other decision-making issues. When I help them, my mother, in particular, my wife says she feels "second" to my parents and that I choose them over her. But why can't I make things a little easier for them as they age? I do my best to take care of her needs as well as my parents' needs. I don't think I'm choosing them over her. I am only trying to honor my mother and father as the Bible commands.

(Wife): I've shared with my husband that sometimes I feel my needs take a backseat to his mother's needs, but he denies that this is true. He argues that if it were really true, he would never have moved out of their house and married me. I see his marrying me only as an indication that he wanted to spend the rest of his life with me, *not* that he was placing me second only to God.

Why can't he realize that I feel as if he's prioritizing me after his mother and that it hurts me and our relationship? His mother's business comes before mine, including our household affairs. He talks to her several times day, every day, but rarely shares a meaningful conversation with me. I feel neglected, unloved, uncherished, insignificant, and lonely. Needless to say, I have resentment building in me toward his mother, who is allowing this to continue.

A: We've talked in detail about Genesis 2:24, which says, *"Therefore shall a man leave his father and his mother, and shall cleave unto his wife: and they shall be one flesh."* Now let's look at another couple of verses, Ephesians 6:2 and 3, which say, *"Honour thy father and mother; (which is the first commandment with promise;) That it may be well with thee, and thou mayest live long on the earth."*

Are these verses contradictory to Genesis 2:24? No. Note the order of things. The first order is always the spouse; your husband's or wife's needs come *first*. Never should it be said by your spouse that your parents get more of you — of anything about you — than your spouse does.

Sir, if you're going to talk every day to your mama, you must talk *twice* the amount of time to your own wife. If you're going to buy something for Mom, you must spend *twice* the amount on your wife. What your parents get from you shouldn't even be close to what your wife gets from you. Your covenant partner and your parents are not even together in the same league.

This issue should never be raised as a question at all. The fact that a question is raised says that something is out of order in the family, and we are talking primarily to the husband, the head of the house. You are out of order. Yes, you're supposed to assist your parents if they need to be assisted, but only *after* you have completed meeting the needs of your family and immediate family — those of your own household.

Also, to clarify what defines a need, the needs of your wife are not what *you* think her needs are, but what *she* thinks they are. If your wife is satisfied that her needs are being met, she should not begrudge the fact that you help your parents. And, again, you *should* help your parents *if* they are unable to help themselves.

Keith Butler Sr.: We both have living parents. If parents on either side of the family need our help, we help them. We *expect* to help each other's parents. But I am not going to assist my parents or Deborah's at her expense. In other words, I'm not going to help them financially, for example, and then tell Deborah she can no longer afford the lifestyle she has become accustomed to. Therefore, the level of assistance provided to the parents on either side of the family is determined by whether my wife's needs are met first, because she is biblically my first priority.

Deborah Butler: Honoring your parents is not just a financial matter. But in defining exactly what it is to honor your parents, let's look at what it is *not*. Obviously, when you're grown, honoring your parents doesn't mean doing whatever your parents want. And it doesn't mean that the wife has to conform herself to what her mother-in-law thinks.

Indeed, the mother-in-law should never comment to her son, especially if it's bad, what she thinks about his wife. That mother is out of order if she does. So honoring parents doesn't mean they get to have their way with your life. Parents who insist on having their way in the affairs of their grown children and their spouses are the ones doing the dishonoring.

Keith Butler Sr.: I would never allow my mother to say something to me that's negative about Deborah. Now my mother wouldn't do that; she never has and never will. But I'm saying that I wouldn't let her if she tried — I would stop her mid-sentence! And I'm talking about *anything* negative about Deborah, even something as seemingly insignificant as the décor of the church. Deborah is the "first lady" of Word of Faith International Christian Center. She is largely responsible for the décor in the buildings. Now my mother may have different tastes in furniture and interior decorating than Deborah does, but that doesn't mean that she can voice her opinion to me about it. If she did, she'd be out of order, and I would not allow it.

You see, honor goes both ways. Yes, you're supposed to honor your parents, but your parents are supposed to honor you and your spouse and your union together. Not all parents honor their children as they're supposed to. That's why it's up to you, as an adult, to guard and protect your marriage, and that includes guarding and protecting your spouse against family members who would vie for time and money that should be spent on him or her.

As we've said before, we decided early in our marriage (even as teenagers, we had that much sense!) that we were not going to fight with each other about something somebody else was doing, including our family members. If we were going to have a "falling out," it was going to be over us, not somebody else. And we have abided by that agreement all these years.

I may not always agree with her dad about certain things, and she may not always agree with my dad. It doesn't matter; we never take sides with our family members against each other. We protect our union, our covenant partnership, as husband and wife.

Don't ever let anyone else come between you and your spouse. And it is your responsibility to see that you don't. You are responsible to God for your spouse — to please him or her first, above all others. If your mother got pleased about something, but your spouse didn't get pleased, you are out of order, *period*. You need to focus your time, money, energy, and efforts maintaining a happy union with your spouse, not with your parents.

Q: What do you do if a spouse takes an out-of-town job assignment for six months and leaves the other working spouse with two young children to care for?

A: First of all, the only way the spouse can ever take such a job assignment scripturally is that you both agree. If you agreed that your spouse should do this, then don't complain when he or she does.

We do not recommend taking a six-month assignment away from your spouse for any reason. The only people who should do that sort of thing are those conscripted by the United States Navy. Those men and women are often assigned to work on carriers for periods of six months at a time. However, in those cases, a person usually knows before marriage that the possibility exists that his or her spouse might not be at home all the time. Therefore, to resent something he or she had foreknowledge of would be wrong.

Now let's talk about other situations in which one spouse wants to leave for six months at a time. Let's say a person receives a great opportunity to work out-of-state and says to his spouse, "It's a great opportunity, and I'm taking it whether you like it or not." That person is operating outside of the Word — outside the perimeters of God's rightness and His way of doing things. He is breaking his covenant with his spouse, and is going to create "hell" in his house for some extra dollars.

Those extra dollars aren't worth it if you've taken that kind of attitude with your spouse or if you've made a decision to leave for a job without his or her full agreement and consent. Your pockets may be bulging when you come home, but "hell" is going to be waiting for you. It will "hell" when you arrive, "hell" when you go to bed at night, "hell" when you wake up in the morning, and even "hell" when you go to church!

You can't buy peace, friend. You need to seriously weigh your priorities in such situations, and, clearly, the Bible shows you the direction you should go.

Q: How do you handle a spouse who buys expensive items for the house on credit without the other spouse's approval and then uses the bill money to pay the creditor?

A: *You don't buy expensive items without your spouse's knowledge and consent, period.* "Yes," someone argued, "but I might need to buy it right then — today. It might be gone tomorrow." Then let it go, because you are in a covenant *together* with your spouse, and agreement between the two of you is more important than some "here-today-gone-tomorrow" deal.

Keith Butler Sr.: My wife is an "expensive" woman — a high-maintenance woman ! And if there's any blame to be assigned for that, the fault should be assigned to me, because I helped make her that way. I wanted to do it, and I'm glad she's who she is.

I'm expensive too! I spend a lot of money on my main hobby, which is hunting. I hunt all over the world, and you know that costs some money! But neither of us spends large sums of money, even when the money is available, without the other's approval. If Deborah told me, "Honey, I think it would be best financially if you didn't take that hunting trip to Africa just yet," then I wouldn't take the trip.

In some countries, certain game is expensive to hunt, because of what it costs to bag and transport it properly. For example, I recently did take a trip to Africa to hunt lion and cape buffalo. I got a lion, and would have gotten a buffalo, but I was over budget. I had the buffalo sited and could have very well taken it down at that instant, but I didn't. I didn't get the buffalo, even though I had traveled all the way to Africa to get one. And the reason I didn't was out of respect for my wife. I knew that if I shot it, I was going to have to spend more money that we'd agreed upon, so I passed it up. When I returned home, she said, "You should have shot it. I wouldn't have minded." (Of course, you know what that means. That means I'll have to take another trip to Africa, and I'm going to find mister cape buffalo when I do!)

You see, this issue of agreeing on large expenditures is a respect issue. When you spend large amounts of money without permission, it is one of the ultimate acts of disrespect you can commit toward your spouse. Money is vital to a marriage, because it is vital to a household. I mean, what can you really do in life without money? Not much, and without it, you ultimately cannot survive. So when you spend without discussion that which is so vital and which belongs to both of you, it is tantamount to spitting in the face of your mate. You are showing utter disregard for the thoughts and feelings of that other person to which you are joined in marriage.

Some people will spend large sums of money without their spouse's knowledge and then act surprised when he or she balks. They think that other person ought to understand. If that's your attitude, you need a reality check. You've spit in your spouse's face, and you have some explaining and some rectifying to do.

Deborah and I sit down and talk it over before we make major purchases. For either one of us to be able to spend large sums of money, we both have to agree. If we can't agree, then the purchase in question gets tabled.

Deborah might want to spend thousands of dollars on new furniture. Well, I might say, "What's wrong with the stuff we have?" But we discuss it and talk it over and try to reach an agreement. I might say, "What's wrong with the old furniture?" and I might have a good point if our furniture is in good condition. But, on the other hand, the décor of the house doesn't mean to me what it does to her, and I have to respect our differences.

I like our home to look nice, but I'm a private individual and my attitude toward new furniture is, "Nobody's going to see it, anyway. Let's just keep what we have."

But I can't force who I am on her, expecting her to be like me or to see everything just the way I see it. She is a woman; I am a man. We are different, and we think different.

Men don't understand women, but have you ever noticed that *women* understand women? You have if you've ever sat with a group of them and heard them talking. One will say something about a man, and the others will say, "Oh, yeah. I know what you're talking about"!

Then you get the men together. One will start talking about women, and all those men will chime in, "Yeah, I know exactly what you mean."

I said that to make the point that as a married person, if you ever start going through the drill where you're expecting your spouse to feel exactly the way you feel and then judge him or her based on your feelings, you need to stop yourself in your tracks! I mean, don't even go there. You'll be frustrated if you do, because you can't make that work.

Concerning the purchase of new furniture, for example, I have to walk in love toward my wife and give in to her desire because I know it's important to her. What's important to me is the lion and the buffalo! So I get to hunt, and she gets to buy some things for the house.

Q: Are means of birth control, such as vasectomy and tubal ligation, acceptable options for Christian couples who have decided they absolutely do not want any more children?

There is a biblical way to judge the acceptability of something such as this with God even when the Bible makes no specific mention of it. You judge it with First Corinthians 6:19: *"...know ye not that your body is the temple of the Holy Ghost which is in you, which ye have of God, and ye are not your own?"* Anything that will do harm to your body is unscriptural. If you know something will harm your body, then it is unscriptural and, therefore, sin. If it does not harm your body, then it is permissible.

So in the case of birth control, if taking the "pill" doesn't do harm to your body, you can take the pill with freedom and liberty. It is not a sin to you. Now the evidence continues to be conflicting on the effects of the "pill," but every woman is different. What might affect one woman one way might affect another woman in a different way altogether.

Years ago when we got married, medical reports said that birth-control pills could cause cancer. So we made the decision not to use the pill. Later evidence came forth that claimed the early reports were erroneous and that the pill was, for all intents and purposes, harmless to a woman's long-term health. Then more recently, contradicting reports have emerged. Some say that it's fine to take the pill; others advise against it.

The risk of many of the possible side-effects of the pill are determined by age, heredity, and lifestyle, such as diet and use of tobacco. It's best to research this information for yourself so you can intelligently make the determination using the guideline of First Corinthians 6:19. When you're not sure, another biblical guideline is to *always follow peace*.

As far as the procedures you mentioned, we would not advise you medically except to say you should consult with your physician and even get a second opinion if you still have questions. As far as we know, a tubal ligation (having your "tubes tied") will not negatively affect your body. However, concerning the vasectomy, there have been some questions arise concerning potential long-term harm. Again, arm yourself with as much knowledge from respectable sources as you can before making a decision.

Q: If the intended goal for sex in marriage is that both parties be mutually satisfied, is it wrong for a husband to require sex from his wife even though they both acknowledge that she is tired and not physically and emotionally prepared for sex?

A: Practically speaking, you need to consider the time of day you usually have sex. A popular survey by a company renown for its expertise in this area concluded that eighty-five percent of American couples have sex at approximately 10:00 p.m. or later. The reason for this time is fairly obvious: Both husband and wife are in a bed together unclothed or partially clothed. For those reasons, ten o'clock at night is a time that is conducive to having sex.

However, there is a problem with that, and this problem is why many couples are having sex problems. Ten o'clock at night is also that time when husband and wife are probably the most physically tired and the most emotionally spent. That is the time they are getting ready to go to sleep. Therefore, 10:00 p.m. is not the optimal time for sex.

According to this survey, the optimal time is somewhere between 2:00 and 4:00 p.m. Someone said, "But that's not practical." Well, what you need to do is plan some of your sexual escapades with your spouse. That doesn't sound romantic, but, really, it is, because it works. We're not saying that all your sex should be planned, but you need to plan to have sex with your spouse at least once a week before 10:00 p.m. Doing that would ensure that there will be sex at least once a week when you and your spouse are not tired. Also, planning sex creates an excitement as you anticipate coming together. You can prepare yourself physically, mentally, and emotionally. All the factors that make for optimal sex will be present: physical and emotional energy, preparation, and anticipation. One time of especially satisfying sex is better than three of four times of attempting romance when one or both of you really aren't interested.

When one spouse repeatedly responds negatively to sex, even when that person is legitimately tired, it can lead to frustration, performance anxiety, and feelings of inadequacy.

This issue of sex is surprisingly like money in that without a plan, you will get haphazard results. So create a plan and work with it — we believe you'll be happy with the dividends.

To answer your question specifically, in general, it's not a good idea to press your wife to have sex when you know she's exhausted and can't participate fully. Now when a man is in his twenties, he doesn't care as much whether she's ready for sex or not. He'll get satisfied, and that's all that's important as long as she's not complaining too much about it. But as a man matures, his wife's satisfaction becomes more important to him. In his mind, it's better to let her get some sleep than to press her, knowing that she's just going through the motions, so to speak.

Now if you're a wife, if you know that your husband was interested in sex last night, you should make sex a priority tonight and make the necessary preparations to take care of him in bed. If he let you rest and take care of yourself the night before while he reined in his desires, you need to, in turn, take care of him. Then both parties are happy.

You see, a man will figure out that if he treats his wife right, she will reward him. But if treats her nice repeatedly with no sign of a reward, he will lose his motivation for treating her nice.

Deborah Butler: On the other hand, if we'll be honest, wives know most of the time when our husbands want sex. So don't wait till the end of the day when you know you're going to be tired. You pick the time sometimes. Your husband may be watching a football game on television; you don't have to turn off the set, but you could walk in front of the screen during a commercial and invite him to a half-time rendezvous. Then you're both fresh, versus waiting until the game is over. And your husband can go back and watch the second half a winner even if his team is losing!

Keith Butler Sr.: But don't complain if your wife is wooing you, and you're choosing your team over a fling with your "good thing"! That's not smart! You need to strike while the fire is hot, so to speak. Record part of the game if need be — I believe that's why God gave us the VCR!

Q: We always pay our tithes and give offerings. Do we need to do anything extra to exercise our faith that God will meet our financial needs and even give us the desires of our heart? I have considered giving additional offerings exclusively as seed sown toward a particular desire and then "naming" my seed to produce the specific harvest I desire. Is this scriptural? My husband thinks that unless the Holy Spirit leads me to give such an offering, I'd just be giving to *get.*

A: Obviously, wherever the Holy Spirit leads you to give is going to be the place of giving where you'll receive the fastest return because you would be giving in the perfect will of God. And you should obey the specific leading of the Holy Spirit. In fact, to *dis*obey such an unction of the Holy Ghost would be a "slap in God's face."

However, a person's first motive for giving must always be that he loves God and wants someone else to receive the blessing of the Word whether or not he gets anything in return financially. Despite what some critics may propagate, I do not teach giving to *get*. I teach giving because a person loves God and people, and because he or she knows that God said you could receive from Him as you're obedient to His Word in the area of giving. There's a big difference in giving with that motive and giving solely with the motive to get something.

First Timothy 6:5 talks about folks who believed that money and financial gain were equated with godliness. But that erroneous thinking should not stop a God-fearing, Bible-believing Christian from sowing financial seed in faith that he will reap a harvest from his giving. A person can give like that, expecting to receive *because God said he could*!

The principle of seedtime and harvest is not man's idea; it originated with God (*see* Genesis 8:22). So it wouldn't be wrong to expect something that God said you could expect.

Keith Butler Sr.: There have been times in our ministry when the budget was short, and we needed a significantly greater amount of money than we had coming in. I'd pray about it and say, "Lord, I know from Your Word that giving puts me in position to receive. That's Your system, but I want to obey You specifically. I don't want to just give money away. I want to seek direction from You and give where *You* say to give." So you could say that while we may not have specifically "named" our seed, we have often given specific seed, believing for a specific harvest.

The Lord will never turn down an offering from you. He won't do it, because giving and receiving is His system. But He will direct you in your giving. He might say, "Give to such-and-such ministry." To obey that is to operate in faith, and when you sow that seed in faith, you can scripturally receive the harvest in return.

A couple of years ago, it became popular to run down to the altar and throw money on it, sometimes as the preacher was ministering. Some people were being led by the Holy Spirit to give in that way. But others were doing the same thing — throwing money on the altar — but they weren't doing it in faith. They were getting caught up in the moment emotionally, throwing money because others were doing it.

Faith is the key to receiving from God. I've ministered in many meetings in which people came down to the altar to give, and there was a mixture of Spirit and emotion involved. In other words, I knew that there were people there who were being led by God to do it and that there were others who were not. Well, I don't ever want to stop the people who are being led to do it, because if I did, I'd hinder their faith and rob them of a blessing. Faith and obedience always reap the blessing of God.

On the other hand, I do want to stop people who are throwing money on the altar for the wrong reason. If I don't try to teach people and help them that way, they're going to give, but they're going to be just giving money away. They're not going to get anything back in the way of a return on their giving.

A minister must have money to function in the ministry, but he or she should want to help people, not hurt them. God has always provided for our needs even when there was no Word of Faith ministries. I didn't enter the ministry for money. When I first entered the ministry, I didn't even think about a salary. Now I receive a salary, but the Board of Directors of our ministry sets it. And if they cut it tomorrow, I'd still show up to preach on Sunday morning — and I'd be smiling.

So giving is good and right, but there are times when you should be led to give certain offerings. Now I'm *not* saying that you have to be led every time you give an offering. No, you should give because the Word says that you should and because you want to sow and be a blessing to the Kingdom of God and to others. However, there are times when you need to check to with the Holy Ghost before doing something that you see others doing. Following peace is one way you can know whether He's directing you to do a particular thing. It is never out of order to obey the Holy Ghost!

The answer to this question can be briefly summed up in the word "motive." God's Word and the attitude of your heart should be your first consideration in giving.

Q: When parents give children gifts (besides money on birthdays, at Christmas, and so forth), should the parents based on the value of the gift received?

A: We taught our children early about tithes and offerings, but we never forced them to do either. Yet they have always tithed and given offerings, and they did it of their own volition. Honestly, we think they've sometimes given more offerings beyond their tithes than we thought they should. At times we've seen them give every dime they had, and we're talking about hundreds of dollars, into helping the poor. We'd asked them why they did it, because we wanted to make sure their reasons were scriptural. They took to heart what they were taught from the Word on the subjects of tithing and giving offerings, but they did not act on that as something we required of them.

We taught our kids the Word, but then we lived by the Word and let them watch us in the situations and circumstances of life. If you as a parent obey God's Word and do what God says to do, your children will follow you. But if you issue mandates to them without teaching them in love and then living it by your example, even if they did obey you, they wouldn't benefit spiritually from it. And they will eventually stop doing whatever it is you're forcing them to do.

In short, your children's money is their money. They should not be forced to tithe or give offerings. They'll learn in time by your guidance and example.

Q: What counsel would you give a wife who wants to support her husband and follow him wherever God leads him, but feels she's not ready spiritually or emotionally to make a major transition and help manage the responsibility of relocating the family?

A: If you as a wife want to support your husband in his calling, yet you don't feel ready even though you're being called upon to do so, somebody has missed God's timing somewhere — you or your husband. It could be that you're more ready than you know. On the other hand, it could also be that you're just not ready to obey. Only you, with God's help, can answer that question.

Keith Butler Sr.: When I was working for IBM and the Lord told me to quit and go to Bible school full time in Oklahoma, Deborah had to make a decision as to whether or not she was going to stand behind me and support me in my calling. At the time, she had only been outside of the state of Michigan once or twice in her entire life. She also comes from a very large, close-knit family. So to give up an excellent job and uproot her from her family, friends, and everything that was familiar to her was going to be a big step.

Deborah balked at first. She suggested that I go on to Oklahoma while she and our son stayed in Michigan for awhile. She was putting off taking that step of faith. But I wasn't leaving without my wife! I didn't want to move hundreds of miles away and get some "Dear Keith" letter in the mail one day!

I told the Lord, "Your Word says that my wife and I are one flesh. So if You can speak to me, and You have spoken to me, You can speak to her as well. You think I'm ready to go;

therefore, since Deborah and I are one, she must be ready to go too. So *You* tell her."

Well, Deborah started praying about it, and the Lord spoke to her to go and be with her husband. So she made the decision and we left. Not only did Deborah go, she enrolled in school with me! Then we found out she was pregnant with our second child, who was huge, and Deborah had to waddle up and down the stairs to her classes. She was a trooper about it. She had our baby over spring break and then brought that baby to her classes! She made the decision that she was going to finish school with me, and she did.

If God is sending the husband away to do something for Him, the wife's job is to pack up and go. Do you as a wife want to hinder or stop the call of God on your husband's life? I hope the answer is no.

What would have happened had Deborah decided not to go? I wouldn't be where I am today, pastoring the churches I pastor and doing the work of the ministry that I'm doing today. We might not even be married, because trouble always ensues in a marriage when a wife snatches her husband's dream from him.

Q: After a wife is divorced from her husband and marries someone else who later divorces her, can she, according to Scripture, be reconciled to her first husband?

A: When you marry someone, he or she is your covenant partner. If you divorce that person and marry someone else, that new person is now your covenant partner. According to First Corinthians 7:11, you should fight to be reconciled to your current husband. More explicitly, it says be reconciled to your mate, your covenant partner, or remain unmarried.

You can't just divorce someone, remarry, divorce again, and go back to your first husband or wife without committing adultery somewhere along the way.

While there are Bible reasons for divorce and extenuating circumstances that sometimes make divorce necessary, generally speaking, we are too quick to opt for divorce in our society today. With the exception of a certain few circumstances, a person should stay with his or her spouse.

Q: What should a person do if his or her spouse has been diagnosed with a terminal illness and the person needing healing has not been taught the Word of God in that area? That is my situation, and now that all hope of natural healing is gone, at what point do I stop ministering to my mate and just begin to comfort my partner and prepare myself for the loss of my loved one?

A: Every person, including every married person, is responsible to God for himself. You cannot make someone you love study the Word, and you can't build his faith for him. If anyone will not hear, believe, and act on the Word, there are natural consequences that will follow, and cases such as this one, the consequences are that the person will likely die.

The faith of the spouse may prolong death for a while, giving that other person time to build his faith. But even if your faith keeps your mate alive, Satan is going to continue to attack, and that person must learn at some point how to stand his ground against the devil and fight for his own life.

Just because a person hasn't availed himself to the Word doesn't mean he is not responsible for the Word that he's rejected. You are responsible for the teachings of the Bible whether you read and study them or not. If you as an individual decide not to follow God, then, ultimately, no one in the long run can avert for you the repercussions of your choice. As a man sows, so shall he also reap (Gal. 6:7).

That may sound hard, and we're not saying that you can't pray that God will strengthen your mate and enlighten his or her understanding according to the prayers the Apostle Paul prayed in Ephesians 1 and 3. But, ultimately, the decision to hear, believe, and act on the Word lies with the individual believer, not with his or her spouse.

Q: **Is there Scripture that gives a person license or liberty to request that doctors *not* try to revive a spouse who's terminally ill and whose organs are beginning to fail?**

A: It is certainly okay for you to direct a physician in this manner if it was the known, express will of your spouse. It is very important to discuss these things and to know the will of your spouse on the matter.

Keith Butler Sr.: I personally would not want to be on a respirator for ten years with my wife struggling all that time to handle that burden.

I mean, God forbid that I miss it and wind up in a coma or incapacitated somehow for a prolonged period of time. But if it happened, I'd want Deborah to give doctors reasonable time, and I'd want her to pray and use her faith. But something that would drag on and on and drain the finances and tax her emotionally is a situation in which I would want her to let me go. I'd want her to let me go on and shout up and down those streets of glory! She could go find somebody else — as long as she knew she'd never find anybody as good as me!

You see, I'm the head of my house, and I have provided for Deborah's future whether I'm here or not. Why? Because I love her. I care about her welfare even in the event I'm not there to take care of her.

I wouldn't want my family to suffer because I wasn't there. It's a man's responsibility to take care of his family financially. In fact, the Bible says a good man leaves an inheritance to even his children's children (Prov. 13:22). Of course, we know from Scripture that if you're going to leave something for your children, you're certainly going to leave something for your wife. In fact, I have money designated for my children, but should Deborah survive me, I have even more money designated for her. That's the way it should be.

But how medical issues are handled should be discussed in advanced so that a person will know how to represent his spouse if he can't represent himself.

I know of an incident in which one spouse was diagnosed as terminally ill, but was determined to stick with the fight, receiving medical treatment until he could activate faith to the fullest and receive from God. Well, as symptoms progressed and the person's condition became worse, the other spouse decided it was too hard to see the person suffer, and gave doctors permission not to revive the patient. That spouse took a lot of offense for that.

In short, your spouse's will is what you want to uphold and communicate to the doctors in the event he or she is not able to do so. Remember, your job is to be a help to your spouse in life. If he or she wants to stay alive, you should help him or her stay alive. But if he or she wants the "plug pulled," then you are free and within your rights to make such a request if you decide to do so.

Q: If I am honestly doing the things I know to do from the Word of God to improve my relationship with my wife, yet she still refuses to have sex with me more than once a month, what should I do?

It is not normal to have sex only once a month. You didn't get married to have sex with somebody twelve times a year! There's a problem here. What we need to do is find out what the problem is, and there could be any number of reasons why this problem exists. (Incidentally, while this question was written by a husband, we have encountered similar situations over the years, and our experience has been that three times as many women than men will have this same complaint!)

Let's explore some possibilities as reasons why your wife won't have sex with you more than once a month.

In general, this problem can arise in a marriage because one spouse is no longer attracted to the other person. When two people get married, there are certain characteristics about them that attract them to each other physically. It isn't all spirit, you know!

Then as the years go by, they can let themselves go. By that, I mean they can physically stop practicing good hygiene. They can stop taking care of their bodies to the point they are no longer attractive.

Certainly when this happens on the part of one spouse, the other spouse still loves him or her, but that doesn't mean the other spouse finds him or her attractive. And that loss of appeal can affect the sex drive.

Now we're talking about an extreme of going from someone who is clean and kept to someone who doesn't care about his or her appearance. We're not talking about unreasonableness in expectations. For example, no one can reasonably expect his or her spouse to look 18 years of age when he or she is 48. But a 48 year-old can remain attractive to his or her spouse in spite of the natural aging process.

Sometimes a spouse can lose his or her sex drive because of other issues in the marriage. For example, stress and pressures affect libido in some people, particularly women. If there are financial pressures, and you're ducking and dodging creditors, you might lose your desire for sex. This pressure does not affect women exclusively in this way. But the most important thing to a woman in a relationship is security, including financial security. If there's no security, she might have a problem being sexually ready for her husband very often.

A man who feels as though he's being pressured on every side sometimes has difficulty performing sexually or even wanting sex.

Also, some people cannot perform sexually when strife is present. That's one reason we said previously to resolve all conflicts before nightfall. It should never be the case that a couple goes days with conflict between the two of them.

And sometimes, sex itself is what hinders some people sexually. In other words, if one spouse wants the other to do things he or she isn't comfortable with, such as oral sex, it can shut the other person down.

It takes communication and, often, counseling to discover the real source of the problem when one or both parties is no longer interested in sex.

Most of the time, the reason one party doesn't want to have sex has nothing to do with the performance of the other party in bed. Remember, we said that sex, especially for women, doesn't start in the bedroom. Sex can be emotional as well as physical, and if there are emotional issues, they will have to be taken care of outside the bedroom before a couple will begin again to find pleasure together inside the bedroom.

Keith Butler Sr.: Years ago I encountered a couple with a similar problem, but in that particular case, it was the women who was complaining that her husband didn't want to have sex with her. As they were talking to me, he communicated with her for the first time as to why he no longer desired her sexually.

As it turns out, this woman had been married before and had told her new husband that her former husband was much larger physically — more endowed — than he was. Then she said, in effect, that she was used to being with a "bigger" man, and she severely criticized his performance in bed. Well, that hurt him and shattered his ego. She might as well have gotten a gun and killed him, because he was dead to her after that. Her remarks destroyed him in terms of his belief in himself as a man. So we know that the things people say to one another can kill the sex drive.

It is not usually normal for a man not to want to have sex. Of course, different men have different frequencies — for example, the older they get, the less frequently they need sex. But it is unusual for a man not to want to have sex. If a man does not want to have sex with his wife, there is probably some unresolved issue between him and his wife that is hindering him. That issue needs to first be exposed and then resolved, and it may require counseling. I guarantee you, a man does want sex; he simply might not want to have it with his wife for some reason. (That doesn't mean he can just go out and get it somewhere else. Men do have control. Many people want to say they don't, but they do; they can control themselves.)

Many times, the subject of problems with intimacy is so personal, for both men and women, that you really need to hear a couple out over a period of time. This issue is so tied to a person's self-esteem that you can't shut him down when he's ready to talk about it. You have to let him talk, and you have to listen to him.

Some people feel they can't talk about problems in their sex life. But if there are problems, and those problems aren't discussed, the marriage is going to be in serious trouble. Men especially don't like to seek counseling, because their attitude is, "I'm a man, and I should never have to divulge what is happening in my life for some other man to tell me what to do."

That's unwise because there's nothing that's going to impact the life of a married man like his wife. If he wants his woman to make him happy, but there are problems they can't resolve on their own, they'd better seek some outside help.

If a man had a car that needed repair, but he couldn't fix it, would he just junk the car and leave it sitting? Would he say, "I'll just catch the bus the rest of my life"? No, he'd find somebody who could fix his car so he won't have to ride the bus. Similarly, he should want to find the right kind of help if his marriage is "broken" and he doesn't know how to fix it.

Q: I have had problems with a bad temper, and when my husband and I argue, I say things that hurt him. It seems I am unable to say the things I feel any other way, and I do believe they are things that do need to be said. Yet I am trying to talk to my husband without losing my cool. However, these "discussions" usually turn into an argument, anyway, because he gets so defensive.

I want to communicate better with my husband so that he won't feel he has to be defensive. I also want to work on my temper, and I've asked the Holy Spirit to help me, but I think I'm missing it somewhere.

Here is the second part to my question: I want to praise and compliment my husband, accepting him the way he is, but sometimes it's hard. There are times I feel like I am "second" in his life. He does not purposely try to make me feel that way, but I still do. I try to tell him how it makes me feel when says and does certain things, but he continues to do them. What should I do?

A (Deborah Butler): First, you need to realize that when you lose your temper with your husband, you damage his ego. So even if what you have to say is legitimate, he's not going to want to hear it, because you're hurting him with your words. He doesn't get the feeling you want to help him at all, so he's not going to be open to hearing from you.

Then when you praise him, he probably doesn't respond like you think he should, but the reason is, he's confused; he doesn't know what to believe. And he has a point. How can you say one thing on the one hand, and another thing on the other hand, and expect to have any credibility?

You need to spend extra time praying in the Holy Ghost so you'll be able to control your temper. *You can't change things in your own flesh or strength, and you certainly can't change them overnight.*

I advise you to seek outside help to help get your thinking straightened out. It's seems to me you're a little confused as to your role as a wife, because it seems you are pushing him more than supporting him. No man is going to take that very well.

Also, you really do have to accept your spouse as he is. You knew him when you married him, and you chose to love him for who he was. Now this is the man you must learn to live with. If you try to make him something different, it will backfire on you; you will make a mess of things.

So seek counseling and be open to the Holy Ghost to help you and change you into the kind of wife you should be. Many times, when we focus on being the right kind of person ourselves, we find we have much less problems with that other person in our lives.

Q: My wife and I recently lost our son during the fifth month of pregnancy. My wife has had a history of having rough pregnancies. We currently have one daughter. Even though I want to have more children, she's afraid due to all the problems she's had in the past.

A: Well, first of all, you don't want a woman to get involved with a pregnancy when she's not ready for it. She has to have total confidence that having another child is what she wants. And if she never reaches that level of confidence, you should thank God for the child that you do have. There are so many couples who don't have any children and would be so grateful to have just one.

If there have been problem pregnancies in the past, that is the area you both need to shore up in with your faith. Your wife especially needs to learn to use her faith, because she is one who would carry their child and then go through the labor and delivery.

The Word of God is clear in First Timothy 2:15 where it says that a woman who has faith and sobriety can be spared those kind of symptoms. But her faith has really got to be strong in her heart and in her mouth, her confession. But if it's not there and doesn't ever get there, you're place is to love her, and if loving her means that one child is enough, then you settle for that one child.

Consider this: Whether you have one child or two or more, when he turns eighteen or so, he's going to leave. Even if he's still at home in body at eighteen, he's left you in his soul. I mean, if you're a father of a daughter, can you remember a time when there was no one else in the world for her but you. You were the center of her universe, and she couldn't think of wanting anyone but you.

But then something happened. One day, you come home from work as usual, and she's gone somewhere with some boy. In other words, the day comes for fathers of little girls that those dads are no longer the men in their lives.

Kids come and go, but you and your spouse are going to be together the rest of your lives. The question of who's more important over the long haul is something to consider if you and your spouse can't agree on whether to have more children.

Q: My husband and I were married five months ago. He has a daughter who resents me and the fact that I married her father. Since we've been married, she has indicated she wants nothing to do with me or her father. Her mother also refuses communication with either one of us and does not want us to call her house. My husband tries to communicate with his daughter by mail and by e-mail, but she refuses to respond. How can we bridge the gap? They are not Christians.

A: The only thing you can do is continue to walk in love toward them regardless of how they act toward you. Actually, if the two of you weren't married yet, we'd say you have no business getting married until that issue has been resolved. But since you're already married, you have to walk in love toward that daughter and her mama. You can pray for them and perhaps you will win them in time because of the witness you are to them.

You can't make others love you. You have to walk in love and love them regardless of how they respond. That love that's in you — the God-kind of love — will get on them because it's contagious. And it will eventually affect them in a positive way.

Q: My wife doesn't work but I do. We decided that she should stay home with our two-year-old child. She does attend classes part time, a few mornings a week. I understand that caring for a young child is a lot of work, but am I insensitive to expect dinner to be cooked more than twice a week?

A: This wife is not performing in her role as a help meet if she is only cooking twice a week. The husband is doing his job; he's bringing home the bacon, so to speak. He's taking care of business, and he should be able to expect, reasonably, to receive from her hands a majority of days each week. Two is not a majority.

Q: My wife is constantly late for just about everything. It has gotten to the point where I would rather go place in separate cars. We have a small child, and I offer to wash, feed, and clothe him so that my wife can have enough time to get ready. But each time I take care of our child, she spends so much time critiquing the way I do things that she wastes time and is still late. I am willing to help, but I don't like being "micro-managed." As it stands now, I am letting her do everything and am living frustrated that we are always late. Please help!

Women generally do have more to do than men. Men get up in the morning, shower, put on deodorant, brush their teeth, comb their hair, and put on clothes. That's it. Then they're out the door. And they can do all of that pretty quick if they want to. But a woman has to shower, fix her hair (which may include any number of steps in order to finish the process), put on makeup, which may or may not include a skin care routine, and dress. And a woman might find any number of things she needs to do along the way. I mean, when she's putting on her makeup, she may decide she needs to tweeze her eyebrows too!

It is a known fact that it takes women longer to get ready than men. So a woman should adjust or adapt her schedule accordingly. Avoiding tardiness is really a matter of logistics. For example, if it's going to take the husband 30 minutes to get ready, and it's going to take the wife 60 minutes to get ready, and they both need to leave the house at 9:00 a.m., she needs to get up at least 30 minutes before he does.

Lateness is never acceptable for men or women. Just because you're woman and it takes you longer to get ready, that doesn't excuse your being late. If you worked for a large company, you couldn't just go in late to work and tell them you're late because you're a woman and it takes you longer to get ready than the men. No, you wouldn't do that. So since you probably wouldn't be late for work, you shouldn't be late for church, either.

If you've had problems with punctuality, make some logistical changes. Get up earlier in the morning or, if possible, delegate certain responsibilities, such as helping the children brush their teeth and comb their hair. As I said, lateness is not acceptable. It's even less acceptable when it's an issue between you and your spouse that creeps up on a regular basis to cause problems to your marriage.

As the pastor of a church, I definitely have to be at the church by a certain time, and I don't have a lot of leeway as to when I can show up. So I expect that if Deborah and I are going to leave for church together, she knows what time we need to be there; therefore, she knows what time we have to leave and what she has to do to make that happen.

Recently, we had a session that we were going to minister together. I woke up early that morning and reached over to where Deborah was supposed to be, but she was not there.

She had gotten up extra early so she could finish preparing for her portion of the session and to get herself ready so that we could be on time. And we were. You see, she had more to do, and she did the responsible thing in making an adjustment so she could take the required time to prepare herself for the day.

So, really, there is no excuse for being chronically late. You should know how long it's going to take you to get ready; therefore, you should make allowance to begin preparing yourself in advance, whether that means getting up earlier or getting yourself and your children up earlier.

Q: What should be the first step for couples who are separated but still love each other?

A: Well, if you're separated and still love each other, the first thing you should do is seek help in getting back together. Since you're separated, obviously you have been unable to resolve issues on your own. If you're already separated, you're going to need some assistance in reconciling, and reconciliation is what you should be striving for.

Q: What do you do if you're separated from a spouse who is not saved?

A: He or she is still your partner! Whether that person is saved or unsaved doesn't change that fact. Neither does it change the fact that you still have to walk according to the Word of God in this situation. You can't just jettison or cast aside your responsibility to the Word and to your spouse because he or she is not saved. First Corinthians 7:14 says that your mate can be sanctified because of you. And First Peter 3:1 and 2 says that the unsaved can be won over by your lifestyle.

So if you're married to an unsaved person, you have to live with and walk with that person. Just don't expect an unsaved person to act like a saved one.

Q: I would like to know how my husband and I should address a situation that involves a child from a previous marriage. My husband is the only parent that is involved with his child's school. He is the only parent that goes to PTA meetings and meets with the teacher. Since his ex-wife, the child's mother, has custody of the child, she should have some involvement too.

A: Well, she certainly should, but whether she does or doesn't shouldn't wrinkle your fur. Your husband should attend those parent-teacher conferences if the child's mother showed or didn't show. Your job is to support him, not to concern yourself with what the other parent is doing. And don't be concerned that there might be issues or feelings between your husband and his ex-wife. He married you, so you should focus on that and on being a helpmate to him.

Q: What is a man to do when his wife keeps bringing up his past mistakes? I've asked God and my wife for forgiveness, and I've repented, changing my behavior. Yet my wife keeps bringing up the past. Help!

A: If your spouse has missed it and has repented, you should forgive and forget, letting the past be the past. If you don't, you could risk driving that person into his or her past behavior. Men especially are reward oriented. If a husband is doing the right thing now, but never feels rewarded for his behavior by his wife, he will become discouraged and quit, and he may possibly revert to wrong behavior.

Keith Butler Sr.: Men are simple; women are a bit more complex. I mean, we men just need to be patted on the head, kissed on the cheek from time to time, and told, "I love you, Baby." We want cooked meals and we're happy. And we are reward-oriented. We want our wives to notice when we are doing the right thing.

If a wife uses a husband's mistakes as a tool to manipulate or control him, eventually he's going to have the attitude, "Why don't you live over there; I'm going to live over here." So wife, don't be unwise. If your husband is sincere and is making the effort for your sake and the sake of your lives together, move on. If you don't, there are going to be problems, and it won't be his fault.

Q: I am a "layman" Bible school student who recently was quoting a verse of Scripture to my wife. She began vehemently disagreeing with me and even got so frustrated, she started saying the "f" word, and I don't mean "faith." What do you think the problem is, and what can I do to try to fix it?

A: Well, first, you *pray*! The first thing that comes to our minds is the question as to why this woman is so angry. Her behavior seems extreme on the surface. She has some deep anger inside, and you need to find out why. We recommend counseling. Even if she won't go with you, you need to seek help. Your pastor or counselor will have some questions that will help the two of you discover the source of her anger. Then you can work from there to try to solve the problem.

Maybe you did something, even if it was inadvertently, to make her stoop to using that so-called "faith" word. At any rate, your wife is a very frustrated person. People usually become frustrated because they've been saying something over and over, trying to get someone to understand something about them or about they way they're feeling. When they don't feel as if they're being listened to, frustration builds, and one day, it comes out of their mouth in the form of "faith food."

Q: What should couples do when neither has the ability to successfully maintain the finances or housework and other household responsibilities?

A: First, we need to know your ages. I mean, are you adults? Part of being grown is taking responsibility to manage your finances and household affairs. If you're not taking that responsibility, it is your responsibility to find someone to help you learn, and there are all kinds of places for that. (But, remember, whatever your source, they will help *you* take control of your own life; they won't do it for you. Discipline can be taught to an extent, but it is predominantly a decision.)

There is no excuse for a person not knowing how to budget in America. There are community colleges, seminars, books, churches, and other non-profit organizations that can assist the person who has missed receiving this valuable training in his life. So the information is available. Once you receive the information, the rest is up to you. You have a decision to make. Budgeting is more about "want to" and discipline than anything else.

It is encouraging that you are seeking help, because if neither of you has the ability to manage finances, without a change, you are headed for the poorhouse. Unfortunately, many people in your position don't recognize that they need to change. They are the ones who will come to the pastor complaining that the Word doesn't work. But there other factors involved in receiving from the Word. You can pay tithes and give offerings, but the Word also teaches responsibility and self-discipline. It also says to do all things in moderation. If you fail to spend in moderation, you will cancel out all the tithing and giving and believing God that you are doing. God is not Santa Claus. He doesn't just say, "Ho! Ho!

Ho!" and dole out presents. No, you have responsibility to manage what you have.

So with all the information that's available, there's really no such thing as not being able to manage money. It's your decision; you can manage it if you want to.

Money is the most important vehicle you have in your life. So if you aren't going to take the time to learn how to manage money, what else in life are you going to learn? You would be taking a step in the right direction to seek some instruction and training on developing and maintaining a household budget.

Q: I no longer desire my husband sexually as much as I used to. I get really upset when he wants to spend "quality time" together, because sex is what he is wanting, and I know it's only going to last for a minute or so. He is the consummate "two-minute" man.

A (Keith Butler Sr.): According to a popular study, the average time its takes for a man to reach ejaculation is two minutes and thirty seconds. The average time it takes for a woman to achieve orgasm is more than five and a half minutes — twice the time it takes for a man. So a man needs to understand that in order to please his wife, he's going to have to take some time to "minister" to her instead of being in such a hurry.

Many men do not know how to warm their wives up. As we mentioned previously, sex begins outside the bedroom. For a woman, kind words and actions help prepare her emotionally for sex. Women are affected by everything that happened in the hours before she and her husband get to the bedroom. Men only count what happens inside the bedroom.

For example, a man can fight with his wife at three o'clock in the afternoon, and at seven o'clock that night, he can be quite ready to make passionate, mad love! His attitude is, "That was then; this is now." In his mind, there is no connection between the incident that happened earlier and sex with his wife later. Conversely, he could "have it out" with his wife and seven o'clock in the morning, and at seven that night, *she* is still hanging on to what was said that morning! She's not ready for sex, and she *won't* be ready until her husband has talked with her (and I don't mean about sex) and resolved the issue.

A woman wants to be talked to about something unrelated to sex. She doesn't want to talk about the two you "getting busy" or "taking care of business." No, if you're just talking to your wife about sex, you haven't talked to her like she's a person yet. You have to ask questions and listen to her as she tells you about what her day was like, for example, or about whatever it is she wants to talk about. And she can tell if you're not listening. You have to show interest and be engaged in her conversation; in other words, you have to *participate* in conversation with her. She has to feel that you care. She also needs to know you're attracted to her and that you love her. Then she'll be ready to go down the path of physical intimacy that you've been ready to travel for some time.

What often happens is, men don't want to take the time to "court" and woo their wives, which is selfish. It's big-time selfishness. He's ready, and he can reach satisfaction in a couple of minutes. His wife can walk across the room in a negligee, and he's ready. So the "warming up" part is strictly for her. It's not his need, but hers. So when he's not interested in her needs and in what pleases her, he is being selfish.

Preparation is very important in successful sexual intimacy (by "successful," I'm talking about what's successful to both parties). And once a couple is engaged in intercourse, a man can hold off ejaculating for a time. He can't hold off for a *long* time, but he does have the power to wait for a time in order to meet the needs of his wife.

These are things that need to be discussed between husband and wife. Sometimes the adjustment that needs to be made is as simple as changing your position when you have sex. For example, a man could perhaps slow down long enough to meet his wife's needs if they assumed a position other than what is called the "missionary" position. Practically speaking, gravity could help him hold off while he is satisfying his wife.

Husband, you have an obligation to make an effort to achieve orgasm with your wife *together* — as close to a tie as possible. The goal should be to "get there" together. That requires some work and effort. Unfortunately, many men simply don't want to do the work. They want the *result* — they want a "hot mama" — but they don't want to invest the effort it takes to warm her up sufficiently. Now if you want a "medium mama," then just invest medium effort. But if you want sexual intimacy between you and your wife to be mutually gratifying and pleasurable for you both, you're going to have to work at it.

A woman has to help her husband by communicating with him. She can't expect him just to know what works for her. And what works for her one time might not work as well the next time, because a woman's body changes depending on the time of the month. But a man will not know this if she doesn't tell him. For example, if he discovers something that heats her up on Monday, he will do the same thing on Wednesday. A man is practical. If something is working, he will stick with it — that is, until he finds it's not working anymore. So his wife needs to communicate with him often so he can know how to please her.

A man's body is constant. His body doesn't change as a woman's does. He doesn't feel what she feels, so he cannot possibly know what she requires unless she tells him.

Despite what Hollywood tries to tell us, a man does not automatically know what he's supposed to do. So if his wife doesn't assist him, he may get it wrong. But "hit-and-miss" sex shouldn't be the goal. A couple can get it right every time if there's communication.

As we've said, sex is important to a marriage. In fact, I think we've overlooked the important role sex plays between a husband and wife. A frustrated, dissatisfying sex life will negatively affect an individual as well as a marriage. For example, people who aren't satisfied sexually can be terrible to get along with. They'll come to church on Sunday with an attitude. The usher might tell them where to sit, and they'll get upset. The real problem isn't the usher; it's something else.

Sexual frustration can manifest itself in different ways depending on an individual's personality. But the bottom line is, married people can become seriously upset when their sex life is unsatisfactory. Therefore, they shouldn't settle for less than God intended in their sexual relationship.

Q: I have been married for nine years, and my husband still has old cards and letters from old girlfriends. This really upsets me. I've asked him to throw them away, but he refuses. He says he wants something to look back on and read when he gets old. I can't relate to that kind of thinking. When we are old, we need to reflect on our own lives together and that of our children and grandchildren, not old girlfriends.

Now that we are both born again and endeavoring to raise godly children, do you think it's okay for him to hold on to these things? I know he doesn't read them now,

nor does he attempt to contact these women from his past. That's not my concern. I simply don't think the cards and letters are appropriate to keep.

A (Keith Butler Sr.): No, I don't think holding on to cards and letters from old girlfriends is appropriate. I had a lot of girlfriends before I married Deborah, but I don't talk about those things. And I'm certainly not going to keep any cards or letters from them. There's no reason to.

And I *sure* don't want to hear about any of Deborah's old boyfriends! I don't even want to go there! Your husband should get rid of the memorabilia he's been holding on to and focus on making and preserving memories with his family.

Q: I am not in the habit of checking my husband's messages from his personal voice mail, but I did so recently by chance and heard a message from a woman saying he should come and visit his child. I confronted him, and he admitted to a relationship with this woman, but asked me to hold off filing for divorce until he could determine whether the child was, in fact, his.

I prayed for guidance and felt led by God to suggest a blood test. The woman was hesitant and indicated she didn't have the money for such a test. However, she continues to be reluctant even after we've offered to pay the full price ourselves.

I need "closure" on this so that we can proceed with our lives. I know my husband has had an affair with this woman, but I need to know whether or not he's the father of her baby.

A (Keith Butler Sr.): We dealt with a case years ago in which a man in the church had been paying money to a woman for support of a child he allegedly fathered. I don't know if it was the message I preached one particular Sunday morning or the convicting power of the Holy Ghost, but she came up to me in tears that morning and confessed that she was taking this man's money under false pretenses.

This woman knew the child was not his. She had collected money from him for seven years to protect the identity of the real father. All three parties were in the church. But more than three people were affected by this woman's duplicity. For example, the wife of the man paying the support was, of course, resentful at having to shovel out money every month for support of another woman's child.

The situation wound up on my desk seven years after the fact, and from that ordeal, it doesn't matter to us what a woman says, we advise blood testing for every case. I tell people, "Don't take it personally. This is business; and the first order of business is — before we proceed any further — we need to see a test result. A woman might be pregnant, and a man might confess, "According to her due date, I am the father, because I was with her at the time she would have conceived." But what he's not seeing is, somebody could have been with her right *before* him, and somebody else could have been with her right *after* him.

We have counseled women in situations who'd slept with three different men in the same day. These things happen, and, unfortunately, they're happening with people in the Church.

So the first order of business, before anything else is discussed or decided, is to test for proof of paternity. Even if after the baby's born, the man says, "Oh, that baby looks like me," we still ask for a test. There is a statistical probability that a baby will look like someone who isn't his parent. And babies change from day to day and week to week. A man may look at a baby and see a resemblance to himself one week, and two weeks later, that baby could look very different.

A blood test makes everything simpler, because you can make an intelligent decision when you know the truth. I mean, it makes a big difference if the woman has to deal with a man paying child support for eighteen years as opposed to having only to deal with an indiscretion. So we have to deal with the facts.

I have a motto with my ministers and that is: *Find out all the facts first before you make a judgment.* If a woman wants money from a man because he has allegedly fathered a baby with her, she needs to be willing to take a blood test — no test, no money. It's that simple.

Q: Please define "separate vacations." I travel alone from time to time to visit my mom, but my family takes a vacation together once a year. Does my trip to my mother's constitute a separate vacation?

Also, I am a stay-home mom. No family vacation is really a vacation to me when I have to continue to minister to the needs of my family. I used to go away for two or three days to visit college roommates or friends without my husband or the kids (I've done this twice in eleven years). It gave me an opportunity to not be responsible for anyone but myself for a few days.

Someone suggested attending women's conferences as a way to get away without it being called a separate vacation. But, again, conferences aren't a vacation to me because there is a schedule that must still be adhered to.

A: Visiting your mom or other relatives isn't a vacation, and attending a conference isn't a vacation. People should have some latitude when it comes to a spouse visiting friends for a very short period of time *that the other spouse approves of.*

Our son married a woman whose family lives in Louisiana, where she is from. When he began dating her, we told him that if he married her, he'd have to let her go see her mama at least a couple times a year. And at holidays, he has to spend time with her folks as well as with us. Last Thanksgiving, our son and his wife went to Louisiana to be with her family. It was the first Thanksgiving he has not spent with us, but those sacrifices are part of being married. Yet spending time with relatives, which we recommend, is not considered a vacation.

Keith Butler Sr.: Everyone needs some special "space" every now and then. For me, that space is in the woods, hanging out in camouflage with a rifle on my lap. Deborah's space might be at her favorite department store for several hours with or without friends. She finds shopping relaxing, and she might spend four or five hours looking around and come home with nothing but a pair of stockings. That's not relaxing to a man. In fact, he might see it as a total waste of time. Conversely, a woman might wonder how relaxing it could possibly be to deal with mosquitoes and other bugs in the woods, to risk being attacked by a bear, and so forth.

Our interpretation of separate vacations would be the wife going to Jamaica, for example, and the husband going somewhere else. That's not healthy to a marriage; in fact, it could be harmful, and we do not recommend this kind of separateness in order to enjoy an little free time alone.

The greatest advice we can give about marriage is advice that the Bible, the Word of God gives: *Getting married should be a decision to love someone else and to meet his or her needs ahead of yours.* If you will put your spouse's needs ahead of yours continually, your marriage should be a happy one.

You can never take a vacation with marriage. You can never take the attitude, "I'm not going to work on this for awhile" and still have a happy marriage. You must always be thinking about how you can minister to your husband or wife.

You can be married for twenty years and have your marriage break up in the twenty-first year if you decide you're through working on it. *The time you stop working on your marriage is when the marriage will begin to deteriorate and will, ultimately, fold.* Marriage is a life commitment of work and blessing — of working together and of sharing the reward of your labor together.

Other Titles By Word of Faith Publishing

Bishop Keith A. Butler

A Seed Will Meet Any Need	BK003
Hell: You Don't Want To Go There	BK005
How To Be Blessed By God	
Making Room for Yourself	BK007
Angels — God's Servants for You	BK010
The Last Week of Jesus	BK020
Success Strategies From Heaven	BK001 (Harrison House, Inc.)
What On Earth Are We Here For?	BK002 (Harrison House, Inc.)

Min. Deborah L. Butler

Establishing Godly Relationships Through Marriage and Family	BK012

Rev. Keith A. Butler II

God's Plan for the Single Saint	BK006

Keith A. Butler II and MiChelle Butler

For PKs Only: A Book for the Next Generation	BK016

▶ The Internet. It has the potential to communicate information and connect people in powerful ways.

Now it is bringing together Kenneth Hagin, Kenneth Copeland, Keith Butler, Jesse Duplantis, Creflo Dollar, Jerry Savelle, Mac Hammond, and many more for something historic... something with exciting possibilities for you, your family, and the world.

THE TIME HAS COME

"Now you can join the online revolution, build your faith, protect your family and be a part of taking the Gospel to the world."

CFAITH.com
▶ YOUR INTERCONNECTED FAITH FAMILY

These well-respected ministries, along with many others, are uniting to connect the global faith family and reach out to others with the life-changing message of faith through the power of the Internet. They are coming together to launch **CFAITH.com**.